Danny Wareham is a psychologist whose work explores the intersection of psychology, leadership, and culture. Recognised as a Global Top 25 Thought Leader in Culture and Top 50 in Leadership, his debut book brings new research in these fields to life through stories that make complex ideas practical and human. He lives in Stoke-on-Trent, UK, with his partner, Charlene.

CONSTELLATION

Leadership reimagined for a connected age

DANNY WAREHAM

FIRGUN

PRAISE FOR *CONSTELLATION*

'Constellation Leadership may well be the leadership of tomorrow. It takes you on a thought-provoking journey through leadership history, relatable case studies, and an invitation to explore the real power of organisational culture.'

Jo Garland
Director, Customer Engagement (EMEA)
the LEGO Group

'Constellation leadership is a wonderful book that shines light on how leading can work collectively. We know that leading is a collective process but struggle to find ways to make that practice tangible and accessible. This book is giving you access to the why and the how of leading by the many. It nudges you to learn and put your reading into practice, which is, to me, a must for any good book.'

Professor Bernd Vogel
Director, Henley Centre for Leadership UK & Africa,
Henley Business School, University of Reading

'The way it connects history, research, and practical insight makes what could be complex ideas accessible, without ever dumbing them down. Reframing culture as a leader in its own right, is a refreshing new perspective that will resonate strongly. *Constellation* will be powerful and relevant for leaders and organisations'

Martin Teasdale
Founder of The Team Leader Community™
& Get Out Of Wrap podcast

'It's so practical, relatable, and beautifully underpinned by research. One of the clearest and most usable explanations I've seen of what actually needs to be true for psychological safety to exist – especially in distributed and hybrid teams.'

Marion Anderson
HR Leader & PhD Researcher in psychological safety
at Glasgow Caledonian University

'Grounded in research yet highly readable, Constellation explores leaderless leadership with clarity and engaging prose, offering fresh insights for navigating today's connected world.'

Melanie Robinson
Deputy CEO
The Institute of Leadership

'Constellation Leadership is a fascinating concept. The book takes the reader on a voyage of exploration, showing how leadership can be reimagined in fresh and thought-provoking ways.'

Judith Germain
Leadership Impact Catalyst and Founder
The Maverick Paradox

'In an age where the contact centre evolves with technology, I love hearing of new approaches to enable individuals to excel within their roles. Constellation leadership definitely gives food for thought and to think about organisation structure a little differently.'

Kate Knowles
Services Director
Contact Centre Management Association (CCMA)

© Danny Wareham 2025

Danny Wareham asserts the moral right to be identified as
the author of this Work in accordance with the
Copyright, Designs and Patents Act 1988.

A CIP catalogue record of this book is available from the British Library.

ISBN: 978-1-83688-797-3

First published in the United Kingdom by
Firgun Publishing
Independent Publishing Network
Business & Leadership Books in 2025
www.firgun.co.uk

Illustrations © Luisa Phillips (luisaphillips.com)

For Charlene.

My rock. My bee. My lobster.

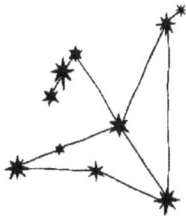

CONTENTS

Culture comes from the Latin *colere*
meaning "to *cultivate*", "to *till*", or "to *care*"

Introduction

Who leads when the leader is not in the room?

*"A great organisation is an organism where all the parts
are connected – not by rigid and irrelevant reporting
lines, but because the organisation is powered by trust:
Trust that each part will do what it is designed to do.
The parts of an organism aren't working together for pay.
They're not pointing the blame at other parts.
They're supporting each other towards a larger purpose."*

I jotted this in a notepad in mid-August 2020, as the world changed around me. At the time, I was struggling with organising my workload, as the COVID-19 pandemic changed approaches within the blue-chip organisation I was supporting.

The initial "let's all pull together" mentality of March, where the UK entered its first lockdown and various areas of my organisation dropped their siloed behaviours and office politics, and worked together to move all employees to a supportive home-working model, had long elapsed. Remote-first was now normalised, support structures were in place, and the UK Government still had no clear plan for how or when restrictions might change.

In this new environment, the familiar tribal behaviours had returned. Siloed mentality; protectionism; defensive decision making. Processes moved at a glacial pace, as multiple departments refocused their energies onto their core roles. Interoperability had practically ceased.

I remember feeling frustrated. We – as a company and as a society – had shown what was possible if we freed ourselves of these social shackles and hierarchical handcuffs. If we had a clear objective and we rallied around each other with common purpose, behaviours, actions and practises, we could each use our own unique skills in support of that purpose.

Somewhat coincidentally, I was remotely delivering a development session to a group of senior leaders focusing on teamworking. One delegate described their role as being like the clichéd swan metaphor: looking calm on the surface but kicking like mad underneath to keep everything afloat. I built on this analogy to open a discussion about management and leadership:

"Managers do things right; Leaders do the right things", I suggested, in an equally clichéd paraphrasing of Peter Drucker[1]. "Management is about operational effectiveness and efficiency. Doing what we do today exceptionally well and looking to improve. Management is the majority of the swan. It improves

---

[1] Technically, this quote is misattributed to Drucker. The original quote was, *"Efficiency is doing things right; effectiveness is doing the right things"*

those leg kicks; the foot positions; the spread of the webbed toes. It keeps the organisation moving forward and on course. Leadership is the swan's head. It plots the swan's path through the river, looking out for debris in the water, opportunities to eat or to mate. It doesn't even think about the legs."

IT DOESN'T EVEN THINK ABOUT THE LEGS.

When you look closely at how living organisms survive, you see an astonishing harmony. Cells specialise, but none of them knows the whole picture. The immune system patrols constantly, identifying threats and sacrificing some of its own to protect the whole. The skin forms a barrier without being told; the liver cleanses the blood without asking permission.

Nature is full of these patterns. This is what fascinated me: in the most successful systems, coordination doesn't depend on conscious direction from the top. It happens because every part, every unit, has absorbed a sense of purpose so deeply that it operates without needing to check back with a central brain.

The various parts of an organism aren't thinking about other parts. Your hands don't think about the lungs that are providing the oxygen needed by the *opponens pollicis* muscle every time you oppose your thumb. Indeed, they don't *know* each other at all.

Each part has a clear, but unconscious, goal: to keep you alive long enough to pass on your genetic material. Every part of you is focused on that goal. What if organisations could be the same, with every part moving in coordinated instinct, like the parts of a living being? If the purpose is paramount, known and understood by all parts of the organisation, surely the organisation would thrive in pursuit of that purpose?

Like an organism, a healthy organisation doesn't rely on just a brain to function. It relies on coordination, purpose, and instinct shared across the system. Yet in most of our workplaces, leadership has been conceptualised as precisely that: a brain at the top of the body, issuing instructions downward and assuming every limb will obey. This is the model we've inherited. Leadership studies, management textbooks, and corporate practices continue to circle back to the idea of the leader as an individual hero: the visionary chief executive, the decisive manager, the charismatic figurehead. Culture, in this framing, is something secondary: a support act, or at best the environment in which leaders lead. But when we reduce leadership to a person with authority, we overlook something vital.

Think about it. How often do you truly change your behaviour because a leader told you to, compared with how often you adjust it to fit with the group around you?

The language we use, our appetite for change or risk, and how gregarious or measured we can be is different when we're with friends versus with family versus with work peers. The unspoken expectations of colleagues, the silent agreements on what's "normal" in a meeting, the unwritten rules of risk and reward all flex us – temporarily – like plasticine.

This cultural influence shapes us far more frequently, and often more powerfully, than a single directive from the top. Culture, not hierarchy, is what governs behaviour when the leader isn't in the room. And the leader isn't in the room most of the time.

Yet this is where the friction lies. Our inherited models of leadership grew up in simpler, more linear times: armies, factories, and hierarchies where instructions could flow downward and be executed with predictability. Today's organisations look nothing like that. They are complex, matrixed, globally connected, and constantly adapting to shifting markets and technologies. A chain of command is too rigid for problems that cross silos, too slow for environments that demand agility, and too narrow to account for the diversity of skills and perspectives now needed. The result is a daily tension: leaders trying to steer through structure, while their people navigate an inclusive reality that refuses to stay in neat boxes.

This gap between model and reality creates frustration on all sides. Executives wonder why their strategic vision doesn't translate into behaviour on the ground; managers feel trapped in bureaucracy while still expected to be nimble; employees juggle competing reporting lines and conflicting priorities with little clarity on whose voice really matters. The system strains under the weight of a leadership model that no longer matches the shape of the work itself.

A NEW WORLD

Meanwhile, the world has changed. Historically, employees might remain in one or two roles for their entire working lives. This was partly due to the societal narrative of loyalty to an employer and partly because employees had to tolerate employer behaviours and values that were incongruent with their own, because of lower social mobility.

Today, employees are more focused on values-alignment, ESG impact and purpose from their employer. Meanwhile, it's never been easier to have a side venture – selling clothes on Vinted, old electronics on eBay, or opening a Patreon, Discord or OnlyFans account – to supplement an income. The message for today's employers is clear: if you cannot provide us with purpose and utilise our passion to make a difference, we will move to somewhere that will.

The wider world has also changed. Society has never had such a variety of information at its fingertips, yet the binarisation of opinions has become normalised. We are conditioned to take sides: "for" or "against," "leave" or "remain," "red" or "blue." Nuance is set aside in favour of simplicity. Political populism has risen, and, in many organisations, we see echoes of the same reflex: leadership that seeks quick, uncomplicated answers to complex, nuanced challenges. Quarterly reports and half-year earnings reviews only accelerate this search for immediacy.

Companies that once embraced the triple bottom line of people, planet, and profit now privilege one dimension above all. Great Man leadership has regained a foothold. Equity, diversity, and inclusion programmes are rolled back or tokenised. Already profitable businesses drive profits higher still through mass layoffs. This societal craving for simplicity creeps into leadership itself. It reduces decision-making to a zero-sum game, creating a mechanised process tree of black-and-white outcomes and predictable levers.

But our world isn't mechanical. It isn't black and white. It is colourful. And it is in that rainbow where our tribal species lives. Diversity and inclusion are not limited to legally-protected characteristics: as a social animal, they're woven through every aspect of our lives.

Despite these truths, organisations continue to pour billions into initiatives that promise to enhance charisma, decisiveness, or presence in individual leaders, as though stronger personalities at the top could solve systemic challenges. Yet the problems we face today are not solved by ever-greater concentration of authority, but by collective adaptability across the system. If culture can suppress dissent, limit risk-taking, and mute innovation, might it not also have the power to enable trust, unleash creativity, and coordinate action?

What if we've been looking in the wrong place? We already recognise culture's influence. None of us are immune. It affects our language, our appetite for risk, our approach to change, and our daily behaviours. It pulls us in ways we may not even notice. What if culture itself could lead?

WHO'S THIS BOOK FOR?

This tension between leadership as a person and leadership as a process is where this book begins. As a social phenomenon, culture has long been studied for its leadership-like influence on groups, but never as if culture itself were the leader.

This book invites you to rethink how leadership works. Whether you are a leadership practitioner, a senior manager, an academic, or are interested in the evolution of leadership theory, this book intends to challenge our existing models and offer an alternative. It aims to start a debate about what it means to lead, and to invite readers to evaluate, expand upon and evolve the ideas suggested within these pages.

In the first part, we'll look at the theories we've inherited: models of leadership, culture, and psychological safety that still dominate organisational life. We'll explore how these inherited models that are rooted in hierarchy, heroics, and positional power may be holding us back.

In the second, I'll share new research in social dynamics, personality psychology, and psychological safety that unveils a different possibility where leadership is not a title or a position, but a process distributed among people, powered by purpose and culture, and expressed in ways hierarchies often overlook.

Finally, we'll explore real-world examples where these ideas are already being practised. We'll travel from the battlefields of eSports to the British Army's response to a global pandemic, and from space shuttle launches to inter-generational cooperatives: there are case studies that show what happens when leadership is not only shared but embedded in culture itself.

This seems timely. Today's world is defined by unpredictability and accelerating change. We face technological shifts like artificial intelligence, environmental pressures from climate change and biodiversity loss, social disruption through involuntary migration and pandemics, and political polarisation driven by globalisation versus protectionism. These are not isolated problems but interconnected, systemic challenges unlike those faced in the industrial era. And yet, we continue to confront them with leadership approaches designed for a different age.

Our world has changed.
Perhaps it's time for our approach to leadership to change, too?

Part One:
Where are we?

01

A HISTORY OF LEADERSHIP:
The pyramid prison

"We shape our tools and thereafter our tools shape us."

Marshall McLuhan
The Medium is the Massage (1967)

It might surprise you to learn that the study of leadership is a relatively new field.

Though we have always had leaders throughout history, the word *leadership* didn't appear as a dictionary definition until 1821, and the first academic research wasn't considered until the middle of the 19th century.

During this time, the Industrial Revolution was at full steam (pun intended) and the most profitable and influential businesses in the world thrummed with the power of coal, iron and hierarchy – at least in the West. Railways thundered, mills spun, and coal mines drove empires, organised under rigid hierarchies and helmed by singular men. These men sat atop a pyramid of productivity, buoyed by the belief that leaders cannot be taught; they are born. They were *Great Men.*

NATURE NOT NURTURE

These great men were revered by other great men. Thomas Carlyle was a Scottish philosopher and essayist, whose writings influenced much of Victorian England's intellectual views. In a series of lectures on heroism, Carlyle argued that society was carried forward by great men and heroes, not by the masses. These men were the "practical realisation and embodiment" of progress, and their attributes of leadership "dwelt in the Great Men sent into the world." The implication was that every great leader is born already possessing the traits that will enable them to instinctually lead. These skills were inherent, not taught. It is nature, not nurture, that creates leaders.

Carlyle's views were widely accepted at the time and for decades later. In 1911, the Encyclopaedia Britannica published a list of historical accomplishments as part of lengthy biographies of great men. In one list, all European people migrations during the Barbarian Invasions at the fall of the Roman Empire (c.300-600AD) were attributed to Attila the Hun, despite him only being alive from c.406-453AD. Attila may have been an impressive leader, but it's especially impressive to lead over a century before you're born and more than a century after your death – and even more impressive still to account for all the migrations of all people during that period.

Still, from the 1840s through to the middle of the following century, Great Man theory dominated our views of leadership and what makes a leader. Sir Francis Galton – the father of personality psychology and pioneer of eugenics (he also coined the terms 'eugenics' and 'nature versus nurture' in 1883) – supported Carlyle's views, writing that the traits that leaders possessed were immutable and could not be developed. Galton's work in social Darwinism, eugenics and biological racism highlight an uncomfortable truth about Great Man theory: If men are born great and greatness cannot be learned, then some men are, by nature of birth alone, better than others.

The idea that one man is better than another purely due to their inherited traits and attributes is one that is easily identifiable as discriminatory at best; bigoted at worst. But, even today, we still see the use of typing tools in personality and leadership assessments to group people together based on shared attributes.

We might recognise that an individual claiming that all people from a specific race or heritage share some inherent attribute that makes them "better" as racist. Yet we continue to accept business models based around identifying individuals as a specific behavioural colour, title or set of letters. It's part of the reason that personality psychologists can be highly critical of these assessments. Their field shares a common father figure in Galton.

EVOLVING THE GREAT MAN

Herbert Spencer, a contemporary of Carlyle, vocally opposed Great Man theory. He argued that individuals are shaped by time, place, race, and society – not born with greatness baked in. It is illogical, he suggests, to think that these traits are inherent in an individual. Surely, some, if not all, of these attributes might be developed, released or learned?

In the early 20th century, *Trait* Theory became more accepted and studied – though Great Man would continue to influence leadership approaches until the Second World War. In this model, we recognise that some traits might be inherent, but many could be learned or enhanced through training, practice and awareness.

The challenge is that no one could identify and agree upon the specific blend of traits and attributes that were required for leadership. In some contexts, being amiable, rapport-building and consensus-seeking was effective. In others, high accountability, robust challenging and conflict management delivered the approach required to create followership. This lack of consensus allowed the Great Man versus Trait argument to continue (at least academically) until the late 1940s.

Only at this point – after over a century of study – did anyone consider that the situation might influence the leader. In 1948, Professor Emeritus of Management Science and Psychology at Ohio State University, Ralph Stogdill, suggested that "persons who are leaders in one situation may not necessarily be leaders in other situations." Leadership research in academic circles tends to move like molasses, it seems.

Despite this (patently obvious?) observation, leadership development courses today – over 70 years after Stogdill's statement – still include trait-based training. Courses on conflict, communication and strategy still dominate leadership syllabuses. HR and business publications analyse the latest trait-based approach you, apparently, need. "What's the most important skill a leader needs?", is a regular question at almost every leadership conference, seminar or discussion panel on the subject, as if building the perfect leader were some sort of recipe.

There is still an underlying, stubborn belief that, if we could just find the appropriate combination of traits and attributes, we could create and develop leaders consistently. If we could mechanise the process, we could roll ready-made leaders off the figurative production line.

But when it comes to leader effectiveness, the situation and context do matter. The oft-cited example of Winston Churchill being a paragon of leadership in wartime but ineffective in peacetime is normally included in a paragraph located about here in any review of leadership history.

This *Situational leadership* doesn't only consider a leader with a more fixed style working in separate specific situations (such as the Churchill example). It also includes the individual leader's ability to adapt their approach to a given situation.

Yet, again, academia finds itself slow on the uptake of this insight, with studies into contextual and situational leadership not being published until 1969, under its original name of *Life Cycle Theory of Leadership*. (It was changed to Situational Leadership in the mid-1970s.)

By this point in our leadership history journey, there is a bit of an elephant in the room. We've considered the leader, their traits and attributes, and whether they are born with them or they are learned. We've thought about the situation that the leader finds themselves in, and whether they are suitable for specific contexts or if a leader can flex their approach to suit a changing environment. But we've not yet discussed the output of leadership: what is it that we're aiming to achieve?

WHAT ARE WE HERE FOR?

Transactional leadership made its first appearance in 1978, and focused on the exchange of knowledge, skills, resources, and effort between leaders and their followers in pursuit of a specific outcome (or set of outcomes).

It relies on a system of rewards that are granted in recognition of performance, and penalties for performance or behaviour below an expected level. In other words, transactional leadership is about a carrot and stick approach in pursuit of a deliverable, measurable output. It is effective, but repeated research studies have shown that it can produce a culture of fear and compliance, rather than commitment.

Over the next decade, explorations into transactional leadership evolved towards a model of *Theory X* and *Theory Y*: X being *transactional*, with managers ruling through consequences and Y being *transformational*, with managers assuming the best of their followers and encouraging their work.

Transformational leadership builds on the premise that people are not simply motivated by rewards (or deterred by punishments), but are influenced by a sense of purpose and personal growth. First popularised by James MacGregor Burns in 1978 and expanded by Bernard Bass in the 1980s, the model focuses on inspiring followers to transcend their own self-interest for the sake of the group or a shared vision. Transformational leaders work by aligning organisational goals with individual values, creating a connection between personal meaning and collective ambition. These leaders inspire and motivate followers to go beyond their perceived self-interests for the benefit of the group through the use of charisma, inspiration and personalised consideration for each follower.

We're almost 150 years into our journey and we've reached the 1980s. Whilst we know that there can be no leadership without followship, only now, as Wham! entered the pop charts and disposable cameras are invented, are we starting to think about the relationship between leader and follower. Questions now turn to consider whether encouraging, nurturing or serving followers is a route to improved leadership effectiveness.

WON'T SOMEBODY THINK OF THE PEOPLE?

Throughout the 80s and 90s, researchers focused on this complexity of interpersonal relationships between leaders, followers, situation, task, values, and environment – in varying combinations. All the while, they'd still not agreed a consensus definition for what leadership actually is. More and more theories were introduced, adding more complexity to the field. Many of these models were re-workings of each other, licenced as proprietary offerings from the explosion of consultants and consultancies that came into being during this period.

Academics grew increasingly critical of the field's fragmentation. The sheer number of models led to what some described as "definitional drift": leadership meant something subtly different in each framework, making comparison difficult and practical application inconsistent. Was leadership about traits, behaviours, relationships, or outcomes? The answer depended on which book you opened.

This theoretical pluralism had some value, as it reflected the richness of leadership as a social phenomenon. But it also left the field without a unifying foundation, fuelling a sense that leadership research was chasing its own tail.

In practice, the gap was quickly filled by consultancies and proprietary frameworks. Leadership development became a booming industry, selling simplified models designed to be memorable, trainable, and scalable across organisations. The approaches of rank-and-yank, forced distribution performance curves, management by objective, management by walking around, the "one minute" manager, 360 feedback, and growth through merger all became part of the leadership zeitgeist at this time.

These frameworks gave managers language and tools, but often at the cost of nuance. The risk was that leadership became less about inquiry and more about branding: a cycle of fads promising the "new key" to unlocking human performance. What flourished was not consensus, but competition – between theories, between providers, and between interpretations of what leadership should mean in modern organisations.

As Ralph Stogdill wryly observed, 'there are almost as many definitions of leadership as there are people trying to define it.' And that was in 1974, before the boom in theories.

LEADERSHIP IN A VACUUM

Research into leadership doesn't happen in isolation. As studies tend to investigate what's occurring in organisations of the time, the research acts as a sort of time capsule or snapshot for the societies of those times.

With the order and efficiency of engineering, industrialisation and mass production, craftspeople were turned into labourers. Time and motion obsession focused on removing inefficiencies from organisations whilst consolidating power and order towards a shrinking minority within those businesses. The pyramid structure became both appropriate and normalised.

Great Man and Trait were the de facto approach when men were creating the machines of industry, requiring great amounts of wealth and power. The class-based elitism of the society of the day fed the narrative that some men rise based on their innate qualities; that some men are innately better than others. These were reinforced through the command-and-control leadership approaches of the First and Second World Wars. In the rationing and infrastructure rebuilding between the wars, and in the crisis management of the Great Depression, it was believed that a form of relatively siloed, controlled management, and hierarchical leadership was required and considered simpler to implement.

In the period of growth after WWII, when situations became more varied and complex, situational and contingency approaches were adopted – and academic research focused on these models. With the rise of individualism and neo-liberalism in the 1980s, transactional and Theory X developed, focused on the measurable outputs of leadership. Transformational and Theory Y emerged as a counterpoint to these outcome-focused approaches, seeking to understand the human element to followship. In these models, the pyramid was sometimes inverted to demonstrate the importance of the frontline employees. But it remains a hierarchy. It remains a pyramid.

Ironically, the boom in proprietary leadership models and consultant-proposed theories, which were designed to limit their use outside of paying clients, drove an increase in academic research. The plethora of available models, variety of businesses (as the Internet started to find its feet), and data to show the measurable impact of the each of the models – plus more powerful computers available to analyse that data – meant that research centres finally had their hands on usable, applied insight to discuss and critically analyse.

In this sense, leadership theory has always been reactive rather than predictive. Academics do not invent models in a vacuum. They observe what is already taking hold in practice and then attempt to make sense of why it seems to work. The consultancy boom of the 1980s and 1990s provided a fertile testing ground, much as the Michigan and Ohio State studies[2] had done decades earlier. What was first sold as neat frameworks for managers quickly became case studies for scholars, who sought to strip away the commercial wrapping and examine whether the underlying ideas had any explanatory power.

This interplay between practice and research is both a strength and a weakness of the field. On the one hand, it grounds leadership studies in lived organisational reality. On the other, it means the discipline often lags behind the needs of the time, chasing after trends instead of anticipating them. The GLOBE[3] study in the 1990s, for example, did not arise from a theoretical void but from the pressing questions of globalising businesses: how do leaders operate across cultures, and what makes them credible in one setting but ineffective in another?

---

[2] The Michigan (Likert, 1947) and Ohio State (Stogdill & Shartle, 1948) leadership studies distinguished between task-oriented and relationship-oriented behaviours, forming the foundation for subsequent behavioural leadership theories.

[3] The Global Leadership And Organizational Behaviour Effectiveness (GLOBE) Project was a major cross-cultural leadership study launched in the early 1990s by Professor Robert J. House to understand how cultural differences impact leadership behaviours and effectiveness across the world.

Leadership theory, in this sense, reads like a chronicle of shifting social, political, and economic priorities: from industrial control, to human relations, to measurable performance, to transformational ideals. Each stage is less a clean break than a mirror held up to its age.

As inclusion has become more of a societal focus, contemporary theories have emerged that consider leadership as a shared or socialised responsibility. Though new to study, this is not a new idea. It was proposed over a century ago.

A FORGOTTEN HEROINE

Seebohm Rowntree inherited a company on the brink of administration, when he succeeded his father as Chairman of Rowntree Mackintosh PLC in 1923. The famous British chocolate maker hadn't recovered from two of its competitors – Cadbury and Fry – merging five years prior and needed to reestablish itself or face collapse.

Lyndall Urwick was hired as a senior manager and tasked with assisting in the modernisation of the company. At the behest of Rowntree, Urwick cancelled a weekend with his wife to attend a lecture given by an American academic – a "gaunt Boston spinster", Urwick unflatteringly described her – he'd never heard of. As he listened to her speak, he found great admiration for her views on leadership and management, remarking that, "…in two minutes I was at her feet, where I remained for the rest of her life." Her name was Mary Parker Follett.

It's difficult to overstate Follett's impact on leadership. Just about every theory today – from trait, relational, distributed, situational, authentic, transformational, servant and pretty much every other model – has been influenced by her studies and she laid the foundation for modern management practices. Outside of academic and leadership purist discussions, she is often overlooked. But her insights into power dynamics, participatory decision-making, and leadership as a relational process make her a true visionary ahead of her time.

Follett's ideas challenged the rigid, hierarchical structures that dominated business and politics in her era. She believed that teams could play to each member's strengths in different instances, and that the mantle of leader could move between team members. But her ideas of creating high-performing teams based on individual strengths and great cultures fell out of fashion, as the planet lurched toward the First World War and the traditional autocratic, command-and-control styles used within the military at the time.

After the war, much of the world was in recession. This only became more acute with the Black Tuesday stock market crash and the Great Depression (1929-1939) in the United States, followed by World War II. In the aftermath of WWII, rebuilding costs, further recessions and rationing continued, as economies struggled with the burden of nearly half-a-century of turmoil. Follett's socialist-leaning, inclusion-based, collectivist views on leadership fell out of fashion and have been largely ignored for almost a century. She died, following an operation, in Boston, Massachusetts in 1933.

Today, echoes of her work can be found in *distributed leadership*, which has become an accepted, practical model in some educational settings. For example, since the early 2000s in England, several individual state-funded schools may join together to form a multi-academy trust. These academies have a centralised governance team that determines matters of budget, curriculum and regulations. However, each individual school maintains a level of autonomy in how those local budgets are utilised, their own recruitment and selection processes, and other devolved powers.

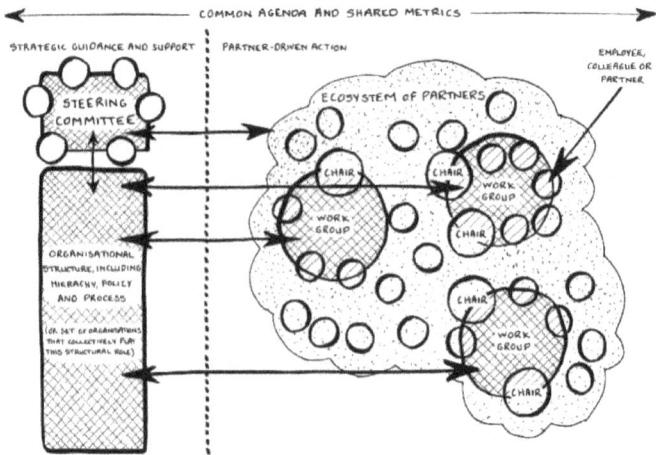

Example of a Distributed Leadership model, with individual leadership within work groups

This devolved, context-dependent approach also isn't quite as recent as we might think. The indigenous Haudenosaunee[4] people of North America recognised individual-centric challenge of finding all leadership skills for all situations in one individual long before the word was added to the dictionary.

In this union of six tribes, a matriarchal leadership protected the culture, determined succession matters and managed day-to-day tribal affairs. During wartime or famine – contexts requiring different leadership skillsets – power devolved

---

[4] Haudenosaunee means 'the people of the long house', comprised of the Mohawk, Oneida, Onondaga, Cayuga, Seneca, and Tuscarora nations. They are sometimes referred to as Iroquois – a French colonial term

to local tribal leaders, who had full autonomy to determine the appropriate course of action without influence from the matriarchy.

As an applied approach, it can be an effective leadership style. However, critics have argued that it is not true leadership but delegation. If we acknowledge that headteachers (and the Haudenosaunee matriarchy) have the ultimate decision in what is and isn't distributed, easing the workload burden of these figureheads through delegation is both probable and likely.

In the educational scenario, teachers may accept "distributed leadership" over "delegation" as a more agreeable description. However, this is not true distribution; the responsibility might be delegated, but the accountability is not.

WHO'S THE MAN?

In nearly two centuries or research, our views of leadership have evolved. To some, leadership is psychological: a list of attributes, circumstances and characteristics. To others, it's sociological: the result of relationships, culture and norms. But the position of leader has always been a person.

The discussion has then focused around whether it is the person's traits and attributes (Great Man, Trait, and Behavioural Styles), their context, situation and/or conditions (Situational and Contingency), or their relationships with followers (Transactional, Transformational, Servant, and Distributed) – or some combination of all of these – that creates the leader.

These models developed alongside the textile mills of the 19th century and the production lines of the 20th. They have adapted to the changes in industries, the rise of individualism and the influence of capitalism on societies. In these contexts, hierarchy was the norm and organisational design was simple and linear. Our researched models mirrored the application of our leadership approaches: academics examined what worked in real-world examples and then reverse engineered those approaches to develop their theories and models. The result is an attempt to understand what works in the practical workplace, so as to replicate it more effectively through study.

But the world has changed since those mills and production lines – even though our leadership approaches have not. Hierarchy, structure and pyramids are still normalised in today's leadership. All models ultimately resemble pyramids, whilst contemporary organisational structures have become increasingly matrixed. This leaves modern leaders finding themselves requiring new skills to navigate managing the cross-functional, multi-disciplined teams working in flattened pyramids with multiple reporting lines, often across geographies, which are common in organisations today.

Faced with these challenges, we look to research for the answer. But these studies are based on what we already have. It's a circular belief of looking at what's working in industry, understanding and isolating more of the tenets that are effective, and then recommending to industry how to utilise those approaches more intentionally.

So, we change our organisational structures, our teams and our reporting lines. We introduce or remove incentivisation. We examine our internal processes, our reward mechanics, and our technologies. We invest in training and consultancy to add to our arsenal of traits and attributes. We take the leadership pyramid, and we flip it upside down, claiming leadership is in service of the frontline. And because we're doing something different, it feels like we're innovating. But we're simply repackaging the pyramid. The pyramid has become a prison.

And yet, after two centuries of models, theories, and frameworks, we still haven't asked the most radical question: what if leadership isn't about people at all?

The answer doesn't lie in a new org structure. It's not found in a recognition programme, a strategic-thinking workshop, or a shiny new communication platform. It's not rooted in our pyramid models – regardless of which way we flip it or how we shuffle its strata.

It lies in a new paradigm. One where the leader isn't a person, but an environment. One where *culture* is the leader.

THE ROLE OF A LEADER

It might feel somewhat bizarre to suggest that culture could provide leadership. Culture feels abstract and ambiguous. It can be difficult to describe, challenging to nurture, and often is viewed as an afterthought: a nice to have once the 'real' business drivers of efficiency, process and operational effectiveness are handled.

Before we can understand whether culture can lead, we need to step back, look at this philosophical challenge from a different viewpoint, and ask a more basic question: what does it actually mean to lead?

Despite two centuries of research and hundreds of theories, models and proposals, we're no closer to sharing a definition of leadership. In the academic sphere, debate even continues over the differences and shared attributes between leadership and management. We also don't have an agreed definition of management either[5]. Consensus is not a word commonly found in academic circles.

We must rely on the applied world – business, organisations and institutions – combined with academic insight, to trace the golden threads that connect the models and help us to identify three stable leadership facets:

1. **Leadership is a person.**

   In every proposed theory, the position of leader is given to a physical individual. In some models, there may be sharing of status between individuals (i.e., distributed leadership). However, the point remains that it is a person or persons.

2. **Leadership sets the direction, vision or goal.**

   In each model, responsibility for determining what or where followers are working towards is defined by the leader. We might refer to this as the vision, mission, purpose or goal.

3. **Leadership informs our unwritten behavioural rules.**

   The accepted and tolerated behaviours, the favoured approaches and decision-making processes are subtly influenced through the social cues and norms of the group – with the leader holding a disproportionate level of influence.

---

[5] When uncertain of definitions, a useful starting point is etymology. '*Manager*' comes from the Latin '*manus*' ('*hand*') into the Italian '*maneggiare*' meaning '*to handle or direct*'. '*Leader*' finds its roots in the Anglo Saxon '*lǣd*' ('*road*') into the Old English '*lǣdere*', meaning '*to travel*', '*to guide*' or '*to go*'. With this context, *Manager* is about doing things well today; *Leader* is about going somewhere tomorrow.

With this view of the common thread of leadership theory, an intriguing question emerges:

If the group are aware of the direction/vision and have an agreed understanding and interpretation of the unwritten rules of how we get things done here, is a person required to be the leader at all?

On first read, this might seem fanciful. Either, we might assume, this is a form of impractical, socialised anarchy or it's a commune of free-loving individuals, sitting around a campfire singing kumbaya and being generally unproductive. It's certainly not the first thing that springs to mind when we think of leadership. It's perhaps more Woodstock than workplace.

EXITING THE PYRAMID

Our view of leadership is moulded around the pyramid. We see it as layers of authority and responsibility, steadily increasing as we travel vertically through the model. In many organisations, our reward and remuneration are explicitly linked to our layer, rather than the value we create: the highest paid is the CEO; the lowest is at the coalface. We might find it unequitable if someone in a strata lower than ours receives a comparable or greater salary.

This is how deeply the pyramid shapes our thinking, even unconsciously, and it is why an apparently leaderless-leadership model might feel alien. But there are examples of this phenomenon all around us.

For example, consider a football team[6]. We recognise that, before a match, there is traditional vertical leadership. Decisions are made about the tactics and strategy, who has made the team, and the objectives of the game. After the match, we also have vertical leadership. This debriefs match performance, provides recognition and takes learnings to develop future training programmes and approaches. But *during* the match, who is the leader?

We may have assigned the label of captain to a player for the game's duration. But, in reality, how much in-match leadership is provided (or required)? The goalkeeper knows what to do, as do the midfielders, forwards and defenders. They've trained for this moment, built and practised the skills needed, and are in a position to perform. Their tactics were understood before the game, and they will not be asked to play out of position: the keeper will not be expected to be a goal scorer; a forward will never be in goal. They know their role, are equipped to do that role, and understand how their role contributes to the team's objective.

In this moment, leadership isn't embodied in a single individual – it's a process. The team knows the goal (no pun intended this time), understands their roles, and adapts instinctively to meet changing circumstances. Leadership emerges from action, not authority.

A similar approach is used by the US Navy SEALS. The primary special operations forces of the US Navy are renowned for their ability to operate in all environments (e.g., the name is derived from SEa, Air and Land) and are trained for a range of missions, including direct action raids, counterterrorism and

---

[6] Soccer for the American readers.

reconnaissance. Within the SEAL teams, there are various specialised roles, such as breachers, snipers, communicators, and assault specialists. Each role requires unique skills and training to contribute to the overall mission.

Prior to an operation, there is vertical leadership: The squad members are chosen, the objectives identified, mission strategy is created etc. Post-operation, vertical leadership processes debrief the incursion, perform lessons learned and recognise performance against the agreed mission parameters and objectives.

During the mission, a dynamic leadership approach is utilised, where members flex between leader and follower positions and relationships, dependent on the situation.

When approaching the beachhead, the logistics expert might be the leader. On reaching the beach and discovering mines, the ordinance technician takes the leadership mantle. Approaching the target location, it might be a designated marksman leading from a sniping position or a breacher (a specialist in forcing entry into fortified locations) that is calling the shots. On breaching, the point man heads the team. Whilst some of these decisions might have been agreed in the pre-operation vertical leadership session, the situation and reactions in real-time are what determines the relationships and approaches on the ground.

In this approach – whether on a football pitch or a SEAL operation – leaders are not seen as individuals in charge of followers, but as members of a community of practice. Each contributes their skills in pursuit of the group's shared goal, adapting their approach and contribution based on the situation, relationships and other members' capabilities. When organisations ignore these principles and cling rigidly to the pyramid, they often sacrifice responsiveness and squander their people's potential.

Of course, in both SEAL teams and sports teams, there may still be underlying hierarchies or formal roles. But the essence of leadership in these moments is not positional power, but responsiveness, relevance, and contribution to purpose.

This is the key differentiator between traditional (pyramid) leadership and shared practices: Vertical leadership focuses on achieving the goal through a set method. Shared leadership focuses on refining the method in service of a shared goal. Rather than the leader being the enabler for the direction, output and approach, the team is motivated by common purpose, supported by an environment of trust. Leadership emerges from team members through collaboration and shared objective.

It's the same approach that occurs in families. Depending on the situation, context and the family member's individual capabilities and experiences, the person taking charge can – and does – flex between members. In some situations, it might be a parent that is providing direction, guidance and informing the appropriate behaviours. But when the Wi-Fi router isn't connecting, their leadership might not be suitable, and we might see the youngest household member step up to the plate.

This approach appears innate and instinctive. We can infer that we're wired for this style of leadership. So why isn't it utilised more frequently in organisations? In a word: trust.

This kind of leadership – shared, situational, purpose-driven – can only thrive in an environment where people trust one another to play their part. Without that trust, we revert to command-and-control, even when it's ill-suited to the work.

Trust plays a foundational role in inter-human relationships. It is a key variable within the research into the proposed model of leadership, and it is deserving of much more attention than we can give it in this chapter. In fact, it underpins whether culture can truly act as a leader in its own right.

For now, let's recap on our understanding of leadership and the common themes that have appeared through our plethora of models and approaches.

Leadership provides direction. Without it – a goal, mission or vision – members bring their own interpretations of where they're heading and end up working toward different ends.

Leadership provides the approach. It sets the terms for how we do things around here. Whether that's a command-and-control type environment, where every action is signed in triplicate before being completed or a laissez-faire style, where group members have more control over their workings without intervention or interfering from external parties, leaders explicitly and implicitly nurture this agreed psychological contract between individuals and the group.

If individuals' interpretations of those acceptable approaches are congruent with each other, we have a culture: the shared behaviours of the group, which inform how we get things done here and help the group to survive.

In our new paradigm, it is proposed that culture becomes the leader. But, like leadership, culture has many definitions and interpretations, both academically and in the applied world.

If culture is to be the leader, it follows that this is a good place to open the discussion on how we define culture, whether there are good, bad or even toxic cultures, and how influential it can be in our organisations.

02

THE CULTURAL CURRENT:
The silent social pressure

"Well. I guess I just followed the crowd at chow time, sir."

Corporal Jeffery Barnes
A Few Good Men (1992)

Imagine a workplace that's energetic and inviting. Everyone's smiling as a puppy bounds around the office. Managers high-five employees as they arrive. On Wednesdays, a huge inflatable cash cube machine – a grab-a-grand booth – is wheeled out, and the week's top performers get to spend thirty wind-whipped seconds snatching gift vouchers out of the air. Everyone dresses casually and Fridays end early so that everyone can head to the bar together.

Does this sound like a place you'd love to work? Congratulations! You're a terrible funeral director!

This is a common challenge with our view of culture: the perception that culture equals fun and happiness. It might *be* fun. But that's not – and shouldn't be – the prime motive of culture or a cultural change programme.

It's often seen as something separate from business and strategy. Something that holds its own lane and is thought about after other more "businessy" considerations have been discussed, such as marketing, operational efficiencies and EBITDA. The famous and (again) misquoted Peter Drucker[7] statement of "culture eats strategy for breakfast" is held up to highlight both the importance of culture and reinforces its position as separate from strategy and business.

But this is incorrect. What Drucker actually said, in an article for the Wall Street Journal in March 1991, was that "culture – no matter how defined – is singularly persistent."

Drucker's published statement offers more nuance. Granted, it's not quite as soundbitey as the breakfast example, but it does provide more practical guidance. By repeating the non-existent quote, we are in danger of viewing the dynamics of organisations as being over-simplified and the result of culture alone: i.e., If we fix the culture, the strategy will follow.

This, too, isn't quite accurate. In the same article, Drucker also laments a similar frustration that "Changing the corporate culture has become the latest management fad. Every business magazine carries articles about it."

---

[7] Technically, this quote is misattributed to Drucker. The original was: *"Efficiency is doing things right; effectiveness is doing the right things."* There's no evidence Peter Drucker ever said the more popular variant. The Drucker Institute has no record of it in any of his works, talks, or interviews. The actual author is unknown, though some credit long-time GE CEO Jack Welch.

This does seem to be a familiar trend even today. Any search of any business article resource will return countless examples of culture and its importance. But these are often framed as if culture change is a panacea. It's the "biggest competitive advantage", "the secret sauce to success" and, as one Forbes' article claims, "you cannot connect and elevate leadership" without focusing completely on the impact and influence of culture.

These statements have some truth to them. Culture generally – and people specifically – are the source of our biggest competitive advantage. But it's not the whole picture and many of these resources miss the point: A corporate culture is worth absolutely nothing unless it is aligned with the company's strategy. Why would an organisation adopt a set of values, assumptions and behaviours unless these also supported its vision?

STRATEGY. STRATEGY. STRATEGY.

In this sense, strategy comes first. Only after we've clearly identified our strategy (the purpose, goals, resources, and channels) can we ask what assumptions, behaviours and values will maximise the possibilities of that strategy's success. Strategy sets the direction. Culture lubricates the movement toward that direction.

Culture without strategy is a slippery mess. Actions and decisions end up unaligned to any clear intention. That might sound fun – indeed it often is – but ultimately it is futile and unsustainable. The business world is paved with the remains of organisations that focused on creating great places to work, but haemorrhaged productivity, profits and people.

On the other hand, strategy without culture is a slog. It's a gruelling hike up the mountain, in measurable pursuit of onwards and upwards; of performance and deliverables. But it barely stops to consider the impact on the hikers, their equipment, their morale, or whether this approach would encourage them to climb future mountains.

Culture is strategy's counterweight. If one misaligns with the other, both will fall. They will eat each other for breakfast. The relationship between the two is not linear; it's cyclical and relational. The cultural assumptions feed and push the strategic goals and they, in turn, shape and hone the strategy. Strategy gives culture its *direction*; culture gives strategy its *momentum*.

GOOD OR BAD?

In approaching culture as something that trumps strategy, we miss a vital point: culture is built on our foundational assumptions about our roles and purposes in our world. In turn, they demand behaviours and values that fulfil those roles and purposes. These foundational assumptions are where cultures help or hinder progress.

If we consider a culture that utilises silos to keep groups separate, encourages low transparency across the organisation, and requires narrow, specialist skills (i.e., you won't do much, but you do it well). This culture also encourages hierarchy, clear lines of responsibility, and has documented rules and processes across almost all areas of its operations. Sound bad? That could be a perfect culture for crisis management. It's the type of culture that creates a high-performing armed services.

If you could lift-and-shift that culture to Google, it would reduce (or perhaps even stop) all innovation. At the same time, if you could photocopy Google's move-fast-and-break-things philosophy for innovation into a nation's armed forces, some borders might change.

Instead of viewing culture as good or bad, these foundational assumptions allow us to approach culture as a strategic tool and to pivot our viewpoint to a simple question: Do the behaviours encouraged by this culture increase or decrease the likelihood of the organisation's strategy being achieved? It is the foundation and the direction of travel required – not the words on a wall – that determine if a culture is matched or mismatched.

One practical way of examining these foundational assumptions, and how they connect to the visible and invisible elements of an organisation, is through a model developed by Gerry Johnson and Kevan Scholes.

The Cultural Web offers a way to map and understand the different forces that sustain a culture, making the invisible more visible. Johnson and Scholes identified six interlinked elements that, together, form the organisational paradigm – the shared assumptions about "how things are done around here."

- **Stories**: The narratives people use to describe the organisation's successes, failures, heroes, villains, and defining moments. These reveal what is valued, what is frowned upon, and what kinds of behaviour get remembered.

- **Rituals and Routines**: The daily habits, events, and behaviours that reinforce norms, such as regular meetings, onboarding processes, or recognition ceremonies.

- **Symbols**: The visual or material artefacts that carry meaning: logos, office design, dress codes, or even the language used internally.

- **Organisational Structure**: How authority, communication, and responsibility are distributed; both the official hierarchy and the informal influence networks.

- **Control Systems**: The measurement and reward systems that signal priorities, from KPIs to bonus criteria to performance reviews.

- **Power Structures**: The individuals or groups with the most influence – not always those with the most senior job titles.

At the centre of these sits the paradigm – the deep-rooted, often unspoken worldview that shapes decisions and behaviour. It is this assumption that provides meaning to a culture.

By analysing each element in relation to strategy, leaders can see whether the cultural "web" is supporting or undermining the organisation's direction. For example, a strategy that prizes rapid innovation will falter if control systems reward cautious risk-avoidance, or if stories celebrate meticulous perfectionism over experimentation.

This is where organisations often misinterpret culture and culture change. The focus is on the visible artefacts of the culture (e.g., the structures, control methods, recognition, and rituals etc.), rather than the underlying and foundational assumption: why do we exist and what are we here to achieve.

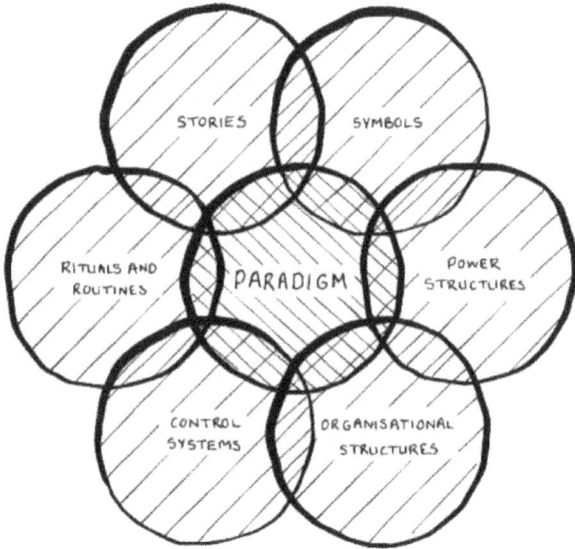

Cultural Web model by Gerry Johnson and Kevan Scholes

When that assumption is misaligned with the strategy, then the behaviours, approaches and decision-making practises will align with the culture first. Culture ends up the more powerful force.

This tension between strategy and cultural assumptions isn't just theoretical. It plays out in vivid ways, sometimes across thousands of employees and millions of customers. Consider the case of Avanti West Coast.

GOING OFF THE RAILS

The customer service on the UK's west coast main line railway was shockingly bad. Over 82% of nearly 3,000 Trustpilot reviewers rated the service from Avanti West Coast as a one-star-out-of-five experience; less than 10% scored a five.

This level of service hadn't always been the norm. When Avanti West Coast took over mainline operating from Virgin Trains in December 2019, Net Promoter Score (a measure of customer satisfaction with a brand) was between 70 and 80 – much higher than the rail industry average of 50. Customer sentiment was high, and train cancellations were low. Virgin were investing in customer experience, and had announced policies that, where there was disruption on the rail network and services were busier than normal, any passengers who couldn't get a seat would get a full refund of their ticket.

On paper, Avanti West Coast and Virgin Trains are almost identical. They operate the same routes with the same trains, under the same procedures, stopping at the same stations. Because staff tenure on the railway is long and their contracts were transferred between employers, many individual employees have worked for both operators. So, why is the customer experience – and the employee experience[8] – so different when everything else appears to be objectively identical? It's the subtle, irresistible influence of the underlying cultural paradigm: the vision and direction of the organisation.

---

[8] At the time of writing, in the 6-years that Avanti West Coast have held the franchise, employees have taken industrial action on eight occasions. During Virgin Trains' 22-year tenure, only one 24-hour strike took place. If you were to meet a Virgin Trains employee in a bar and ask, "Where do you work?", they might proudly reply, "I work for Virgin." The same question from an AWC employee might receive a more detached response: "I work on the railway."

Virgin Trains recognised that no one chose to travel by rail for fun; they were going somewhere. That might be to meet friends, visit family or travel to work. Perhaps it was to go to the airport, a job interview or university. But it certainly wasn't because someone was really in the mood to get on a train. So, they set out to be *the holiday before your holiday*.

With this as the underlying belief, the accepted behaviours, actions, decisions, and approaches encouraged by the culture supported that paradigm. The view was that the customer would own any information. This transparency kept customers informed of connection trains, platforms for their journey and weather reports for destinations. Employee recognition was designed around customer experience feedback. Technology investment was focused on that experience, and ensuring every customer arrived refreshed and ready for their reason for travel.

Avanti West Coast have a different underlying belief. They aim to *run a railway that generates prosperity and pride, right across the nation.* "Prosperity" includes having a fiduciary responsibility to its shareholders and ensuring that they are a safe pair of hands for investors. There's nothing inherently wrong about this belief: AWC is a commercial business and creating return on investment is part of that responsibility. However, the encouraged behaviours and approaches driven by this underlying belief are aligned with a focus on operational effectiveness, efficiency and cost management.

If a customer travelling from London to Manchester fell ill, Virgin Trains might ask the network control office for an emergency stop order for the next station – even though it's an unscheduled stop. AWC, perhaps, would not, as the cost of delay-repay compensation for the other 500 passengers arriving late might outweigh the benefit of customer experience for the poorly traveller.

The underlying paradigm – the implied reason for existing – can completely change an organisation, even when the machinations of the business are identical. It sets the tone for what is tolerated and accepted versus what is not. It encourages or suppresses decisions, risks and actions. Its influence will nudge strategy off-course.

London's Metropolitan Police service's underlying belief is that "We are law enforcement". In May 2023, Police Commissioner Sir Mark Rowley announced that officers would no longer attend emergency calls related to mental health incidents. Whilst there was a public outcry, when we consider the underlying belief, the decision is aligned with their culture – even if we might have personal, moral objections to the decision. That same paradigm shapes other behaviours too, from the disproportionate use of stop-and-search powers on certain demographics to a focus on compliance and control over care and prevention.

How different would the behaviours, actions and decisions of the Met be if that underlying belief were, "We are here for public safety"?

IF IT LOOKS LIKE A DUCK

When we think about culture, it's natural for our minds to go to pizzas, perks and parties. We have dogs in the office, flexible working and standing desks. There's beanbag furniture, full bean coffee, and rewards that make the bean counters proud. Culture, we might feel, is about a great place to work. But that's not quite accurate. What we're really seeing is what psychologists call *artefacts*.

In psychological research, an artefact[9] is something that looks like evidence of a cause but is actually the result of an external distortion. In organisations, we see the same: behaviours or symbols that look like proof of culture but are really caused by something else. For example, we might see smiling individuals in an office and think that the culture encourages employee happiness. However, those smiles may be purely due to us being expected visitors and some enthusiastic line manager encouraging their people to smile. Correlation is rarely causation – and artefacts are rarely evidence of what our culture is subtly influencing.

Artefacts are simple to observe. They show up in behaviours and actions; in language and practices; in risk approaches and in decisions. But observing behaviour in isolation provides poor cultural insight. It's like judging someone's dancing without hearing or understanding the music that's playing.

Within this lies a challenge: In psychological processes, if it looks like a duck, walks like a duck, and quacks like a duck, sometimes it might not be a duck. It might be something else simply demonstrating duck-like behaviours.

Focusing on artefacts as if they were causal results of our underlying cultural influences can be problematic. Causation and

---

[9] Note on "artefacts." In some cultural frameworks – like Edgar Schein's – artefacts refer to visible signs of culture: behaviours, rituals, language, etc. In this chapter, the term is used in its research sense – something that looks like evidence but is actually caused by an external factor.

correlation are not synonyms[10]. This is a phenomenon that has been studied for over a century and is still pertinent today.

QUACKING AWAY

It was one of the most significant manufacturing locations in the United States. Straddling 100 acres and employing over 45,000 people at its height, Western Electric's factory in Cicero, Illinois produced telephones, cables, and transmission and switching equipment for the expanding telecommunications industry.

Employee roles were highly specialised, and their outputs were precisely measured. They needed to be. Punch-and-die tool making is a specialised and precise process. One error could have huge ramifications for a client's timekeeping records and affect their employee wage calculations.

The production line approach to manufacturing was established, but still in its infancy. In 1913 – just ten years prior – the Highland Park Ford Plant had introduced the new technology, which utilised employees in highly-specialised, highly-repetitive and highly-efficient work. In the decade that followed, it had been honed for efficiency across multiple industries. But there was a challenge: that efficiency had started to stall. There was only so much inefficiency that could be removed from the mechanical processes. William J Dickson, head of the Department of Employee Relations at Western Electric, asked for help in understanding how the human processes might be made more effective and improve production.

Dickson approached Elton Mayo. The son of a civil engineer, Mayo was an industrial researcher and a psychologist,

---

[10] Case in point: Everyone who believes that causation and correlation are the same eventually dies.

who had already established himself as an expert in mental philosophy and organisational theory. Mayo sent his research assistant, Fritz Roethlisberger, to undertake the analysis at the Hawthorne plant and to experiment with ways to improve the factory's productivity rates. Between 1924 and 1927, many experiments were undertaken, investigating factors such as rest periods, shift length, payment systems, and management approaches. One of the first experiments considered production line lighting, to identify if there was an optimum luminosity or brightness for productive work.

An interesting – and unexpected – result occurred. When lightbulb brightness was increased, productivity increased. When the light source was dimmed, productivity also increased. And when there was no change to the lighting levels, but researchers had been present in the factory, productivity – you guessed it – increased. This became known as the Hawthorne Effect; named for the factory where the experiments took place.

This effect is often used to show the impact of observing employees. Making a small change in an organisation or team (i.e., changing a manager, introducing a new process etc.) can result in a small improvement in performance or behaviours. But the spike is not sustainable, and performance returns to its pre-change level shortly afterwards. It's also a litmus test for leaders and consultants who might suggest changes to a business' processes and practises, claim the short-lived performance improvement benefits, and have left the organisation before the return to pre-Hawthorne Effect levels.

Artefacts might be evidence of our culture, but they aren't the culture itself, are open to bias and might be instructed behaviour – such as the manager letting their employees know that a researcher is visiting the factory.

These artefact behaviours return to a base level. That base level is likely to be the cultural norm for that behaviour. Rather than cultural change, this is climate change.

Climate refers to the shared perceptions and feelings employees have about their workplace at a specific point in time, while culture is a deeper, more enduring set of shared values, beliefs, and norms that shape behaviour over time. Climate is more easily changed and influenced by immediate factors like leadership style and recent (even intraday) events. Culture is more deeply rooted and evolves more slowly.

Behaviours and approaches that are culturally informed are influenced and sustained by the underlying belief. This is an often unwritten, implied assumption about the nature of the social group and why it exists. In organisational terms, we might call this a vision. That vision provides the direction; the cliché North Star for us to head towards.

We can then think of culture as being like the wind. Though it is invisible, it's effects are real and powerful. When it's blowing with you, it's plain sailing. But when it's blowing across or against you, everything is a little bit harder.

But, for that cultural wind to blow with you, you must know where you're trying to get to. This is why many culture change programmes fail. Not because of a lack resources, effort or imperative, but because of a focus on the artefacts instead of the underlying belief. Changing our organisational structure, management layers or processes without changing that belief means that cultural wind will soon blow us off course – if, indeed, we recognised what that course was to begin with.

Thinking of culture not as a nice-to-have afterthought, but as a core strategic partnership, is fundamental to leadership. Culture is the group's behaviours, which should increase the likelihood of the organisation's strategy succeeding. The behaviours of a successful Fintech are different to the behaviours of a successful funeral directors – even when both sets of employees really enjoy a pizza.

Those pizzas might help to make a great place to work; as might perks, puppies and pension contributions. But culture is not about creating a great place to work; it's about creating a place where great work is done.

When great work is done, purpose and passion intersect. Individuals feel that what we do matters, that we make a difference, and that we are working toward something meaningful. This, in turn, creates a great place to work. Starting with creating a great place to work might result in great work; but this is correlation, rather than causation. Many great places struggle to deliver great work.

Culture can be the wind in our sails or a storm that drives us onto the rocks. What happens when cultures become mismatched and head towards toxicity? And how can organisations find their way back to safer waters?

LEADERSHIP AND TOXICITY

Despite two centuries of debate and countless theories, one thing has remained consistent: we've always assumed leadership requires a person in the role. Yet culture – something that feels less tangible – often exerts even greater power over behaviour than a supervisor ever could.

We recognise that our own behaviours, decisions, approach to risk, language, and our actions are all informed by the social norms of groups that we share membership with. The cultural influence on the group (and we ourselves) cannot be understated. Culture establishes what is acceptable and safe; it suppresses the improper. It encourages how we get things done around here. Humans are built for group conformity and culture informs us how to behave when the leader is not in the room – which is most of the time.

Yet our views of culture are skewed. It is associated with fun and frivolity – or described as toxic, when it doesn't feel happy/fulfilling/[insert superlative here]. But workplaces are ecosystems. What's toxic for one person might be energising for another. Some thrive in the urgency of an investment bank; others feel suffocated by it. A start-up's chaos might exhilarate one engineer and exhaust another. A culture cannot be toxic to all any more so than a tree can be toxic to every animal in the forest.

X (formerly Twitter) has been publicly derided as a toxic workplace. However, Elon Musk has been clear about his expectations of employees, mandating a 40-hour-a-week return-to-office approach, and explicitly asking employees to "work long hours and at a high level of intensity." Only employees that had "exceptional performance" would be considered as "passing the grade." The edict was equally explicit: Commit to the new demands or find a new job[11].

---

[11] Note: There is a separate conversation about whether a culture is appropriate for what your organisation is attempting to achieve. Does the culture encourage the behaviours that support your organisational strategy? With the X/Twitter example, Musk is walking his talk. The day-to-day experience is aligned with what the organisation claims is expected. However, it could be argued that this encourages behaviours that are individualistic and competitive, which reduce

After the cultural shift towards these "hardcore" work expectations under Musk's leadership, many decried the environment as toxic. And for many people, it absolutely was. But for others – those who shared those values around long hours, relentless focus, and radical risk-taking – it became a place of belonging. For these individuals, it isn't toxic; it's thrilling.

What creates the sense of "toxicity" is not the work itself. It's the gap between what is promised (or perceived as promised) and what is actually delivered. It's the difference between what we say we're about and what the reality the day-to-day experience reflects.

In psychology, this is often referred to as the psychological contract. It's an unwritten, emotional agreement between an individual and their employer. It's the understanding – sometimes explicit, but more often unspoken – of what both sides owe each other. When the psychological contract is honoured, even demanding environments feel fair. People know what they're signing up for. When it's broken, even the best perks can't compensate for the emotional breach.

This is why workplaces that preach collaboration but reward ruthless individualism might feel particularly poisonous. Or why organisations that trumpet "work-life balance" while quietly expecting weekend emails create such deep resentment. The damage isn't just about workload or hours. It's about incongruence between the internal tension we feel when our values and our environment no longer align.

Leon Festinger's *Cognitive Dissonance Theory* explains that human beings experience psychological discomfort when

---

collaboration and innovation – two factors that are likely important in a tech company their behaviours conflict with their beliefs. This incongruity fuels the internal tension that drives withdrawal, cynicism, and eventually, burnout.

This dissonance isn't just about values. It also violates basic psychological needs. According to *Self-Determination Theory*, people need autonomy, relatedness, and competence to thrive. When cultures say they "support autonomy" but act controlling or they claim to be "safe communities" but encourage individualistic competition, this violates a deep psychological need and can be interpreted as toxicity.

Consider individuals working in Human Resources. Generally, HR practitioners expect to be creating places that are people-focused, safe and fair. That's their understanding of the psychological contract. But the reality is that the role is often more focused on protecting the employer, mitigating risks to them – rather than the employee – and managing reactively. It's no wonder HR teams often face some of the highest rates of stress and burnout. It's why they often move from company to company as teams; there's safety in numbers.

The problem isn't toxicity; the problem is (mis)alignment. We each experience and process the world differently. Psychologists call this *subjective humanism*, which emphasises the individual's unique and personal interpretation of their experiences and reality. It focuses on the subjective meaning an individual gives to their world, rather than adhering to objective, universal truths. Everyone sees the world differently.

This isn't just philosophy. Research into *Person-Organisation Fit* consistently shows that alignment between personal and organisational values predicts engagement, performance, and retention, while misalignment predicts frustration, withdrawal, and attrition.

How we experience the world is unique to each of us – including how we experience toxicity and environments that we might call toxic. The real challenge for organisations isn't to be "non-toxic". That's a meaningless aim, given that we each experience it differently. A better approach is to be clear and honest about who we are, what we value, and how we operate – and then to actually demonstrate those values.

This approach takes intentionality and awareness. It takes effort. Many of the incongruencies between those values and the reality are unintentional and innocent. Culture lives in these unspoken norms: what gets praised, punished or ignored. As social animals, our brains are constantly searching for cues from our environment and others around us to determine what's safe, acceptable and allowed.

These norms are often subtle, but they are hugely influential. They're what culture practitioners are trained to spot, identify and address. Like a medical doctor noticing the nuance between symptoms and the over-looked signs of a condition, culture experts identify patterns in these symptoms and bring clarity and purpose to the approach to address the root causes of those symptoms. Purposeful organisational culture requires clarity.

To create clarity, we need to intentionally surface those hidden norms and focus on what encourages behaviours that support the organisation's goals and strategy.

LIVED, NOT LAMINATED

Culture is created by everyone within the group. It's a myth that culture is solely created by the leadership – but leaders are incredibly influential in setting the tone for what is and isn't acceptable. Leaders illuminate or cast shadows on our cultural panorama; as MIT Sloan's professor Edgar Schein pointed out, what leaders focus on gets culturally amplified. How leaders praise, punish or ignore behaviours sends powerful signals. When these signals conflict with the organisation's stated values, the values become distorted and are translated into unintended languages.

Values are lived, not laminated. They must be more than posters. They must shape day-to-day behaviours and should be exemplified in the actions, decisions and approaches of our leaders. For example, if we value collaboration, do the reward and recognition mechanics identify individual contribution or team results? Leaders model the invisible rules – for better or for worse. If someone demonstrates a values-aligned behaviour, do we actively recognise (and reinforce) it, or do we ignore it because "that's part of their job"?

But we must also be cognisant that values are not virtues. We often treat values as universally good. But they are subjective, context-dependent, and sometimes even in tension with one another. A value like honesty might be admirable. But, in the wrong context, it can strain relationships. If your partner asks how they look in a new outfit that you feel is unflattering, do you keep to that value or show diplomacy? Values must be interpreted through human nuance, not moral absolutes.

Similarly, having a value of "respect" might seem uncontroversial. But whose respect are we referring to? In New

Zealand, it is a cultural faux pas to lean or sit on a surface where food is served. Yet how many modern UK office designs have standing tables to have informal 121 discussions over a quick sandwich?

A friend[12] has a core value about his dependability. Raised as the eldest child in a single-parent family, he was always told that there was nothing he couldn't do. He should rely on himself, carry others and be there for friends. Loyalty and dependability are paramount. There are times when this value is a superpower; particularly in tough situations where grit and resilience are required, or when others need his support. But it also makes it much more difficult for him to ask for help. There are many occasions when he argues with himself in the shower for taking on too much and becoming emotionally stretched. We cannot fill from an empty cup and this value is not always a positive in every context.

When considering organisational values, it is not the words on the wall that are important. In fact, merely having values as single words or simple, subjective statements can be counterproductive. They can highlight what we don't currently do, providing a glimpse into an optimistic future state of the organisation. If a company espouses a value of "collaboration" or "teamwork", there's a high likelihood that the company does not currently demonstrate either value. In one study, nearly 90% of corporations cited "ethical behaviour" or the word "trust" in their communications about their organisational values. If an organisation has trust as a value, it probably has larger challenges to deal with.

---

[12] This is definitely not the author. Definitely.

A case in point is Boeing. Once the largest commercial aircraft producer in the world, boasting a market share of over 90%, Boeing set the standard for aviation safety and quality (another Boeing value), and followed their guiding principle to "do the right thing." Even with competition from French competitor Airbus, Boeing dominated the industry throughout the 80s and 90s. Then came the merger.

In 1997, after delays by the European Commission in approving the merger, Boeing joined with McDonnell Douglas. Almost immediately, it became clear that there was a clash of cultures between the two organisations. Boeing's engineers – who valued trust and doing the right thing – found themselves at odds with the operational efficiency, profitability and accounting focus of their McDonnell Douglas counterparts. Corporate headquarters was separated from the Seattle-based production line and relocated 2,000 miles away to Chicago. Ethics and safety seemed to be of less importance, as the internal pressures from supervisors and external influences in the market focused production on cost-saving and speed of delivery.

Many highlighted safety risks. Ed Pierson raised concerns. The former US Naval officer joined Boeing in 2008 and became a senior manager at the Renton factory in 2015. Pierson highlighted a shortage of parts and test equipment for legally required assessments. But, with work backlogs growing to the point that unfinished aircraft were being stored in the employee car park, his protestations fell on deaf ears. He pleaded for the production line to be shut down to allow for issues to be addressed. Senior executives refused – despite Pierson highlighting that military operations had been halted for far less.

"The military is not a profit-making organisation", was the reasoning from senior management. In this statement, we see the unwritten norms and true values manifest. Trust, safety and quality were to take a backseat to profitability, efficiency and delivery schedules.

Two months after Pierson retired in August 2018, Lion Air Flight 610, travelling from Jakarta to Pangkal Pinang, plunged into the Java Sea, 13-minutes after take-off. The incident killed all 189 people on board. Just seventeen weeks later, Ethiopian Airlines Flight 302 also crashed, just 6-minutes after take-off. 157 people perished aboard the same model plane: the Boeing 737 Max 8. The 737 Max fleet was grounded, whilst investigations into the causes were conducted.

In the subsequent investigations, a new software function in the flight control system – the Manoeuvring Characteristics Augmentation System (MCAS) – was identified as the cause of both incidents. MCAS software was intended to protect pilots from inadvertently flying at too steep an angle and stalling the aircraft by pushing the nose down. When a sensor failed, this system forced the aircraft towards the ground.

Crucially, this new software had been intentionally omitted from Boeing's operating manuals and training. For at least a year prior to the Lion Air crash, Boeing were already aware of the issue with MCAS and with a secondary system concern that would warn of sensor failing. But, by withholding the information and categorising the new software as an update rather than as a new system, the Federal Aviation Administration's certification of the aircraft was expedited, allowing Boeing to deliver aircraft to customers more quickly.

Profitability was deemed a higher priority than pilot awareness and training.

Throughout the 737 Max 8 affair (and to the present day), the values of "Trust" and "Safety & Quality" remain emblazoned on Boeing's walls. But, in their push to maximise sales, reduce costs and increase the speed of delivery to the client, Boeing had strayed from the values that they had previously lived and breathed. Demonstrating their values had brought them success; Disregarding them cost more than money. The accidents and 20-month grounding cost Boeing an estimated $20 billion in fines, compensation and legal fees, with an additional $60 billion lost from over 1,200 cancelled orders and 347[13] people lost their lives.

WALKING THE TALK

When organisations stop walking their talk – when the day-to-day actions don't reflect the vision and espoused values – cultures can drift away from their purposeful alignment to the strategy. However, their influence on how we do things around here remains and can actively work against the organisation's identity.

When Amazon acquired Whole Foods for $13.7 billion in 2017, it was hailed as a bold fusion: the precision of data-driven operations meeting a values-led, decentralised retail culture. But the collision of identities that followed revealed how even well-resourced integrations can unravel when cultural misalignment goes unaddressed.

Whole Foods, once celebrated for its decentralised, high-trust, and employee-empowered ethos, was quickly reshaped

---

[13] In addition to the 189 people aboard Lion Air Flight 610 and 157 aboard Ethiopian Airlines Flight 302, a rescue diver died during recovery operations in the Java Sea.

under Amazon's tight, process-driven model. Reductions in perks like gainsharing and employee recognition, tighter central control over inventory and shelving, and the imposition of compliance checks turned former team cohesion into frustration and disengagement. Employees described a loss of meaning and autonomy, with many saying "Amazon has changed the company so much that I can't recognise Whole Foods anymore"

Morale plunged. Benefits vanished. Store managers faced a tide of resignations, as employee benefits and flexibility disappeared. Amazon's scale and systems enabled lower prices and improved logistics, but at the cost of diluting the culture that had once driven customer loyalty – and those former strengths eroded quickly. The breakdown in alignment led to employee disillusionment and rising unionisation efforts, including the first successful vote at a Philadelphia store in January 2025, where workers cited understaffing, shrinking hours, and declining benefits as major concerns. Whole Foods ultimately lost its place on Fortune's "Best Companies to Work For" list for the first time in two decades – symbolic of a broader erosion of its original identity.

When values lose meaning or consistency, they don't just fade – they can backfire. In misaligned cultures, those values can also become weaponised. One blue chip organisation in the Techcoms sector advocated for a value of "speed". The encouraged behaviours were intended to stun customers with the speed of execution, action, and resolution of issues. But, in the day-to-day lived experience of employees – where culture is created, nurtured, developed, and realised – the value quickly became a complaint. When a laptop password reset took an hour, cynical comments such as "I thought we operated with speed around here?" could be heard. Complaints about project delivery times, bonus announcements and even how quickly ID card-activated security gates opened to allow employees access to the building all became normalised. A well-intentioned value had become a basis for criticism.

This is not to say that values do not have a place in organisations. By recognising their subjectivity, individual interpretation and contextual benefits, values can provide the behavioural direction that helps the organisational climate and also provide a common language to articulate what is and what isn't acceptable within that environment.

So, what's the alternative? If leadership isn't about telling others what to do, what is it really about?

FROM FOLLOW ME TO FARMING

The true role of leadership is not to lead people, but to lead environments. To model and create the optimum conditions for success, so that individuals can utilise their strengths towards a shared objective. This view is similar to how a farmer operates.

A farmer doesn't grow the fruit; the plants do that themselves. Instead, the farmer starts with understanding each plant, the soil it's in, the nourishment it receives, and then helping it thrive based on those circumstances. It's not glamorous. Often, it's the mundane, daily, repetitive care – not a quarterly burst of watering or pruning – that makes the biggest impact. Any farmer will tell you that successful cultivation doesn't start with the fruit (the outputs); it starts with the environment. Leadership is the same.

When leaders create the wrong environment – one that's not conducive to the plants thriving – crops can fail, weeds can grow and trying to harvest anything useful becomes futile. But when leaders are unclear on the environment or their behaviours and approaches don't demonstrate the agreed values and uphold the psychological contract, the incongruence can become toxic for individuals.

Toxicity is not a failure of kindness. It's often a failure of alignment and clarity. When leaders shape environments where values and behaviours match purpose, culture becomes a true strategic asset and people engagement[14] is a side effect.

ENGAGEMENT AS A RESPONSIBILITY

When discussing people engagement – particularly in an organisational context – it is often framed as a lever for business: driving productivity, innovation, and performance. Research supports this. Higher engagement correlates with stronger results: from higher sales and revenue growth to fewer accidents and reduced absenteeism. But the impact of purposeful engagement extends well beyond the balance sheet.

Studies show that when individuals feel their work is meaningful and connected, they are more likely to contribute positively to their communities, from volunteering to small acts of neighbourliness (i.e., putting bins out, taking in parcels or trimming a shared hedge). By contrast, a lack of fulfilment at work is associated with higher rates of domestic violence, mental health interventions, and family breakdown.

Engagement isn't just a business differentiator. Organisations "rent" employees from their families and their

---

[14] I prefer 'people' rather than 'employee' engagement, as the language is more inclusive. Senior leaders – including C-suite – are also impacted by purposefully engaging and aligned cultures.

communities. When they keep their promises, people are returned stronger, more connected, more alive. When they break them, the damage ripples far beyond quarterly reports, and into classrooms, kitchens, and communities.

Now that we've completed our tour of the history of leadership and the influence of culture, in the next chapter we'll consider a new model of leadership. One that respects the dynamic relationship between culture and strategy. This model builds on the importance of a cohesive vision and congruent behaviours in creating purposeful cultures, and shows how culture itself can do what no single leader ever could: guide the group consistently – not only when no one is watching, but when no one is instructing.

03

LOOK TO THE STARS:
Creating constellations

"When the best leader's work is done the people say,
'We did it ourselves.'"

Lao Tzu
Tao Te Ching (6ᵗʰ Century BCE)

Before the compass and the sextant, sailors relied on the stars. Not just a single bright point in the sky, but entire constellations.

Each star had its purpose: some marked true north, others signalled the changing seasons, and some warned of hidden coastlines. No single star was sufficient to find safe passage. It was the relationships between them – the patterns they formed – that guided the voyage.

Imagine leadership working in the same way. Instead of one fixed point directing every move, it can emerge as a constellation: a shifting network of people whose strengths become visible at different moments, depending on where you are on the journey. In the right environment, this distribution of responsibility and accountability can be incredibly powerful and fulfilling for everyone involved. We are greater than the sum of our parts.

Traditional leadership models evolved in relatively stable times. But the challenges facing organisations today are more complex, interdependent, and unpredictable than those of even a generation ago. Climate change, global pandemics, rapid technological disruption, and political populism cross borders and disciplines. No single leader, however capable, can carry the insight or legitimacy needed to respond to them alone. Leadership that emerges from the collective is better suited to navigate this kind of systemic turbulence.

This is where Constellation Leadership departs from simple distributed practice. The problems leaders face are less like chess – where a single grandmaster can outthink the opponent – and more like ecosystems, where countless factors interact. Constellation Leadership treats culture as the binding fabric that allows a group to draw on its full range of intelligence. The strength is not in one heroic leader but in the collective pattern, where expertise and perspective surface when most needed.

In Constellation Leadership, each professional is recognised as an expert – a star in their own right – surrounded by other professional stars. The approach is to create dynamic groupings of these stars – constellations – assembled purposefully to share and achieve a goal. At any given moment, a star's particular strengths may come to the forefront, guiding the group when they are most needed.

Just as sailors needed not only stars but the knowledge to interpret them, Constellation Leadership relies on something deeper: a cultural fabric that helps individuals align, trust and act as one when the moment demands. Today's emerging research builds on studies into distributed leadership and explores the conditions that allow the leadership function itself to be filled by that purposeful, catalysing cultural fabric. This is not an exercise in academic vanity; the benefits of distributed models consistently outperform more traditional approaches across every HR output and measure, including team cohesion and consensus, confidence, trust, and levels of member satisfaction.

While Constellation Leadership introduces something new, it doesn't appear freshly formed from nowhere. It shares important foundations with distributed leadership, a model that has already reshaped how many teams think about power and accountability.

Distributed leadership is defined as the practice that emerges in the interactions between leaders and followers, rather than being a function of the leader's actions alone. Unlike vertical models, performance is a method, not a goal. The model asks, "What can I do to contribute towards the goal?" rather than "Let's achieve that goal."

It is underpinned by a shared strategy and objective, which orientate the group. Usually, an external steering committee determine the objective(s) and provide strategic guidance/support, and an in-group Chair ensures the smooth execution of the team's responsibilities.

This description is unwieldy and overly academic. In practical terms, distributed leadership occurs relatively frequently in larger organisations – though we might not recognise it by this name. An example might be a *Scrum* within Agile project management methodology.

STARRING IN A PROJECT

Broadly, project management approaches can be divided into two families: *linear and sequential* or *iterative and flexible*.

Linear approaches, such as the Waterfall model, are structured: each phase is completed before the next begins. It's like an assembly line in a car factory (i.e., body assembly, engine installation, painting etc.), with each stage finished in sequence. This works well when the end product is clearly defined and unlikely to change.

Iterative project management, such as Agile, breaks work into shorter cycles with continuous feedback. This approach is better suited to projects where requirements are unclear or likely to evolve. Waterfall offers a clear roadmap and predictable timelines, making it ideal for large-scale change with fixed definitions and well-defined phases. Agile, on the other hand, delivers faster changes, early risk detection, and improved stakeholder satisfaction, as the close, continuous involvement of customers ensures the final product aligns with their needs and expectations.

In Agile methodology, iterative milestones are delivered by a small group of subject matter experts – a Scrum team – in short cycles called Sprints. A Sprint typically lasts one, two, or four weeks. During this time, the team works from a fixed to-do list (the sprint backlog) agreed at the start of the cycle. No additional requests are added once the sprint begins, which helps focus effort, avoid scope creep, and ensure efficient delivery.

Crucially, the Scrum team determines what goes into the sprint backlog. They choose their own goals from the broader product backlog, aligning them with the project's overall priorities. It's like the team stepping into a room, closing the door, and working uninterrupted until the sprint ends, emerging only when the work is ready to be reviewed.

Selecting team members, deciding the deliverables, agreeing on working practices, and playing to individual strengths during the sprint are all decisions made within the team. In this sense, leadership during a sprint is distributed.

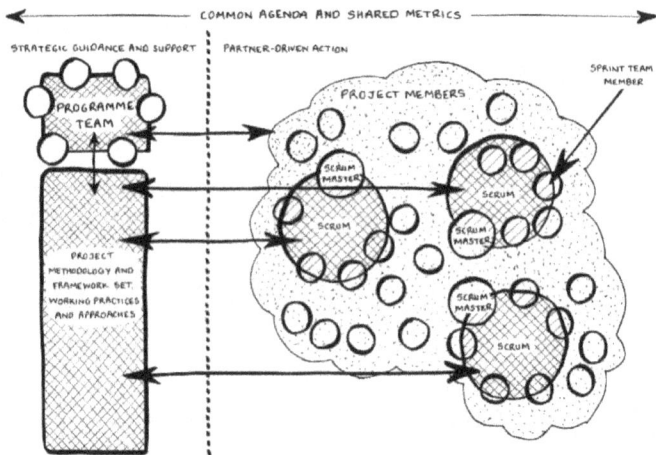

Example of the Distributed Leadership within an Agile Scrum context

Overall responsibility for the project sits with the Product Owner, who liaises with programme stakeholders to establish priorities and define requirements. But once a sprint begins, the Product Owner steps back. A temporary leader – the Scrum Master – ensures the agreed methodology is followed, supports the team, and protects them from disruption.

Before the sprint begins, leadership follows a traditional, vertical pattern: the Product Owner works with the Scrum team to agree membership, objectives, success measures, and duration.

After the sprint concludes, this vertical structure returns for review, reflection, and backlog planning.

Inside the sprint, however, leadership shifts into a distributed form. Here, decision-making is collective and anchored to the pre-agreed objectives, and leadership becomes a shared responsibility, shaped by the expertise of the team members and supported by the Scrum Master's servant leadership facilitation. The Scrum Master's role is not to direct, but to enable the team's autonomy and protect the conditions for collaboration.

Another example might be our previously suggested soccer match. When a free kick is given on the edge of the opponent's 18-yard box, there is no discussion between the team players. Each member knows who the star is for that moment – the person with the most suitable experience, skills and attributes for taking the kick.

In this scenario, leadership isn't formally assigned but emerges organically. Each player understands who will step forward, because the team has built implicit trust and clarity about roles, and recognises – often without explicit instruction – who is most suitable in that moment. Leadership during the match has become distributed.

While distributed leadership provides a powerful framework for collective action, Constellation Leadership takes this further. Here, culture itself becomes the guiding force that determines which strengths shine when. This is possible due to a variety of factors, including levels of team competency and trust, group membership, and individual capability – factors that we'll examine in more detail in the research discussion.

WHEN STARS ALIGN AND SHINE

Constellation Leadership has no Scrum Master; no in-group Chair; no steering committee. There is no traditional leader position within the team. Instead, the group orient around an objective, determined through their shared interpretation of the organisation's vision, purpose and/or goal. This shared interpretation forms the underlying cultural paradigm: the reason for the group's existence and purpose, which influences the behaviours, decisions and approaches within the constellation.

Just as the stars in the night sky shift subtly over time, so too do the constellations of leadership within a team evolve. Leadership is not a fixed role assigned to a single individual but a fluid and dynamic pattern, with different members stepping forward at different moments to guide the group. One star may shine brightly during the problem-defining phase, another during execution, while others may take the lead in connecting perspectives or managing conflict. This shifting constellation is not random but emerges from a foundation of trust, clarity of purpose, and shared cultural norms.

Such fluidity demands self-awareness and adaptability from all team members. The ability to recognise when to lead, when to support, and when to step back requires a culture that embraces flexibility without ego. This emergent flow of leadership strengthens the team's resilience, resiliency[15], and

---

[15] In English, resilience and resiliency are synonyms. They are separated here to describe two different facets of the same word separately: the resistance to trauma and its impact (resilience), and the speed of response to that trauma or impact (resiliency). It can be conceptualised as resilience being the natural resting heart rate and resiliency being the heart rate recovery time to that resting level after exertion.

capacity to navigate complexity, enabling it to respond swiftly to new challenges or changes in direction.

To understand why this model succeeds where traditional hierarchical leadership might falter, it helps to view teams through the lens of systems thinking. Teams are complex adaptive systems where leadership is an emergent property arising from the interactions among many individuals, rather than the directive of a single leader.

Like a flock of birds moving in harmony without a designated leader, leadership in a constellation emerges from ongoing local interactions – conversations, decisions, collaborations – that collectively shape the group's path. The culture and shared goals act as navigational forces, guiding the team while allowing space for individual initiative and innovation.

This approach depends on clear boundaries and shared norms to maintain coherence. Without a guiding cultural fabric, distributed leadership risks descending into fragmentation or inertia. But with those cultural conditions in place, the team self-organises, continuously adapting and innovating in response to its environment.

In other applied leadership models, this underpinning cultural belief is rarely explicit. Instead, the objective or target (i.e., a specific measure, key performance indicator or outcome) is identified, and its delivery becomes the reason for the group's direction. However, individual group members will bring their own subjective interpretation of not only *how* those specific goals should be achieved but *why* they should be achieved. The objective's motive is open to misinterpretation – even when the objective is explicit and specific.

In larger groups with different responsibilities, resources or contributions towards the objective, these (mis)interpretations can naturally encourage siloed behaviours. This is because we're wired to be energy efficient.

THE LAZY APE

Our brain comprises only 2% of our body weight but uses over 20% of the energy we consume. Anyone that's tracked their calorie consumption with a smart watch will notice that you often use more calories during sleep than when you do during exercise. Your brain is a hungry organ. But it evolved in a time of scarcity and has remained relatively unchanged since. That evolutionary wiring is designed for a calorie-deficit, hand-to-mouth, life-on-the-savannah existence and our biases act as mental shortcuts that help conserve energy.

The late Nobel Prize winning Israeli-American psychologist Daniel Kahneman termed these cognitive shortcuts Heuristics. On the surface, these approaches to data, stimuli and problem solving might feel pragmatic and objective because they are "good enough" most of the time. Psychologists refer to this as *face validity*.

Validity (in all its research forms) is about confirming that what we're claiming to measure is actually what is being measured. For example, if you were to ask, "Do you agree that our company is the best place to work?", you might think that the answers would indicate that your company is or isn't the best place to work. However, there are three core issues with the question from a researcher viewpoint.

Firstly, it's leading. The phraseology encourages respondents to answer positively, leading to a response bias.

Secondly, it's vague. The term "best" is subjective and can mean different things to different people. Is it best salary, culture, leadership style? Finally, the scope is limited. It assumes that the respondent will evaluate the company as a whole, rather than their local area, line manager, team or network. Psychologists would say that the question has low construct validity and content validity but has high face validity[16].

Face validity occurs when something seems correct or credible on the surface – even when it's not objectively true. It refers to the degree to which an assessment or test appears, at a glance, to measure the variable or construct that it claims to measure. In other words, face validity is about appearance, not accuracy. A tool can feel intuitively right while being technically or empirically flawed.

We have over 170 cognitive biases that have been identified, studied and understood. Yet psychologists still don't fully understand how the interplay between these, our personalities, social norms, learned behaviours, coping mechanisms, and other processes affect our individual behaviours – let alone our approaches when in complex groups, such as businesses and organisations.

The reality is that many of the decisions we make are shaped not by conscious deliberation, but by unconscious shortcuts and mental habits. These systems don't rely on logic, objectivity, or rational evaluation. As Kahneman observed, we are "blind to our blindness" and "generally overconfident in our opinions and our impressions and judgments."

---

[16] I won't get overly pedantic and go into the nuance of the specific types of validity. Let's just say the responses won't be objectively accurate for researchers – even if they feel accurate to the participant.

It is this tendency toward face validity that keeps organisations clinging to debunked theories and repackaged myths. From the idea that 10,000 hours of practice guarantees mastery to the persistence of viewing group brainstorming sessions as the best way to produce innovation. Despite repeated disproof, bad science continues to thrive in leadership training because it fits our mental models. It feels like it might be true.

Learning preferences is a particularly stubborn, but thoroughly debunked, theory that remains part of corporate training programmes. It might appear to be a recent addition to corporate approaches, but it's actually been around since the 1920s.

Early educational psychology proposed the idea that we have specific sensory modalities: set ways in which the body perceives and processes sensory information. With five key senses – visual (sight), auditory (sound), kinaesthetic (touch), olfactory (smell), and gustatory (taste) – this VAK/VAKOG model falsely assumes that people have dominant sensory modalities for learning. This idea gained momentum as a model in the seventies to the nineties, largely due to people's awareness of Neuro-Linguistic Programming[17] (or NLP) and modalities being a key facet of practitioner training.

In a comprehensive review of the learning styles research, Harold Pashler and his colleagues found that there was no reliable evidence that teaching according to learning styles improves learning outcomes. A separate large review of 13 different learning styles models, including VAK, found that none were backed by strong evidence. They noted that while the

---

[17] NLP is a subject possibly deserving of its own discussion, such is its own mix of science, mythology and prevalence in the corporate world

concept of learning styles sounds appealing, the empirical support for tailoring teaching to learning preferences was largely absent.

But, while there's no evidence supporting learning styles, educators, trainers and leaders continue to use them because they offer an appealing, simple framework for categorising individuals and organising learning strategies. This is simply an example of how confirmation bias and heuristics lead to the persistence of ineffective practices, even in the face of scientific evidence.

Our mental architecture evolved to prioritise speed and simplicity over slow analysis. People still find comfort in horoscopes, outdated assessments, and pseudoscientific models because our cognition actively encourages it. We are capable of rational thought, but only when we choose to be rational. Our default wiring is for ease, energy efficiency, and bias.

Conscious cognition takes effort. It's why you feel exhausted after a day of active listening, problem solving and other energy-intensive tasks. To conserve effort, we categorise and simplify. Stereotyping is one such form of cognitive efficiency. Heuristics – our mental shortcuts – omit full analytical processing and instead offer quick judgments. This efficiency can be helpful, but it can also lead to distortion and exclusion. One consequence is out-group homogeneity bias.

This bias describes our tendency to believe that members of a group we are not part of (the out-group) are more similar to each other than the members of your own group. It's the view that they (the out-group) are alike, whilst we (the in-group) are diverse and complex. The result is silos. The Customer Service team believes the Sales Function will sell anything to anyone, regardless of appropriateness. The Sales Function believes the Customer Service team has no commercial acumen and gives away gestures of goodwill with no understanding of how to run the business fiscally. Everyone hates Finance.

When the objective becomes the central determinant of the group's reason for existing – rather than simply the output – the cultural paradigm is established. Acceptable behaviours are informally inferred, and silos become less influential. (Though there's no guarantee everyone will suddenly love Finance).

Research into Constellation Leadership shows there is an added benefit. It has been estimated that up to 85% of an individual's skills are not utilised in their current job description or day-to-day role under traditional leadership models. But because the group is oriented around a high-level objective, rather than the narrow, pre-defined attributes of their role, each person is liberated to use their full suite of skills, experiences and approaches in achieving that objective, regardless of the arbitrary identifiers of job roles or individual objectives. Constellations permit our stars to shine.

In crises, rigid hierarchies tend to slow response, as decisions must pass upward for validation and downward for execution. By contrast, when culture itself guides behaviour, decisions can be made locally and immediately without losing coherence. This agility is why distributed and constellation approaches are more resilient in moments of extreme change. Whether that's a pandemic demanding rapid workplace adaptation, or a climate emergency forcing industries to innovate faster than regulation alone can dictate, these collectivist approaches outperform their hierarchical counterparts.

DRAWING THE CONSTELLATION

When the purpose is clear and the rules (both implicit and explicit) of 'how we get things done around here' are understood by group members, Constellation Leadership can provide an effective and natural approach to leadership. We see this in the world today.

For example, if an earthquake occurs, the purpose becomes clear for all; *we must save lives*. We might find physically fit individuals are the first to start moving rubble and rescuing people. Well-connected individuals might be on their phones, arranging emergency help. Medically trained individuals would be tending to the injured.

Yet no one has formally organised this response. There's no traditional leader providing mission statements or direction. Everyone understands what needs to be accomplished, and everyone knows how they can best contribute towards that shared objective – and, importantly, feels they have permission to do so. This is not just the in-the-moment volunteer response to the disaster itself. After the September 11th attacks, New York City crime reduced and the increased social altruism (i.e., helping neighbours, reduction in crime etc.) continued for several weeks post-event, as people coalesced around purpose and impact. The social norms – the culture – temporarily set the expectations for an entire city's behavioural approaches.

Another striking but smaller scale example is the 2010 Chilean miners' rescue. Trapped nearly 700 meters underground for 69 days, the miners' survival and eventual rescue were possible because leadership was distributed across a constellation of experts: engineers, doctors, drill operators, officials, and the miners themselves. No single person led the entire effort. Instead, individuals stepped forward as circumstances demanded, bringing their expertise to bear at the right moments.

Igor Proestakis was a 24-year-old field engineer who had travelled to San Jose on his own to offer help. He identified a little-known hammer technology that could cut through rock quicker than the other drills, and suggested its use to the senior engineers. Felipe Matthews and Walter Véliz listened to Proestakis, and a few days later, three concurrent plans with three different drilling systems we put in to action. In just seventeen days, contact was made with the trapped miners – and it was Proestakis' idea (plan B) that reached them first. Four days later, the final miner, team leader Luis Urzúa, was lifted in the rescue capsule and reunited with his family.

This shifting leadership pattern, held together by a shared purpose and a culture of trust, psychological safety and adaptability, enabled an extraordinary feat of coordination and innovation under extreme uncertainty.

However, these are exceptional, extreme scenarios with high-stakes goals. In crisis situations, there is also a tolerance of responsibility. If someone moved rubble that resulted in further injury or death, the ramifications are likely to be less severe than if a member of an organised, professional operation completed the same activity (i.e., If a Medecins Sans Frontieres or emergency service first responder's actions led to further injury, they might be prosecuted.) And, of course, our team of amateur rescuers are also self-selecting. This rarely happens in organisations.

But these lessons extend beyond disasters. If we revisit the example of an Agile project, we can see parallels between the leadership approach in the semi-distributed Sprint phase and

Constellation Leadership. However, the sprint team members will likely have been identified based on their roles, experience, skills or relationships to stakeholders or previous projects. The constellation of individual stars has been predetermined for the scrum.

The original research does not consider whether predetermined teams or self-selecting members are more suitable for this model. However, it still allows us to ask: under what conditions could the Scrum Master (i.e., the traditional leader) be removed from the Sprint process, and the team's performance remain unaffected or even improve?

This might sound as though by removing the Scrum Master, we're removing the leader. But Constellation Leadership is not leader-less. The leadership role is no longer a person; culture and a shared goal orientate the team, its approaches, its decision making, and its behaviours. Culture has become the leader, directed by the shared goal.

There is also a societal (some might argue generational[18]) shift. Employees entering the workforce today are less willing to accept authority based solely on title. They expect transparency, shared purpose, and the chance to contribute meaningfully. Constellation Leadership speaks directly to this expectation, showing that leadership is not something handed down but something lived together, anchored by culture.

So how does this idea hold up when it's more than just theory? In the next section, we'll look closely at the research study that examined Constellation Leadership in action: Its

---

[18] We must be careful not to over-simplify these individual expectations into broad generational attitudes. Whilst we might instinctively believe that different generations have different expectations (see: face validity), studies have found that there is greater variety within generations than between generations.

structure, the research approach used, and what the findings reveal about unlocking the full potential of teams.

Part Two:
Another way

04

THE STUDY:
Unlocking cultural influence

"The only thing of real importance that leaders do is to create and manage culture. If you do not manage culture, it manages you."

Edgar Schein
Organizational Culture and Leadership (1985)

Within the right environment, the distribution of responsibility and accountability can be incredibly powerful and fulfilling for all group members. We are greater than the sum of our parts.

Evidence of this is hidden around us in plain sight. Wikipedia, for example, is a self-governing network of contributors focused on creating the world's most accurate encyclopaedia. Although the platform has an owner[19], a board, and internal employees, the power of the network ultimately decides what is and isn't publishable. Its volunteer membership determines how to challenge inaccuracies, and how to self-police when contributors or outside factions act in ways that conflict with its purpose:

"To benefit readers by acting as a widely accessible and free encyclopaedia; a comprehensive written compendium that contains information on all branches of knowledge."

This kind of collective, culturally driven leadership can also be seen in other contexts, from the rapid coordination in natural disaster responses to something as everyday as family Wi-Fi dynamics, where shared understanding determines whose work takes priority when bandwidth is scarce, or who steps into the role of IT support when the router fails.

Constellation Leadership removes the reliance on a single leader and instead uses purpose and culture as enabling factors. Team members are encouraged to lean into their individual strengths to deliver against a clearly defined objective. In applied settings, such as Agile projects, the Sprint team itself becomes a constellation: a purposeful grouping of individual stars, each contributing in unique ways to a shared outcome.

Even in this semi-distributed structure, however, vertical leadership persists. The Scrum Master provides guidance,

---

[19] A note on ownership. Wikipedia was founded in 2001 by Jimmy Wales and Larry Sanger, and has been hosted by the non-profit Wikimedia Foundation since 2003. It is not "owned" in the traditional commercial sense, but it is governed and maintained via that foundation.

protects the team from external influence, and ensures the Agile methodology is followed. But what would happen if the scrum master were removed?

RESEARCHING CONSTELLATIONS

The first academic study into Constellation Leadership set out to explore how these principles might function in real-world contexts, and assess the overall impact of the theoretical model.

As leadership (as a general term) provides a direction and influences working approaches, these constituent research question aspects must be considered more closely. For example, how does a sprint team define "project delivery success" in a leader's absence? Is this influenced by tenure, trust or talent?

In teams with high capability, competency and commitment, does the scrum master's approach enhance the delivery or are they an observer? Would removing the role have any effect and if so, what?

Before data collection began, the research paradigm and methodology were established. A paradigm provides the philosophical foundations of a study: assumptions about reality, knowledge, values, and ethics. Setting this out in advance ensures transparency, justifies methodological choices, and shows how new insights contribute to existing theory.

For this study, two complementary perspectives were adopted:

- An **interpretive paradigm** considers reality as socially-constructed and interpreted by different people in different ways. It looks to understand how people make sense of the world and helps with discovering multiple subjectivities and suits the anecdotal, qualitative data analysis.

- Group participants were anticipated to have varying views and interpretations of distributed leadership models and Agile. The **radical humanist paradigm** is subjectivist and adopts a critical perspective on organisational life. This subjectivist approach emphasises human consciousness, and focuses on articulating the sociology of change and potential.

Given that Constellation Leadership is a proposed model, *deductive thematic analysis* was chosen. This allowed themes to be identified that either supported or challenged the theory. Thematic analysis provided a systematic but flexible way to work with qualitative data.

The first phase of research used it to identify patterns from group interviews and panel discussions, which then informed the answer options in the second phase of data collection.

The study centred on three guiding questions:

- Does the definition of success vary between individuals, and if so, how?

- Are there preferred leadership approaches during the Sprint phase, and do patterns emerge across groups?

- Under what conditions could the Scrum Master role be removed without harming performance – and possibly even improving it?

In short: under what conditions can culture itself become the leader?

Agile project practitioners from a wide variety of industries and experience levels (including both civilian and military backgrounds) took part in the study. Their insights were analysed against three key components of the Constellation Leadership model:

- **Purpose & Goal**: orienting the group with a clear sense of mission and outcome

- **Organisational Culture**: the rituals, behaviours and shared norms that shape how people work together

- **Ecosystem of Partners**: the dynamic, ad hoc relationships that allow individuals to co-create and support one another in pursuit of the shared objective

A striking theme emerged from participants with military experience. When asked whether a Scrum Master could be removed from a Sprint, their response was immediate: this was already familiar. While civilian participants debated the idea from multiple angles, military voices described it as standard practice under the philosophy of *Mission Command*.

Mission Command centres on achieving the objective rather than following detailed instructions, empowering individuals at all levels to make decisions in line with the wider mission. One participant explicitly linked this to the idea of removing the Scrum Master:

"[after removing a leader] the team are now self-evaluating and they're testing out new scenarios and they're, essentially, getting the evidence and discussing it and deciding what to do about it. They should fly."

This connection highlights how Constellation Leadership echoes an established, field-tested philosophy in high-stakes environments. It suggests that, under the right conditions, organisational culture and shared purpose can replace traditional leadership roles – not only without detriment to performance, but as a catalyst for autonomy and innovation.

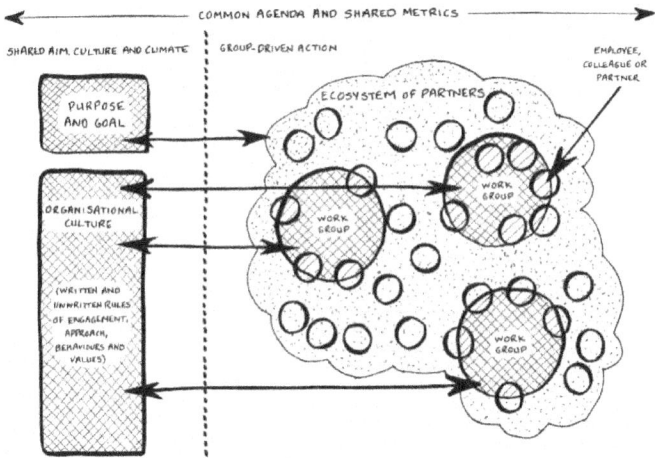

Constellation Leadership model

For Mission Command to be successful, a common goal or outcome is required. This aligns group members towards that objective and identifies what constitutes success. But what is success in low-risk, low-stake contexts? To understand how this plays out in real-world settings, we return to the research.

WHAT IS SUCCESS?

The Japanese philosophy of *Shu Ha Ri* conceptualises of the stages of learning on the road to mastery. It's often applied to martial arts, but it also holds relevance for leadership and team dynamics, describing the journey from rule-following to rule-transcending.

In the *Shu* (follow) stage, the focus is on learning the fundamentals, techniques and basic principles of a discipline. It's about imitation and strict adherence to established practices and traditions. In the *Ha* (break) stage, learners begin to question and adapt. Understanding of the underlying principles starts to allow them to modify or even break the rules. It's about experimentation and finding exceptions to the established norms through critical thinking and innovation. In the *Ri* (transcend) stage, individuals act intuitively, drawing on internalised knowledge and experience, without being bound by rigid structures and approaches. This is the path towards mastery.

This philosophy was echoed in the research on Constellation Leadership, particularly in how participants defined success and approached leadership within Agile sprints. Experience emerged as a key variable.

For participants with less than one year of Agile experience, success was typically defined in transactional terms: completing backlog items, meeting deadlines, and following process. As experience grew, so did the depth of interpretation. Success became less about quantity and more about quality of work delivered and of collaboration. For these participants, a successful Sprint was one in which the team dynamic improved, interpersonal learning occurred, and the output aligned more closely with purpose than process.

The study also revealed clear quantitative trends. Less experienced participants overwhelmingly defined success in transactional terms (i.e., meeting deadlines and completing backlog items), while more experienced team members prioritised shared, team-based outcomes such as collaboration, learning, and alignment to purpose. Interestingly, non-civilian participants (e.g., military and emergency services personnel) exhibited shared success orientation regardless of experience or organisation size, highlighting the stabilising effect of established high-trust cultures.

A similar evolution was observed in leadership preferences. Less experienced team members favoured directive, supportive approaches; project veterans preferred autonomy and minimal intervention. It seems that individual stars within a constellation expect autonomy and to be free of what they perceive to be interference

None of this is especially surprising. In most skill-based disciplines (particularly those with structured frameworks like Agile) beginners expect and benefit from clear targets and closer supervision. As competence builds, so does confidence in ambiguity, and the desire for autonomy increases. However, the study revealed three insights that go beyond this expected developmental arc.

First, experience is not judged solely by duration or level of technical familiarity, or even objective proficiency, but by perceived embeddedness within the group. In commercial organisations, "highly experienced" often meant 4-8 years of

Agile practice. Yet if someone with four years of experience had only recently joined the team, their contributions were treated as if they had less than one year's experience. In these cases, transactional goals reappeared. Experience, it seems, is not just accumulated, it must also be recognised and relationally earned. To repurpose a disclaimer from mortgage and investment adverts: past performance is not to be treated as an indicator of future performance when you're new to a team.

Interestingly, this perceptual bias was absent in non-civilian contexts such as military or emergency services. Regardless of tenure or background, individuals were trusted to deliver against group objectives and were granted autonomy from the outset. Here, a shared cultural expectation of mutual accountability appeared to override assumptions based on familiarity or time served.

This – once again – invokes the philosophy of Mission Command. Mission Command participants understand why and what, rather than receiving overly detailed instructions. This focus on intent unites the team around a common objective, irrespective of individual tenure or technical seniority. Whether newly joined or long-serving, team members are oriented toward the same outcome, enabling autonomy within a shared framework. By prioritising a well-articulated purpose over accumulated experience, trust is established relationally rather than granted on tenure.

A foundational principle of Mission Command is freedom of action, which depends on a culture that encourages initiative and collaborative decision-making across ranks. In environments where organisational culture reinforces contribution, individuals feel empowered to act autonomously in pursuit of shared goals.

The prevailing culture of collective ownership and mutual accountability enables individuals to step forward and lead when needed, regardless of how long they'd been part of the group.

The second key insight is that organisational size shapes both success definitions and leadership preferences.

In organisations with fewer than ten employees, high levels of autonomy were common, and group members focused on the quality of the work produced. As organisations grew towards 150 employees, a preference for defensive leadership emerged – leaders who could shield the team from external pressures and interference. Beyond 150 employees, autonomous leadership returned, but with a notable shift: quality of output became less of a focus, replaced by an emphasis on transactional delivery.

This pattern is perhaps unsurprising. In smaller organisations, individuals often perform cross-functional roles, necessitating broad capability and granting natural autonomy. A single HR representative, for instance, might handle payroll, recruitment, grievances, and even lend support in finance or front-of-house. In larger organisations, these responsibilities are typically divided across multiple specialised roles. Specialisation should, in theory, enhance competency. But this is counterbalanced by the sheer size of the group.

The Scrum Master's influence mirrored these dynamics. In mid-sized teams, their impact on behaviour waned; in larger teams, procedural guidance regained importance. Once again, these patterns resonate with Mission Command. Freed from detailed oversight, team members act with initiative, guided by trust, cultural norms, and a clear sense of purpose. Non-civilian participants consistently preferred autonomy, demonstrating how culturally embedded trust can override assumptions tied to tenure or experience.

Civilian teams eventually embraced this approach, but only after prolonged exposure. Data suggest that around eight years of experience were needed for civilian members to anticipate successful outcomes without a Scrum Master. In high-trust, culturally embedded environments, autonomy was granted from the outset; in lower-trust or newly formed teams, it had to be earned relationally.

Finally, human relational limits shaped these dynamics. Once groups exceed roughly 150 members, shared understanding and peer accountability diminish, and measurable outputs dominate. Cross-functional roles in smaller organisations appear to support autonomy and relational trust. But as size increases, specialisation alone cannot compensate for the relational gap.

Success definitions also shift from collaborative and qualitative to transactional and measurable, reinforcing the delicate balance between experience, trust, autonomy, and group size.

HOW BIG IS TOO BIG?

While increased role specialisation in larger organisations can improve competency, it does not fully offset the relational trust lost as groups expand. Trust and mutual understanding, rather than technical skill alone, remain critical for the distributed leadership model to function effectively.

So, what happens when mastery is achieved, autonomy is granted and yet the group grows beyond the cognitive limits of Dunbar's Number?

Proposed by British anthropologist Robin Dunbar, the concept suggests that all primates can maintain stable, meaningful social relationships providing the group size is below a certain threshold.

This cognitive limit is not about recognition or acquaintance (e.g., we can remember many more faces and names), but about genuine relational depth: knowing how someone is likely to react, understanding their values, and having a shared context for trust and cooperation. Beyond this threshold, coordination becomes harder, informal trust weakens, and social cohesion tends to fragment. Communication moves from relational to procedural, and behaviours that once flowed organically begin to require policy, hierarchy and surveillance.

Dunbar's research didn't start with people. He observed similar cognitive constraints in other primates, such as chimpanzees, whose group sizes rarely exceed 50–60 individuals. When numbers grow beyond this, groups often split into smaller units to maintain cohesion. What's striking is that the same principle holds in human settings, from hunter-gatherer tribes to modern businesses. Below 150, mutual accountability, informal norms, and peer-to-peer trust can carry a great deal of weight. Above that, cohesion often becomes conditional and dependent on formal structures, KPIs, and predefined responsibilities.

The group's centre of gravity shifts from who we are together to what each of us does. In this light, it is perhaps unsurprising that participants in larger organisations placed less emphasis on quality and collaboration and more on completion and compliance. The constraints of human cognition shape not only our relationships, but the very culture of work itself. The result is less shared context, more siloed thinking, and a reversion to measurable transactions over collaborative depth.

This cognitive constraint is more than theoretical. The software company Basecamp offers a cautionary tale of what happens when organisations scale beyond their relational bandwidth.

For years, Basecamp operated with a small, tightly bonded team and a famously flat structure. With under 60 employees, decisions were informal, disagreements resolved relationally, and the culture prioritised calm, purpose-driven work. But as the company grew towards 100, cohesion faltered. Conversations that were once candid became polarised. Cultural tensions, particularly around political and equity issues, spilled into daily operations.

In response, leadership introduced blanket policies designed to neutralise debate, inadvertently stifling the very openness they once championed. The result was a mass departure: over a third of employees resigned. What had once been sustained through mutual context and trust now required policy, structure, and control. The shift was not just about headcount. It marked a transition from shared culture to managed compliance, a classic symptom of surpassing Dunbar's cognitive boundary.

By contrast, W. L. Gore & Associates (the company behind Gore-Tex) took a different route. Founder Bill Gore observed early on that once a team exceeded roughly 150 members, interpersonal familiarity eroded, coordination slowed, and bureaucracy crept in. To counter this, the company implemented a simple but profound rule: no single office or plant should grow beyond 150 people. When that threshold was reached, the team would split into two, each operating semi-autonomously. Leadership was informal and earned through credibility rather than role title, and each unit maintained its own rhythm and relationships.

This design mirrored the mutual accountability seen in non-civilian groups like emergency response teams, where cohesion and purpose override hierarchy. Gore's deliberate adherence to this principle has helped sustain innovation, trust, and psychological safety, even as the organisation has scaled globally.

This principle isn't limited to manufacturing or military settings. Amazon – a company renowned for its scale and speed – enforces a similar design constraint. Founder Jeff Bezos famously introduced the "two pizza rule": no team should be so large that it cannot be fed with two pizzas. While the metric is tongue-in-cheek, the intent is strategic. Smaller teams reduce coordination overhead, promote autonomy, and maintain focus. They are less prone to groupthink and more likely to hold one another accountable. At Amazon, the rule became a mechanism for scaling innovation without losing agility. It keeps teams close enough to trust each other, challenge ideas, and move fast.

Whether capped at 150 or kept small enough for lunch, the principle is consistent: above a certain group size, the human brain begins to struggle and collaboration falters when group size exceeds the capacity for trust, context, and mutual visibility. Leadership must either restructure to preserve relational depth or compensate for its absence through increasingly rigid mechanisms of control.

This phenomenon appears to be recognised within non-civilian organisations. In the British Army, a company – a group of soldiers commanded by a major or captain – usually consists of 100 to 150 soldiers. Beyond this size, intentional compartmentalisation is created within battalions (typically a grouping of a headquarters, a support company, and three or more rifle companies), with each company assigned specific responsibilities and orders. A similar approach to limiting groups to under 150 is also utilised in the US Army, Soviet Armed Forces, and numerous military services around the world, to mitigate the impact of reduced relational depth.

The effect is not inconsequential. As relational ties weaken, so too does psychological safety, which undermines the very conditions required for innovation, learning, shared accountability, and trust. To achieve a comparable level of trust in one another's capabilities – as is seen in military contexts – the study's data suggest it would take up to eight years in a commercial organisation.

However, if the group is larger than 150 people, those performance benefits are lost entirely, and the team's outputs become transactional.

Even if the culture of an organisation is purposeful and aligned to organisational strategy, with high-trust and psychological safety, the findings suggest that the performance differentiation provided by Constellation Leadership can be undermined through the organisational size.

This has practical ramifications for organisational development, resource & planning, and within estate design decisions for those organisations.

Yet group size and perceived competency aren't the only factors influencing the success of Constellation Leadership. What also matters is how teams behave under pressure – especially when things go wrong. In tightly bonded groups, where trust runs deep and the shared mission is paramount, a different kind of culture emerges: one that tolerates imperfection in the moment for the sake of progress in the long run. This isn't about excusing failure but about absorbing it. Effort is redistributed, the plan adapts, and momentum continues. These behavioural norms form the cultural glue that replaces command-and-control leadership when the constellation must reorganise on the fly.

THE TOLERANCE OF FAILURE

"If the chap next to me gets slotted, we don't abandon the mission." This candid response from a British Navy Commander who contributed to the research reveals a core tenet of military leadership: when something goes wrong – or, in this case, a team member is removed from the mission – the remaining members adapt and continue. The mission remains paramount.

But the quote carries more nuance than first appears. It implies an acceptance that replacements (whether individuals or improvised approaches) may not perform at the same standard as the person being replaced. This isn't about tolerating mediocrity. It reflects a pragmatic culture that values the objective over perfection. Success is defined by outcome, even when the path deviates and ideal conditions no longer apply.

One of the most famous examples of this cultural flexibility is NASA's Apollo 13 mission. When an oxygen tank exploded en route to the moon, the original objective was replaced with a new one: get the crew home alive. What followed was a masterclass in distributed, adaptive problem-solving. Across mission control, engineers worked against the clock, trusting each other's expertise, improvising with limited materials, and operating on incomplete information. No one paused for perfect data or deferred to hierarchy by rote. They acted with urgency, clarity, and trust. As one engineer later said: "We didn't have time to assign blame. We had a job to do."

Apollo 13's success wasn't the product of flawless execution, but of cultural conditions that made resilience possible. While the stakes at NASA were extreme, some organisations have embedded similar cultural flexibility into everyday operations.

At Pixar, story development is famously iterative. Directors and writers share early, rough versions of their work in "brain trust" sessions. These sessions are not to seek approval, but to receive unfiltered feedback from trusted peers. When the production of Toy Story 2 began to falter, large portions of the film were scrapped mid-production. Rather than point fingers, the team pulled together in rewriting, reanimating, and re-recording under intense deadlines. The pivot worked, not because of rigid planning, but because of deep trust in each other's creative judgment and a shared commitment to story quality. Here, failure wasn't final but part of the process.

This pattern also emerges in smaller organisations. When employees wear multiple hats, perfection in every role is neither expected nor sustainable. "Good enough" becomes a legitimate benchmark. This is not in a defeatist sense, but as a recognition of what the team needs most at a given moment. As one respondent put it: "When you're in a small boat, you can tell who's looking around and who's rowing – even if they're not a natural rower."

In these contexts, trust and visibility, not flawless execution, keep the constellation aligned to the overall mission.

THE GLUE OF LIFE

Trust is the glue of shared leadership models. It shapes design, performance, and group dynamics, forming a mutually reinforcing cycle: higher trust strengthens effectiveness, while mistrust undermines new approaches.

As seen in Mission Command, trust is not granted on reputation but earned through shared experience, reinforced by integrity and competence. This mutual trust allows individuals – regardless of tenure and even when a required skillset might be suboptimal – to exercise disciplined initiative without fear of reprisal. This atmosphere allows culture and context, rather than a designated leader, to guide performance.

Given the influence of trust in both leadership and project management contexts, it was anticipated to be a significant factor in the application of Constellation Leadership in the study. But what is trust?

It might seem like a simple question. Indeed, most academic studies of trust treat it as a collection of stable components. Scholars and practitioners have tried to pin trust down through frameworks: some emphasise ability, integrity and benevolence; others stress consistency, compassion or connectedness. Blanchard prefers an alphabetical ABCD, while Brené Brown offers BRAVING. Yet despite the acronyms, consensus remains elusive.

An area that is missing from these components is context or situation. You might trust a friend to answer the phone at 3am in an emergency, but not trust them with money or organising a social meet-up, as they never to repay a loan or arrive on time.

Trust is not only about ABCD or BRAVING. It considers specific contexts, relationships and situations.

The Constellation Leadership study found that, as the context and expectations of the outcome and the cultural norms of the group were established, perceived capability became an indicator and variable factor in the project's success. In practice, once a group aligned around a shared purpose and cultural norms, perceived capability became a proxy for trust: that shared objective *increased* the perception of trust within the team.

Research area	High trust / experience	Low trust / experience
Definition of project delivery success	Shared, team-based objectives	Individual, transactional objectives
Does shared leadership link to project delivery success?	Accepted. Perception that if conditions are optimum, this is how sprints should be completed	Alien. Perception that distributing leadership would not work, as leader needs to be directive
Do the Scrum Master's own leadership approaches enhance project delivery success?	Scrum Master is seen as a passive enabler, sharing objectives and approaches with the team	Scrum Master is seen as instructional and directive, setting individual objectives and tasks
If Scrum Master's role was removed?	Little to no impact for single or multiple sprints	Sprint would be unsuccessful in all examples

Summary of research question areas and participants' views

ADDITIONAL INSIGHTS

Beyond experience, tenure, and organisational size, the study surfaced three further dynamics that shaped perceptions of success and leadership:

1. Cognitive bias observations

Participants' self-assessments revealed clear patterns of cognitive bias. Less experienced team members often overestimated their contribution to project success, reflecting a classic instance of *illusory superiority* bias (sometimes described in research as the Dunning-Kruger effect).

In contrast, highly experienced members tended to underestimate their own impact, particularly when embedded in high-performing teams. These patterns were more pronounced in civilian contexts, where individual accountability is less tightly embedded within established cultural norms. Recognising these biases is critical for teams seeking to calibrate autonomy and guidance: overconfidence can encourage misaligned priorities, while underestimation may inhibit initiative even in capable individuals.

2. Specialisation, trust, and performance interactions

Specialisation emerged as a double-edged sword. In smaller teams, cross-functional roles naturally facilitated trust and autonomy: team members observed competence directly, reducing the need for formal oversight.

In larger, highly specialised teams, however, visibility into individual capability declined. Performance became increasingly dependent on procedural norms rather than relational trust. Output quality was not as valued as following protocol. The study indicated that shared purpose and clearly articulated objectives could mitigate some of these risks, but only when paired with deliberate mechanisms to maintain visibility of capability and contribution. Trust, once established relationally, acted as a force multiplier, enabling autonomous decision-making even when formal oversight was limited. But its absence in highly specialised, large teams constrained performance and reinforced transactional behaviours.

3. Perceived capability as a proxy for trust

One of the most compelling patterns in the research was how team members' perception of one another's capability acted as a practical proxy for trust. In distributed leadership models, where oversight is limited and autonomy is valued, the ability to rely on colleagues' skills and judgment becomes central to performance. Rather than formal roles or tenure, trust emerged as a relational and context-dependent metric, informed directly by observation of competence and past behaviour.

In smaller or cross-functional teams, capability was highly visible. Individuals could observe one another completing tasks across multiple domains, creating a tangible sense of reliability. This observation reinforced psychological safety and encouraged initiative. Trust in organisations is strongly shaped by perceived ability, integrity, and benevolence, but in practice, the ability component often dominates when outcomes depend on autonomous decision-making.

As teams scaled or specialised, however, capability became less immediately observable. In highly segmented environments, individuals relied on reputational cues, performance metrics, and formal communication channels to gauge competence.

Previous research has established the link between trust and risk-taking in organisational settings. This study revealed that when perceived capability was high, team members were willing to assume shared responsibilities, make independent decisions, and even step into leadership roles temporarily. Conversely, where capability was uncertain, behaviour became more cautious, transactional, and dependent on formal authority.

Notably, perceived capability also interacted with organisational culture. In high-trust environments, assumptions about competence could be made more confidently, and mistakes were interpreted as learning opportunities rather than failures. In contrast, in lower-trust or newly formed teams, individuals required explicit verification of competence before delegating authority or assuming risk. This aligns with the conceptualisation of trust as "confidence in competence" within a social system: trust is socially constructed and continuously reinforced through observable action.

The implication for Constellation Leadership is clear: building and maintaining trust requires deliberate attention to visibility of capability. Practices such as transparent communication of skills, regular demonstration of contribution, and mechanisms for peer feedback are essential. When capability is observable, autonomy is supported; when it is obscured, hierarchical oversight and transactional measures reassert themselves. In other words, perceived capability serves as both the glue and the lubricant of distributed leadership, enabling teams to act as a cohesive constellation rather than a fragmented collection of individuals.

The insights from this original research can be broadly summarised as follows:

- Under predicable conditions, teams can self-form, self-organise, self-manage, and self-police

- Those predictable conditions must consider the overall goal (specific) or vision (aspirational) to align members

- Where these teams form, outcomes exceed traditional leadership success measures, with a focus on shared performance (i.e., quality, team growth, learning)

- Experience can be a proxy for trust, when social connection and individual member's perceived competencies are high

- The group size can undermine the group's success

- Non-civilian groups have a head start on civilian groups, due to the systemisation of goal creation, pre-mission planning, and both implicit and explicit cultural norms

Together, these findings underscore the complex interplay of human cognition, social perception, and organisational design. They suggest that teams seeking to apply Constellation Leadership must not only calibrate autonomy and guidance based on experience and tenure, but also remain attentive to cognitive biases, structural pressures, and the relational architecture of their members.

WHEN CULTURE LEADS

Constellation Leadership does not remove the need for leadership; it redistributes it. It shifts authority from a single node to the collective – but only under specific conditions. When teams are small enough to know one another's strengths, when competence is visible rather than assumed, and when trust is reinforced through daily interactions, leadership becomes situational, mutual, and dynamic.

The research makes clear that this model does not scale infinitely. There is a cognitive ceiling – roughly around 150 people – beyond which relational depth begins to erode. As relationships thin, trust is no longer personal but procedural. Cultural norms lose their grip, and process steps in to hold things together. At this point, autonomy declines, psychological safety reduces, and performance becomes transactional. The constellation collapses back into hierarchy or ambiguity.

The success of Constellation Leadership depends less on removing hierarchy and more on replacing it with something more resilient: shared purpose, mutual accountability, and a culture that values contribution over control. In one research case, the removal of a team's formal leader resulted not in confusion, but in clarity. The team reorganised itself instinctively, guided by internalised norms, peer respect, and a common goal. This wasn't leaderless chaos, but emergent order.

This model finds large-scale expression in the Chinese appliance giant Haier, which undertook a bold reorganisation in the 2000s under CEO Zhang Ruimin. Instead of growing the business through centralisation, Haier dismantled traditional hierarchies and reorganised into over 4,000 autonomous microenterprises, each made up of fewer than 100 people. These microenterprises are accountable for their own profits and losses, and choose their own leaders based on performance and peer alignment. Units form contracts with each other internally and create a marketplace of services within the business.

Haier's radical decentralisation reflects the same logic seen in smaller constellations: that clarity of purpose, trust in local decision-making, and close-knit teams outperform sprawling structures. Culture and purpose do not scale by decree, but by replication. What Haier engineered through structural decentralisation, others in this study achieved through lived norms. In military units, through ritual and shared mission. In creative studios, through feedback and standards of craft. In Agile environments, through rhythm and retrospection.

Ultimately, Constellation Leadership is not a rejection of leadership. It is a different shape of leadership. It is a model in which leadership is not centralised in a person, but is distributed through relationships. It thrives in environments where culture is purposeful, the goal is clear and there is permission for each member to contribute towards the objective, without fear of ridicule or reprimand.

While the research confirms that Constellation Leadership can outperform traditional models under the right conditions, organisations don't operate under controlled circumstances. Trust, autonomy, and shared purpose must be built, often in environments where habits, hierarchies, and human biases resist change.

The patterns revealed in the research illuminate how Constellation Leadership can emerge when the right cultural and structural conditions align. These findings offer more than an abstract framework; they show the potential for teams to lead themselves with clarity, purpose, and resilience. Yet frameworks alone are not enough.

Constellations form only when each star is both distinct and part of the whole. Understanding the system is not enough. We must also understand the elements within it. Leadership – whether distributed or traditional – is lived through people, and people bring with them unique personalities, motivations, and needs.

That means turning our attention from the patterns in the sky to the nature of each star itself. To understand how Constellation Leadership takes root, we must first step closer to the human side of the equation.

05

THE YOU FACTOR:

Personality & individual differences

*"It is not our differences that divide us.
It is our inability to recognise, accept, and
celebrate those differences."*

Audre Lorde
*The Master's Tools Will Never Dismantle
the Master's House (1979)*

Forty-eight inches was the winner. It dwarfed the losing team's paltry performance, which barely broke the twenty-seven-inch mark. And it wasn't the first time this had happened.

In attempt after attempt, the team consistently outperformed their rivals, constructing the tallest tower using twenty sticks of spaghetti, a yard each of tape and string, and finishing with a marshmallow on top in under eighteen minutes. But the consistent winning wasn't the most impressive part of the story. What made it remarkable was the comparison: the losing team was made up of CEOs, Harvard graduates, and high-flyers in the business world. The winners were eight years old.

The task was part of Tom Wujec's now-famous "Marshmallow Challenge," where teams compete to build the tallest freestanding spaghetti structure. The children didn't win because they were secretly budding engineers or because they had some hidden technical knowledge. They won because they worked in a way that adults – particularly high-achieving adults – rarely do. They experimented early. They tested often. They adapted quickly. Their process was playful but purposeful, free from the need to defend personal ideas or protect reputations.

The CEOs, by contrast, fell into familiar patterns. They spent time discussing strategies and negotiating roles, often treating the challenge as a problem to be solved through planning rather than learning. When they finally tested the marshmallow, it was too late to adapt if the structure collapsed (which it often did).

In the space between those two approaches lies an important truth about leadership and performance: diversity in thought, style, and method is not enough on its own. It must be coupled with an environment that embraces variety in thinking, curiosity, inclusion, and psychological safety.

Research into team dynamics shows that the role of verbal interactions within the group play a critical role in both performance and satisfaction. Groups where some members spoke more than others tend to achieve higher task success and satisfaction, because ideas are tested and refined rather than left theoretical. Individual members were also more satisfied with the communication process within the group.

In teams where most or all members spoke, the average level of anger and frustration was higher. This had an impact on individual personal satisfaction, which negatively influenced their contribution and cooperation levels within the group. People become passengers in the process.

The high-status adult groups of MBA students, lawyers, CEOs etc. often spent more time jockeying for position, protecting their reputations, and sticking to rigid plans. Their more homogeneous thinking styles led to slower adaptation and less innovation. The children didn't waste time posturing for status or debating who was in charge. They jumped straight into speedy experimentation, learning by doing, and openly building on each other's ideas without fear of criticism.

The difference wasn't intelligence. It wasn't resources. It was the way each group worked. The CEOs' approach reflected a narrow range of behaviours: more cautious, more concerned with preserving standing, less willing to risk failure in plain sight. The children's approach was an unselfconscious blend of rapid testing, shared ownership, and genuine openness to ideas. It was Constellation Leadership.

We often assume the most capable groups are those with the sharpest minds or most impressive résumés. In reality, the advantage lies with teams whose personalities, thinking styles, and ways of relating cover the whole problem space – and whose environment makes it safe to use them.

THAT'S SUCH A RED THING TO DO

In Constellation Leadership, the relationships between individuals, the wider group, together with the overall culture, inform the approaches to the dynamic, ad-hoc fluidity of the model. Understanding the individual differences – the personalities – of each member and having the self-knowledge to recognise how these influence how we experience and process the world can greatly influence the model's success.

What makes us unique as individuals often lies beneath the surface of our actions and decisions. Humans have always been fascinated by this puzzle of personality, which shapes who we are, how we behave, and the ways we connect and interact with one another. This curiosity spans cultures and eras, revealing a deep-rooted desire to understand ourselves and the people around us more clearly.

Throughout history, many attempts have been made to categorise and explain personality. Some approaches were grounded in observation and early science, while others relied more on philosophy, tradition, intuition, or simple guesswork. Together, these efforts form a tapestry of approaches, each contributing pieces to the complex picture of human individuality – though not always in useful, productive or accurate ways.

The first documented theory of personality dates back to around 500 BCE. Hippocrates II of Kos[20], the classical Greek physician and philosopher, proposed that personality was based on varying ratios of bodily fluids, or "humours": blood, black bile, yellow bile, and phlegm. This idea was expanded about 600 years later by Galen, another Greek physician and philosopher, who linked these humours to four temperaments: sanguine (warm-hearted and cheerful), phlegmatic (slow, quiet, and shy),

---

[20] Alcmaeon of Croton (possibly a student of Pythagoras) wrote about humours to describe the chemical systems regulating human behaviour around 510BCE. Hippocrates, dubbed the 'Father of Medicine', was the first to propose a link between humours and personality.

choleric (energetic, fiery, and passionate), and melancholic (fearful, depressed, and sad).

Galen's work highlighted the interconnectedness of mind and body. He explored how physical ailments could affect mental well-being and vice versa. Imbalances in the humours were thought to cause specific personality traits and even illnesses. His treatments aimed to rebalance these through "opposite" remedies. For example, yellow bile was thought to be hot and dry, so it could be treated with something cold and moist, like cucumber.

These humours were translated over centuries and geographies to become elements (i.e., fire, air, earth, water etc.), seasons, biblical figures, Hogwarts houses, animals and more. Today, you can complete a personality assessment that categorises respondents as a beaver, winter, Moses or Hufflepuff.

Humourism[21] was the grand unified theory of medicine for nearly 2,000 years, until it was definitively disproven in the 19th century. But it's influence on personality and character traits still remains in some fields today. It's not a coincidence that many of today's categorisations of personality are reflected in the colours of blood, yellow bile, black/blue bile, and phlegm.

HAPPY BIRTHDAY. YOU'RE STUBBORN

Around the same time that Hippocrates was suggesting personality could be changed with bloodletting, dry spices or cucumbers, Babylonian astronomers were looking to the stars.

---

[21] There is new evidence that suggests that the concept of humours has earlier origins in Ancient Egypt, Mesopotamia, or within Indian Ayuveda medicine, which used three or four humours and elemental identifiers

For nearly two millennia, observations of planetary movements and their links to events on Earth laid the foundation for both modern astronomy and astrology. By 500 BCE, the Babylonians had established a system of twelve signs, each occupying 30 degrees of sky to coincide with their 12-month calendar. Unlike today's zodiac signs, this system was not used to identify individuals' traits but as a predictive model for society: "Mars is rising? Prepare for war!"

When Alexander the Great conquered Babylon, Greek scholars gained access to Mesopotamian star charts, and astrology, astronomy, and philosophy began to intertwine. Where Greek culture and Near Eastern customs combined, Hellenistic astrologers like Claudius Ptolemy developed horoscopes. Ptolemy's *Tetrabiblos* became the manual for Western astrology, describing the structure of the heavens, the houses, aspects, and planets, and their supposed influence on constellations and, by extension, on individuals' behaviours, actions, and decisions on terra firma. One simple data point (your birthday) was now used to predict personality.

This evolved into the recognisable horoscopes still found in nearly every newspaper and magazine today, despite their clear lack of scientific validity, reliability, or accuracy. Our innate need to understand how we relate to one another and to interpret and predict each other's behaviour, often overrides our demand for objective accuracy.

SLOPING FOREHEAD? HOME, YOU GO!

"Maybe it's not the ratio of different bodily fluids or the position of celestial bodies on the day you were born that determine your character, temperament and personality. Maybe it's the shape of your head?" This thought preoccupied[22] Franz Joseph Gall and, by 1796, he had started lecturing on organology (the isolation of mental faculties) and cranioscopy (the observation and measurement of the skull).

Gall proposed a set of principles: the brain is the organ of the mind, divided into distinct parts, each responsible for a different aspect of mental acuity. The larger the part, the more that brain "muscle" was developed and the stronger the faculty. Because infant skulls are soft and harden over time, Gall believed external bumps could reveal internal strengths. It was an interesting and imaginative hypothesis, but one as inaccurate as birthdates and bile ratios.

Unfortunately, *phrenology* – the pseudoscience of measuring the cranium to determine character, personality and mental abilities – was hardly a fringe idea. Though loudly debunked in the 19th century, it was still used as part of some countries' education and immigration policies almost until the First World War.

For example, in the early 20th century United States the suffragette movement had gained traction. Many women campaigned for equal working rights as well as equal voting rights. In 1900, less than 20% of women (and fewer than 5% of married women) were classed as gainfully employed outside the home. By 1910, over two million women were working, and within a decade this had increased five-fold. This led to a reduction in women available for domestic, child-caring, and religious activities. Nannies and nuns were needed.

---

[22] There is zero evidence that this was a preoccupation or a specific thought. But given most of the "evidence" in this section is also conjecture, it felt natural to partake in some of my own.

Enter phrenology. Women with low foreheads and a small occipital bone (the rear of the skull) were considered artistic. Meanwhile, women with a large occipital bone implied greater submissiveness and suitability for child-caring and religious duties – and they would score more favourably on immigration applications than their low-foreheaded counterparts.

Today, phrenology survives only as novelty resin busts, car boot sale bric-a-brac, and the occasional antique shop curiosity[23].

WHO IS THIS "YOUNG IAN?"

At the turn of the 20th century, a Swiss medical student and budding paleoanthropologist left Basel for Zurich. In his youth, he had dreamed of becoming a Christian minister. But work as an assistant at Basel University's Anatomical Institute, combined with recent discoveries of *Homo erectus* and Neanderthal fossils, sparked a fascination with humanity's evolutionary past. He began to wonder whether an ancient layer of that past was echoed in the modern psyche. His name was Carl Gustav Jung.

Jung had no time for phrenology, but he did consider astrology essential to understanding subjects like alchemy. While he never claimed outright belief, he noted that horoscopes often "coincided" with patterns in personality and behaviour. Unlike the culturally specific Western zodiac, Jung proposed twelve

---

[23] Phrenology is having something of a contemporary revival in neuroscience research into personality: it is hypothesised that different personality traits are localised in different brain areas. Researchers have found that the areas responsible for positive emotions and reward are larger in extraverted individuals. The brain regions involved in irritability and anxiety are larger in individuals high in neuroticism. The skull measurement aspect might be debunked, but phrenology, it seems, is not completely dismissible.

universal archetypes – primordial patterns of the collective unconscious, shared and expressed by all humans across the globe. These symbolic expressions arose from biological instincts and sought fulfilment in each person's life.

From these ideas grew the first personality "typing" models. These are systems grouping people by shared traits into categories. Quiet, reflective, shy[24] individuals were labelled introverts; gregarious, energetic ones, extroverts. Typing models today include the Myers-Briggs Type Indicator (MBTI), Insights Discovery, and Strength Deployment Inventory (SDI), among many others.

The most widely used of all, however – DiSC, completed over a million times a year – owes more to William Moulton Marston than to Jung.

THE WONDER(WOMAN) OF TYPING TOOLS

Marston is an intriguing character. Educated at Harvard and graduating Phi Beta Kappa – the oldest academic honour society in the United States, whose recipients include 17 US presidents and 136 Nobel laureates – Marston was a screenplay writer, inventor, psychologist, educator, actor, self-help author, essayist, and the creator of the comic book character Wonder Woman. He might also have been a tad kinky.

In 1928, Marston wrote a book entitled 'Emotions of Normal People.' The book was a defence of many sexual taboos and, save for a review written by Olive Byrne in the Journal of Abnormal and Social Psychology, it was widely ignored. The

---

[24] The word 'shyster' describes someone who acts in a disreputable, unscrupulous or unethical way. "Shy" shares the same etymology and the original description painted introverts as untrustworthy, scheming and self-interested

book did, however, introduce the idea that people could be categorised along two axes, based on their task versus people focus and their outgoing versus reserved natures, producing four behavioural types:

- **Dominance**: the active use of force to overcome resistance in the environment;

- **Inducement**: the use of charm to tackle obstacles;

- **Submission**: the warm and voluntary acceptance of the need to fulfil a request; and

- **Compliance**: the fearful adjustment to a superior force

Marston described these DISC behavioural types as people's sense of self interacting with their environment, based on whether an individual feels their environment is favourable or unfavourable and whether they perceive that they have control or not.

This is all very innocent, so far. So where does the kinky label appear? In his book, Marston describes a type of masculine freedom rooted in anarchy and violence, and an opposing feminine notion, which he labels "Love Allure". This, he argues, leads to an ideal state of submission to a loving authority. In other words, Marston suggests that every man's underlying desire is to be lovingly dominated by a woman.

He lived in a throuple with his wife, Elizabeth, and his polyamorous partner, Olive Byrne (the reviewer of his book, which was based on her own doctoral research). He gave the world Wonder Woman – complete with dominatrix attire and a Lasso of Truth. And he invented the systolic blood pressure test, now paired with the polygraph, where you are strapped down and – like Wonder Woman's lasso – unable to resist. Finally, the original D in DiSC was the urge to dominate. The S? A longing to submit.

The DiSC model, as personality specialist and psychometrician Nikita Mikhailov wryly observes, probably has more use in the bedroom than the boardroom.

And yet, despite its enduring popularity, DiSC shares a problem with almost every personality "typing" tool: it tries to fit the messy, shifting reality of people into neat, fixed boxes.

Typing models provide accessibility and ease of use at the expense of stereotyping respondents. This *nomothetic* approach generalises personality and behaviours into broad groupings, sacrificing complexity, nuance and individualism from the discussion. It asks, 'What are the similarities between us?'

By contrast, an *idiographic* approach starts with the individual and builds outward: 'What is unique about the individual?' Additionally, the models on which typing tools are based lack objectivity, accuracy and, in many cases, are classed as pseudoscience.

This approximation of personality and its associated behavioural predictions might have been suitable for the industrial age, when leadership theories, production lines and organisational design valued predictability over individuality. In those contexts, personal nuance was not the point; consistency was.

The search for something more rigorous would eventually push researchers toward approaches rooted in language, data, and measurement. But replacing pseudoscience with statistics did not erase the biases of the time. Scientific measurement does not guarantee scientific neutrality.

One of the first to try was a Victorian polymath whose restless curiosity ranged from weather maps to fingerprints, and whose influence on personality science would echo for more than a century: Sir Francis Galton.

CHARACTERISTICS CLING TO FAMILY

Born in 1822 and a half-cousin to Charles Darwin, Sir Francis Galton approached human nature with the same urge to classify and measure that defined his era's science.

Victorian Britain (c.1837–1901) was an age of rapid change. The First Industrial Revolution (c.1760–1840) had already transformed production through mechanisation, chemical manufacturing, and the rise of factories. The Second Industrial Revolution (c.1870–1914) brought mass production, standardisation, and new efficiencies. The population was booming, and with it came a fascination with measurement, order, and classification – of machines, nature, and people. Galton thrived in this environment. Even in a century rich with inventors, explorers, and theorists, he stood out: publishing nearly 350 books and papers, founding the field of differential psychology, creating the first weather map, inventing the dog whistle, pioneering the statistical concept of correlation, and developing fingerprint analysis for forensic science.

Galton's interest in anthropometry – the measurement of human variation through biometrics, genetics, and psychometrics – was central to his work. Unlike Darwin, who sought to understand evolution as a record of change over time, Galton looked to apply the principle of natural selection to contemporary society. His belief that society could be "improved" by encouraging the reproduction of those with desirable traits, and discouraging that of others, made him the founder of eugenics as well as a pioneer of personality science.

When we recognise that both personality psychology and eugenics share the same parent, it becomes easier to understand why many psychologists are wary of models that classify people into groups based on perceived common traits. Beyond questions of accuracy, validity, or reliability, the historical shadow is hard to ignore. Like the Great Man Theory in leadership, Galton's worldview carried an implicit hierarchy: that some individuals were inherently superior to others, by birthright alone. This tension – between the scientific impulse to understand personality and the ethical dangers of how such knowledge is used – would continue to shape the field in the decades that followed.

Galton's fascination with classification eventually turned toward language itself. If the traits that matter most in human interaction are important enough, he reasoned, they will leave their imprint in the words we use. He believed that these words could be mined for clues about the traits that shape personality. This idea, later called the *lexical hypothesis*, proposed that the most significant personality differences would become encoded in everyday speech over generations. If a characteristic mattered enough to influence human interaction, people would have found a word for it.

Everyday speech becomes a shared cultural ledger of the ways we notice, evaluate, and compare one another. Galton began sifting through the English language for these descriptors, convinced that by mapping the words, one could map the mind.

This seed of an idea would later be cultivated by American psychologist Gordon Allport and others. The premise was deceptively simple: the more vital a personality trait is to our lives, the more likely it is to be encoded in our vocabulary. From this vantage point, language was not merely a tool for describing personality, but a historical archive of human priorities, perceptions, and prejudices.

One of the most widely accepted psychology frameworks for describing personality that is based on the lexical hypothesis is the Five Factor Model, often called the FFM, Big Five or OCEAN model. It breaks personality down into five broad dimensions: *Openness to Experience*, *Conscientiousness*, *Extraversion*, *Agreeableness*, and *Neuroticism*.

Each dimension represents a spectrum along which individuals vary, influencing everything from creativity and diligence to sociability and emotional resilience. For example, high Openness encourages curiosity and innovation, while high Conscientiousness supports organisation and reliability. Extraversion shapes how we seek social interaction and external stimuli; Agreeableness reflects cooperativeness and empathy; and Neuroticism relates to emotional stability and appetite for risk and reward.

There is, of course, far more nuance and complexity to the model. Each dimension contains several component facets, each a spectrum in its own right. For example, Extraversion includes the facets *warmth, gregariousness, assertiveness, excitement-seeking, activity* and *positive emotions*. An individual might score highly across most facets of Extraversion but low on gregariousness. They would be classified as extraverted overall, but in practice might still prefer solitude and avoid large social gatherings. Another extravert scoring low on positive emotion and low in negative affect (a facet within neuroticism) might appear reserved and apathetic.

With thirty facets nested within the five dimensions, if each were categorised simply as high or low, the possible combinations of traits exceed a billion. And keep in mind that these facets are not switches with a high/low result: they are spectrums that demonstrate the uniqueness of all individuals.

Understanding where people fall on these dimensions is not about putting them in boxes, but about recognising how diverse personalities contribute to shared goals – and how that diversity enables the psychological safety that let those eight-year-olds build their winning tower.

SO, YOU'VE GOT A PERSONALITY

At this point, it might feel as though our journey has taken something of a detour away from leadership and that this focus on personality distracts from culture. Yet culture can be seen as the collective personality and personalities of a group. By deepening our understanding of the interpersonal and individual differences, it is possible to transform team members' relational frustration into fascination.

One way to see this is through a project team. Imagine two people tasked with delivering a complex, high-stakes piece of work:

Riya is an energetic, idea-rich connector who scores high in Openness to Experience and Extraversion, but lower in Conscientiousness. She thrives on exploring new ideas, engaging stakeholders, and rapidly generating creative options.

Daniel is methodical and dependable, scoring high in Conscientiousness and Agreeableness, but lower in Openness. He excels at detailed planning, managing timelines, and keeping processes on track, favouring tried-and-tested methods over experimental leaps.

In the early stages, Riya's imaginative thinking helps the team see possibilities others might miss. Daniel's structured approach turns those ideas into actionable steps, anchoring creativity in feasibility and risk management. Together, they balance vision with execution, creating a powerful combination when the environment encourages mutual respect and curiosity about each other's approach.

But in a culture that lacks psychological safety, those same differences can breed friction. Riya may see Daniel as rigid and resistant to change; Daniel may see Riya as chaotic and unreliable. Without trust and a shared understanding of how their traits complement each other, their strengths become derailers: ideas stall, timelines slip, and both retreat into defensive patterns.

Now picture a different pairing:

Alex and **Morgan** are warm, collaborative extroverts, both scoring high in Agreeableness and Extraversion, but lower in

Openness and Neuroticism. They build rapport quickly, and their meetings are full of easy laughter and swift consensus.

In a predictable, low-risk environment, they're effortless to work with: harmony is preserved, conflict is rare, and morale stays high. But on a complex project requiring fresh solutions and rigorous critique, their similarities become a liability. Both tend to preserve harmony over challenging each other's ideas. Their low Openness means they rarely explore unconventional options, and their optimism can lead them to underestimate risks. Flaws in the plan may go unexamined until late in the process, when changes are harder and costlier.

Here, shared traits limit the cognitive "surface area" of the team. Without deliberate structures that introduce dissenting perspectives, the project risks becoming an echo chamber. In Constellation Leadership, recognising when a team's profile is too uniform allows leaders to intentionally bring in complementary voices. This is not to create conflict for its own sake, but to ensure the problem space is fully explored.

This is where Constellation Leadership thrives. However, diversity in cognition, style, and personality is only an advantage when the cultural environment makes it safe to share, combine, and challenge those differences; the same conditions that let those eight-year-olds outbuild the CEOs.

The history of personality assessment is littered with instruments that flatten the richness of human behaviour into rigid boxes. Typing tools can be tempting (they offer neat labels and simple categories) but they often sacrifice the nuance that makes people unique. Additionally, the basis for their psychometric accuracy is questionable. More robust frameworks, such as the OCEAN model, give a fuller, evidence-based picture of personality. But even these should be treated as a starting point, not a verdict.

In Constellation Leadership, the value lies not in pinning down a colleague's "true" personality, but in using these tools to start quality conversations. A shared language for differences helps teams explore how each person's strengths, preferences, and blind spots might shape their work together. Done well, this moves personality from a label to a lens, opening up understanding and collaboration.

When a team's personalities are too similar (as in the Alex and Morgan example), the comfort of agreement can quietly eclipse the challenge of critical thought. In those moments, it's not just diversity of personality that's missing, but diversity of perspective. Without the cultural safety to question, dissent, and explore the uncomfortable, teams can drift into the quiet conformity of groupthink, where harmony is prized over truth. In friction is where the fortune lies.

In the next chapter, we'll explore how groupthink takes hold, why even high-performing teams are vulnerable to it, and how to build the psychological safety that keeps agreement from becoming an echo chamber and create the fuel that powers Constellation Leadership: trust.

06

THE WE FACTOR:
Team psychological safety & trust

*"The key ingredient to building trust is not time.
It is courage."*

Patrick Lencioni
The Five Dysfunctions of a Team (2002)

On the open plains, danger rarely announces itself. It prowls. It circles. And when the lion finally moves, the herd of zebra reacts not with chaos but with unity. They press together, black and white stripes blurring into a single mass. To a predator's eye, the herd becomes one. The individual disappears. Safety, in that moment, is sameness.

In boardrooms, businesses and creative teams, a similar instinct takes hold. Under the pressure of deadlines, dissent, scrutiny etc., teams often tighten their formation. Harmony becomes a goal in itself. Ideas that stray too far are quietly ushered back to the centre.

It isn't laziness or fear. It's a deeply human drive for cohesion: survival instincts dressed in strategy decks and PowerPoint slides. This is *groupthink*.

THE ZEBRA KNOWS

Social psychologist Irving Janis coined the term groupthink in 1972 to describe decision making that prizes consensus over critical evaluation. Its symptoms are familiar: illusion of unanimity, suppression of dissent, self-censorship, and pressure on outliers. Even intelligent, well-meaning groups – such as those behind the Bay of Pigs invasion or escalation in Vietnam – can make irrational choices when conformity outweighs candour.

The psychology is straightforward. Humans are social beings hardwired to seek inclusion and avoid exclusion. Disagreement risks discomfort, so silence often wins. The result is not just poor decision-making, but a narrowing of cognitive bandwidth.

Personality plays a role. Agreeableness (one of the OCEAN traits) captures warmth, trust, cooperation, and conflict avoidance. Highly Agreeable individuals may defer to authority or conform to group norms, even in morally questionable situations. Rioting mobs and radicalised terrorist groups, surprisingly, contain above-average levels of Agreeableness. What looks like loyalty can also be complicity.

Most workplaces don't suffer catastrophic groupthink; they experience a subtler version. Meetings where ideas go unchallenged. Presentations greeted with nods, not questions.

Teams that call themselves "aligned" but quietly agree not to rock the boat. This politeness masquerades as psychological safety.

Marion Anderson, a HR leader and PhD researcher in psychological safety at Glasgow Caledonian University, warns that organisations often mistake surface harmony for the real thing. "Too many organisations conflate 'niceness' or 'positivity' with 'safety'," she explains. "Safety emerges when every voice has a real chance to shape outcomes."

This distinction matters. When safety is low, language itself changes: slogans replace sincerity, and jargon covers for a lack of honest debate. Anderson has seen this in her own studies: "In teams where safety is low, you hear more group-speak and less originality. Corporate clichés and cult-like phrases crop up as armour."

True safety is not the absence of friction but the trust that disagreement won't fracture the group. As Anderson puts it, "Sameness can look like safety but is actually suppression." Groupthink thrives not because voices are loud, but because too many go unheard.

DON'T SCARE THE ZEBRA

The lesser-discussed dimension of groupthink is its intensification under perceived threat. Just as zebra close ranks when a lion is near, human groups often become more homogenous when they feel under siege.

This response has evolutionary roots. In threatening situations, reducing variability and increasing coordination can be lifesaving. In the modern workplace, though, this defensive reflex can become counterproductive. When a team is facing a merger, a reputational risk, or even just scrutiny from senior leadership, it may respond by doubling down on conformity. Differences are smoothed over. Dissenters are marginalised. The group seeks safety in similarity.

In practice, this might manifest as a culture of meetings-before-meetings, where we reduce perceived threat through gaining individual views and consensus before addressing the group.

This reaction is underpinned by social identity theory, which suggests that people derive part of their self-concept from group membership. When the group feels threatened, individuals are more likely to identify with the in-group and less likely to tolerate internal deviance. Even well-intentioned team members can find themselves policing the boundaries of acceptable opinion.

In organisations with traditional leadership approaches, the structures, processes and protocols of the business can run effectively when everything is going well, and threats are few. But when there is change, stress or perceived danger, groupthink can become a blockage to the organisational machinery.

In contemporary workplaces, groupthink can be reinforced by multiple factors: hierarchy, remote working, and the unspoken norms of organisational culture. Digital collaboration tools can compound the issue. In video calls, it is easy to mute a dissenting voice. In Slack threads or Teams chats, agreement can be signalled with a thumbs-up emoji, and dissent left unexpressed. A cursory look at Zoom reveals that almost all of its instant reactions available to respond in-meeting are positive (i.e., thumbs up, celebration animation, floating hearts, clapping etc.).

Moreover, the culture of positivity that pervades many organisations, while well-meaning, can discourage healthy challenge. Leaders may say they want innovation, but reward stability. Team members may say they value diversity but resist discomfort. In such environments, groupthink thrives not through overt coercion, but through ambient pressure.

WHEN CULTURE TURNS CULTISH

If groupthink is the muffled hush of a herd too anxious to stray, then WeWork in its prime was a carnival at full volume. Balloons, slogans, and tequila shots at all-hands meetings created the atmosphere of a perpetual festival.

Employees were told they were not just leasing desks but transforming humanity. Investors were not simply funding office space; they were underwriting a spiritual movement. Adam Neumann, the founder and figurehead, cast himself less as a CEO than as a prophet. And in the electric glow of his vision, few wanted to be the one who turned off the music.

At the heart of WeWork's rise was an insistence that belief was more important than evidence. Optimism, in moderation, can be energising. But at WeWork, positivity hardened into dogma. Staff describe how criticism was interpreted as betrayal. "Negativity" wasn't just an unwelcome attitude; it was a threat to belonging. Meetings resembled rallies, where chants of "We" drowned out doubt. Employees quickly learned that those who raised concerns about spiralling costs, chaotic operations, or dubious side-projects were not celebrated truth-tellers but branded as cynics, obstacles to progress.

This climate reflected what psychologists call *affective culture*: the shared emotional norms of a group. At WeWork, the dominant affect was exuberance. Joy was demanded, not just encouraged. Neumann's charisma became the emotional thermostat of the organisation, setting a temperature so warm that discomfort had no place to settle. The result was a workforce fluent in the language of enthusiasm but increasingly tongue-tied when asked to voice disquiet.

This relentless (toxic) positivity paved the way for groupthink. The company's mission to "elevate the world's consciousness" became a collective article of faith, immune to rational challenge. To question the wisdom of ventures like WeLive (co-living) or WeGrow (a school for children) was to reveal oneself as an outsider, a non-believer. Psychologists note that groupthink thrives in conditions of high cohesion, strong identity, and an external sense of threat. All three were present here. WeWorkers defined themselves against sceptics on the outside world, bonded through their devotion to Neumann's dream, and rallied together to drown out criticism with more slogans, more energy, more "We."[25]

Inside such echo chambers, reality bends. Financial losses were reframed as "investments in growth." Reckless expansion became "proof of ambition." Even the mechanics of everyday communication reinforced the illusion. Company-wide emails echoed with grandiosity and public celebrations rewarded employees for passion rather than prudence. Dissenters either fell silent or quietly left, stripping the organisation of the very cognitive diversity that innovation requires.

---

[25] This is as good a place as any to remind ourselves of the psychological definition of a cult: "a group characterised by extreme devotion to a person, idea, or goal, often accompanied by manipulative and coercive control tactics." *Cult* is derived from the Latin *cultus* meaning *worship*

WE(DON'T)WORK

WeWork's downfall was not simply cultural theatre; it was also structural misalignment. The organisation's systems – communication, rewards, and leadership rhetoric – pulled employees further from reality. Internal communications broadcast inspiration from the top but left little room for dialogue from below. Rewards celebrated zeal over operational discipline: those who drank deepest from the cultural Kool-Aid were most visible, while those who quietly ensured buildings ran smoothly remained invisible.

Most damaging was the widening chasm between vision and reality. On the surface, employees were promised community, creativity, and purpose. On the ground, many experienced long hours, unclear accountability, and a business model that was little more than office subleasing with glossy branding. This gap created what organisational theorists call cultural dissonance: the psychological strain of living in a workplace where official values and lived reality diverge. Such dissonance is corrosive. Some employees masked it with forced cheer. Others exited quietly. By the time financial markets scrutinised the firm's attempt at an IPO in 2019, the mask could no longer hold.

The company's valuation collapsed from $47 billion to a fraction of that within weeks. Neumann was ousted. Thousands lost their jobs. In retrospect, the signs of collapse were obvious: a flawed business model, unchecked spending, governance failures. But the deeper lesson lies not in the numbers but in the culture that kept employees and investors from acknowledging them sooner.

WeWork is often framed as a parable of hubris or financial excess. Yet it is equally a study in how organisational culture can become a hall of mirrors. Toxic positivity silenced the sceptics, whilst groupthink amplified the believers. Misaligned systems rewarded conformity to a dream rather than confrontation with reality, and the result was not only a failed IPO but a workforce betrayed by the very culture that once promised them belonging.

WeWork shows how easily organisations can mistake positivity for progress and consensus for truth. To counter this tendency, leaders must actively design for dissent

GROUPTHINK'S KRYPTONITE

The antidote to groupthink is not conflict for its own sake, but deliberate space for productive dissent. Amy Edmondson's work on psychological safety offers a foundation: teams must feel safe to take interpersonal risks. But safety alone is not sufficient. Teams also need structured ways to disagree.

In vertical leadership, this might be through assigning roles or designing programmes that legitimise dissent. The "devil's advocate" approach is one example, though it must be used carefully to avoid tokenism. More effective still are red teams, whose role is to critique a proposal as if they were an opposing force. These strategies externalise challenge and reduce the interpersonal cost of disagreement.

Another approach is to increase cognitive diversity. This goes beyond demographic diversity, and includes diversity of experience, training, and perspective. Teams with greater cognitive diversity tend to generate more creative solutions – but only when their environment supports open exchange. Without inclusion, any diversity is stifled. Inclusion is the route to diversity – not the other way around.

This is where Constellation Leadership offers a more effective tool against groupthink, where a degree of tension is not a problem to be solved, but a sign that the group is doing important work.

Groupthink is not just a failure of decision-making. It is a failure of courage. The courage to challenge, to question, to step slightly out of line. Constellation Leadership holds the space in which those questions can be safely explored.

Innovation rarely emerges from the centre of the herd. It begins at the edges, where the view is clearer, the risks greater, and the possibilities far wider. Constellation Leadership offers a proxy for this innovation and ideation, through its naturally fluid, ad-hoc and dynamic relationships built on trust.

Yet dissent without trust is just noise. Zebras scatter if they cannot trust the herd to close ranks again. In human groups, the same rule applies: disagreement can only fuel innovation if it rests on the foundation of trust.

WHO'S GOT MY BACK?

Trust is not a management innovation, nor a fashionable leadership competency. It is older than agriculture, older than cities, and quite possibly older than language itself. For most of our evolutionary history, human survival depended less on individual strength than on the assurance that others would stand guard, share food, and defend the vulnerable. A lone hunter could not sleep unless he believed his companions would keep watch. A child could not thrive unless the group cooperated to provide both protection and nourishment. Trust was the invisible bond that allowed fragile individuals to become resilient collectives.

Anthropologists argue that this capacity for trust distinguished humans from other primates. While chimpanzees and gorillas largely restricted cooperation to close kin or narrow dominance hierarchies, early humans extended it further, forming groups that could exceed Dunbar's famous number of ~150 relationships. The evolutionary leap was not physical but social: an ability to recognise trustworthiness beyond blood ties and to sustain cooperation at scale.

This was not simply a matter of belief or choice. Trust functioned as a biological signal. It's the body's chemical, instinctive response to another's intentions being aligned with one's own safety and wellbeing. To trust was to detect that someone else would act in ways that reduced, rather than heightened, our vulnerability. Over millennia, those who could sense and reciprocate trust outcompeted those who relied only on suspicion or brute force. A band that fractured under mutual doubt was less likely to hunt successfully, defend territory, or nurture its young than one bound together by reliable reciprocity.

Evolutionary psychologists suggest that human cooperation scaled precisely because we could reward trustworthiness and punish betrayal, even at personal cost. Reputation became a survival mechanism. To be seen as untrustworthy was to risk exclusion, which in small-scale societies often meant death. What we now describe as "social capital" was once a literal lifeline.

Neurobiology reinforces this story. Acts of care, reciprocity, or fairness release oxytocin, strengthening the emotional bonds between individuals. This is not metaphorical:

it is chemical. Our brains have been wired to associate trust with safety, to reduce stress hormones when we detect reliability, and to trigger alarm when signals of betrayal appear. Cortisol spikes when trust is broken, narrowing attention, heightening vigilance, and preparing us to defend ourselves. In other words, trust and mistrust are not abstract concepts but deeply embodied states, shaping perception, cognition, and behaviour at the most basic level.

The implications for modern organisations are profound. Workplaces may no longer be about hunting or foraging, but the same circuitry governs how people collaborate. When colleagues follow through on commitments, when leaders act consistently, and when processes feel fair, our neurobiology registers these cues as security. We relax, broaden our attention, and take risks that fuel innovation. Conversely, when promises are broken, when information is withheld, or when favouritism distorts fairness, the same neural pathways that once signalled physical danger activate. Creativity collapses into defensiveness. Difference begins to feel dangerous rather than generative.

This helps explain why trust is foundational to distributed forms of leadership. In Constellation Leadership, authority is not centralised but dispersed; initiative is expected to arise from multiple points in the system. Such a model can only function if individuals feel buffered by the group, confident that stepping forward will not leave them exposed. Without trust, autonomy feels like abandonment, and uncertainty breeds vigilance and withdrawal. With it, autonomy becomes empowerment. The group acts as a safety net, allowing individuals to experiment, dissent, or innovate without fear of social isolation.

In environments where trust is thin, even small deviations from the norm feel threatening. Employees keep ideas to themselves rather than risk criticism. Teams cling to consensus rather than expose fault lines. Leaders tighten control rather than risk delegation. The system contracts inward, prioritising safety over progress. Trust does not merely lubricate collaboration; it determines whether difference is weaponised or harnessed.

In a Constellation Leadership context, trust is less an optional virtue than the operating system itself – largely invisible when it runs smoothly, but instantly disruptive when it crashes. This is why leaders who underestimate the role of trust so often find their initiatives faltering, not because the strategy was wrong, but because the social fabric could not carry it.

Importantly, this understanding reframes trust not as blind faith but as calibrated risk. Early humans did not trust indiscriminately; they developed subtle cues to detect honesty, reliability, and shared intent. Gossip, story, and ritual all emerged as cultural technologies for transmitting reputational knowledge to determine who had proven themselves, who had betrayed, and who could be counted on in times of scarcity. Modern organisations deploy similar mechanisms: performance histories, peer feedback, transparent communication, and visible follow-through. What differs is scale and context, not the underlying logic.

If cooperation beyond kinship was humanity's original competitive advantage, then cultivating trust remains our most vital organisational challenge. The same forces that allowed small bands to thrive now determine whether teams, companies, or entire networks can innovate and adapt. Trust signals that "someone else has my back." In Constellation Leadership, that signal extends across nodes of the network, allowing leadership to arise fluidly where needed, without collapsing into suspicion or control.

Yet while trust has deep evolutionary roots, the conditions in which it is cultivated have shifted dramatically. For most of human history, trust was forged face-to-face, in shared spaces where intentions could be read through gesture, expression, and presence. Today's organisations often operate without that constant co-presence. Teams span cities, countries, and time zones; colleagues may know one another primarily through a webcam or an email signature. The very cues that once allowed us to detect reliability and safety are attenuated or absent.

If trust is humanity's operating system, the question becomes: how does it run in a world where physical proximity is no longer guaranteed?

TRUST IN A DISPARATE WORLD

The field of proxemics, introduced by Edward T. Hall, studies how people use physical space in communication. Proxemics research indicates that appropriate physical proximity can enhance comfort and trust in interactions, while inappropriate distances may lead to discomfort and reduced trust. But it isn't the distance that seems to be the moderating factor; it's eyesight.

Modern research confirms the point: trust diminishes as physical distance grows. Not because people become less trustworthy at a distance, but because our brains evolved to read subtle, in-person signals when judging intent. Eye contact, facial cues, and body language give constant reassurance that others are attentive, engaged, and safe to approach. Without them, we fill the gaps with doubt. Experiments show that when partners are physically separated, even simple tasks like sharing resources trigger suspicion and guarded behaviour.

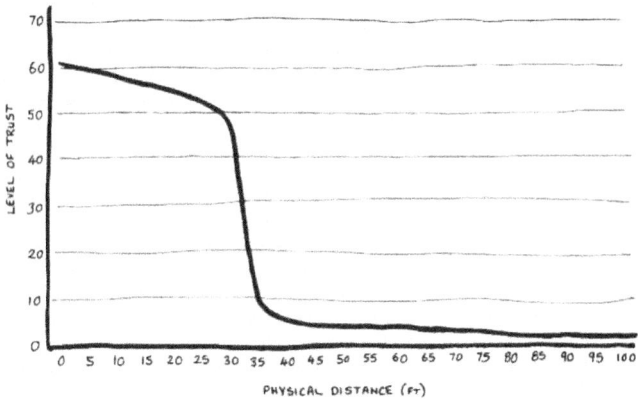

Physical distance and its relationship with trust

Interestingly, this distance impact can be mitigated in some instances. Where remote working individuals who score highly on Openness to Experience – a personality dimension in the Five Factor Model – are shown a photograph of another individual or even an image of their workstation, trust does not diminish from the previous in-person levels.

We're uncertain of exactly why this happens, but it may be that the activation of visual imagery in the brain is related to trust formation. The ventromedial prefrontal cortex (which plays a part in generating mental images), the posterior cingulate cortex (which is involved in memory retrieval and visualisation), and the temporal-parietal junction (which helps us understand the intentions and perspectives of others) are all utilised in in-person trust formation and in our visualisation of others.

This helps explain the tension in hybrid and remote work. Organisations often mistake visibility for trust: if leaders can't see people working, they worry that effort is lacking. The result is a reflex to add more monitoring, more check-ins, and more processes. Instructions for cameras on, core hour working, and mandatory days in the office are expected to mitigate the perceived challenges that hybrid appears to introduce. If we could just find the right combination of processes, then the conundrum would be solved.

Ironically, in trying to make work more visible, these processes often send the unintended message that trust is lacking. Where there is a change to what we can predict, what we can control or what we perceive as being fair, these approaches can cause threat responses in others – and trust never thrives under threat.

BRIDGES, NOT BINOCULARS

The challenge of distributed work is not only distance but distortion. Screens, emails, and instant messages function like binoculars: they magnify certain details while cropping out the wider context. A pause in response may be nothing more than a Wi-Fi delay. But without facial cues or shared space, it is easily misread as hesitation, doubt, or dismissal. Over time, these small distortions accumulate, turning routine ambiguity into mistrust. When a team is split by geography, we don't need binoculars; we need bridges.

The organisations that have been most successful in embracing hybrid working have done so through building these bridges intentionally. Rather than attempting to replicate the in-office experience online, they focus on what truly matters: the outcomes, the processes, and the signals that support trust and collaboration. They leave behind limiting beliefs about presence, visibility, and proximity, and instead leverage the unique advantages of both remote and in-person working practices.

For example, many of us instinctively believe that open collaboration fosters creativity and that in-person interaction is the path to innovation. This assumption often underpins arguments for returning to the office, even part-time. But the evidence does not fully support this view. Traditional brainstorming sessions frequently stifle dissent (a powerful catalyst for creativity) and encourage conformity. As early as 1972, Irving Janis identified that dominant voices in groups tend to shape discussions, suppress alternative ideas, and lead to less innovative outcomes. This is the essence of groupthink.

Hybrid working can counteract these dynamics. Studies show that remote environments allow individuals to develop ideas independently before collaborating, enhancing overall creative output. Freed from group pressures – fear of criticism, dominance of certain members, or social loafing – individuals generate a broader range of ideas, fostering deeper, more original thinking.

Automattic exemplifies this approach. The owner of the blogging platform WordPress.com operates in 95 countries, with a fully-remote workforce speaking 120 different languages. Their job interviews are conducted via SMS.

At first glance, this method may feel alien; perhaps even risky. But there is method in the apparent madness. Automattic aims to:

"Democratize publishing, commerce, and messaging so anyone with a story can tell it, anyone with a product can sell it, and everyone can manage their communications from a single source."

The company empowers people to communicate in ways that suit them, and its hiring processes reflect the skills it truly values: clear, concise written communication across a distributed, asynchronous environment. SMS, not role-play exercises or in-person tasks, is the best way to surface those abilities. They would glean no useful information from group interview exercises in building spaghetti and marshmallow towers.

GitLab, another fully-remote software company, offers a complementary example. With over 1,300 employees worldwide, GitLab relies on exhaustive written documentation, structured asynchronous workflows, and clearly defined decision-making processes. This approach ensures that every team member, regardless of location or time zone, can understand priorities, contribute meaningfully, and feel a sense of agency. By codifying expectations and communication norms, GitLab turns the potential distortions of distance into transparent bridges for collaboration.

Other organisations are experimenting with hybrid models in similarly intentional ways. The principle remains: start with the outcome you want, then design processes, touchpoints, and physical or virtual spaces that enable it.

One of the key determinants of successful distributed teams is a shared vision: a clear sense of the collective difference each individual makes and the goals they are working towards. In Constellation Leadership, this principle is foundational. Defining what success looks like, and then creating the environment in which trust can flourish, is a mutually reinforcing cycle. Practices that build trust enable distributed leadership to emerge, and leadership that emerges in this way, in turn, deepens trust.

PSYCHOLOGICAL SAFETY IS A JOKE

Let's get this out there early: you're not funny. You're also not attractive, charismatic, or trustworthy. And while we're at it, we can add reliable, persuasive, charming – or any of their antonyms – to that list.

This isn't a character assassination. You're not evil, unconvincing, unwelcoming, dull, or ugly either. These attributes aren't determined by the individual. They are relational. Others decide whether we are funny, attractive, or trustworthy. Comedy is subjective because it depends on the audience; beauty is in the eye of the beholder. Trust, charisma, and psychological safety work the same way: they exist only in the perception of others.

This is why comedians spend so much effort "working the room" at the start of a routine. They introduce themselves to establish identity, signal credibility, and interact with the audience to discover shared reference points. Without that relational groundwork, the jokes fall flat. Comedian Jimmy Carr captures this neatly:

"If you make a film and no one goes to see it, it's still a film. If you compose a song and no one listens, it's still a song. If you tell a joke and no one laughs, it's just a sentence."

The same words, phrasing, and delivery can either land or flop depending entirely on the audience. The relationship transforms the sentence into a joke.

Leadership works the same way. A leader without followers is just someone out for a walk. Trust, influence, and psychological safety are not given – they are perceived, decided, and co-created by the team. Without that relational foundation, even the best intentions, skills, or authority have limited impact.

Like comedians, leaders can hone their craft. They can develop tools, techniques, and behaviours that increase the likelihood that their audience (i.e., team members) will respond positively. They can practise awareness of cues and signals, adapt their delivery, and reflect on feedback.

Rehearsal. Delivery. Awareness. Feedback. Reflection. Development. Improvement. It's the iterative cycle that underpins both comedy and leadership.

This relational focus matters because it shapes the psychological environment. Just as shared laughter or understanding builds rapport, leaders' interactions build (or fail to build) psychological safety. Social influence theory explains the mechanism: perceptions of trust, competence, and credibility emerge through relational cues, shaping whether team members feel safe to speak up, challenge assumptions, or experiment.

In Constellation Leadership, there is no single figurehead guiding the team. Authority doesn't reside in a person, but in the network, in the culture, and in the shared understanding of mission. This raises a crucial question: how do we cultivate psychological safety when there isn't a visible leader to model it, enforce it, or signal it?

SAFETY WITHOUT A LEADER

Psychological safety, like humour or trust, is relational. It isn't granted by someone in power; it emerges from the interactions between team members. Each individual continuously interprets whether it is safe to speak up, to take risks, or to challenge prevailing assumptions.

In hierarchical teams, a leader can shortcut this process: their behaviour and explicit signals create a sense of safety. In Constellation Leadership, safety must be co-created, distributed, and reinforced culturally. Without a central figure, the culture itself must carry the weight of psychological safety. Norms, rituals, and shared practices become the scaffolding upon which trust and openness are built. Every interaction – how feedback is requested, how mistakes are treated, how ideas are acknowledged – contributes to the perception that this is a safe space to participate fully.

This shift requires deliberate design. Teams must make explicit what behaviours, communication patterns, and responses signal safety. They must attend to micro-interactions as carefully as leaders in traditional structures attend to their own signals of authority or reassurance. In essence, the "leader" is the system itself: the culture, the agreements, and the shared practices that continuously convey, "Here, your voice matters; here, it's safe to engage."

Below, we explore eight practical approaches to nurturing distributed psychological safety, focusing on how interactions, shared rituals, and reflective practices can signal safety consistently in an autonomous, leaderless team. Each approach emphasises relational negotiation: safety emerges through the team's collective awareness and fluid coordination rather than being granted by a formal leader.

1. Make norms explicit – then evolve them

In Constellation teams, norms aren't enforced from above; they are co-created and continuously negotiated. Explicitly discussing how members prefer to communicate, make decisions, and provide feedback signals that everyone's comfort and participation matter.

But norms are not static rules. They evolve as members experiment, observe each other's responses, and adjust. For instance, a team might start with an agreement to respond to asynchronous messages within 24 hours, then collectively refine that as they discover patterns of workflow that support psychological safety.

Example:
Before starting a new project, the team collectively lists communication expectations: response times, preferred channels, and rules for constructive disagreement. As they work, they notice some members feel rushed in synchronous meetings and adjust the norms to include asynchronous updates. Everyone feels heard, and safety is strengthened by the shared agreement.

2. Ritualise feedback loops as relational moments

Structured check-ins aren't just mechanical exercises. They also become relational signals that vulnerability is accepted and noticed.

In a fully autonomous team, each participant is simultaneously leader and follower in these moments. Daily stand-ups or retrospectives provide repeated opportunities to observe how openness is received: who speaks, who listens, who responds with support.

Over time, these interactions form a web of trust, where everyone can safely raise uncertainties or propose novel ideas.

Example:
During a daily stand-up, a team member admits they're stuck on a design decision. Instead of offering immediate solutions, peers share similar past struggles and encourage experimentation. The recurring ritual signals that admitting uncertainty is safe and valued.

3. Normalise transparent mistakes as a shared practice
Without a figurehead to model error-handling, the culture itself must support learning through failure. Teams can openly share missteps, discuss what was learned, and highlight "near misses" collectively.

Psychological safety arises when members see peers stepping forward vulnerably and being met with curiosity rather than judgment. In this way, the team collectively signals: taking intelligent risks is safe because the network holds each member.

Example:
A misconfigured release causes minor downtime. The team holds a brief review, collectively analysing what happened without blaming anyone. The member who made the error

openly shares their learning, and the network celebrates the improvement in process, reinforcing that risk-taking is safe.

4. Encourage peer recognition and micro-acknowledgements
In distributed leadership, recognition flows laterally. A quick chat message celebrating a helpful insight, an emoji acknowledging support, or a verbal "thanks for stepping in" during a meeting reinforces that contributions are noticed and valued.

These small, relational gestures build a culture of mutual validation, where safety is reinforced continuously through peers rather than conferred by authority.

Example:
During a hybrid brainstorming session, a quiet team member contributes a critical insight. Peers immediately acknowledge it verbally and in chat. These small recognitions signal relational validation, encouraging continued engagement and openness.

5. Build transparent decision pathways
Ambiguity can undermine psychological safety. Even without a leader, the team thrives when everyone understands how decisions are made and why. Shared decision logs, collaborative prioritisation boards, or visible rationale for choices provide the scaffolding for relational trust.

Members know when and how to step forward, when to yield, and when to propose alternatives, reducing the anxiety of hidden agendas or unclear expectations.

Example:

Faced with conflicting priorities, the team uses a shared decision board outlining options, who proposed them, and the reasoning behind each choice. Everyone can see the rationale and know when it's their turn to step in or defer, reducing uncertainty and fostering trust.

6. Map influence dynamically, not hierarchically

Influence in a Constellation team shifts fluidly based on expertise and situational need. Visualising areas of knowledge, responsibility, and influence helps team members navigate interactions safely.

Example:

During a technical impasse, the team may naturally follow a member with relevant expertise; once the issue is resolved, leadership recedes, and influence disperses again. Safety arises when everyone understands these relational cues and can step in or back without fear of overstepping. Members understand when to lead and when to support, strengthening relational safety.

7. Design asynchronous interaction as relational scaffolding

In hybrid or remote environments, clear communication structures preserve relational trust. Detailed updates, documented rationale, and structured channels allow team members to respond with awareness of context and intent.

Just as a comedian adjusts delivery to audience cues, team members observe reactions, calibrate responses, and signal respect and attentiveness. Psychological safety is supported by these conscious relational adaptations across space and time.

Example:
A team member documents a proposal for a cross-time zone decision, providing context, reasoning, and questions for feedback. Peers respond thoughtfully over hours, adapting their input based on cues from the original post. Safety is preserved despite distance because relational context is clear.

8. Reflect and evolve continuously as a collective practice
Safety in autonomous networks is emergent, not static. The team must periodically reflect on interaction patterns, norms, and feedback mechanisms. Facilitated retrospectives, anonymous surveys, or collective sense-making exercises allow the group to observe how relational cues are functioning and make adjustments.

By treating psychological safety as a living property of the culture rather than a fixed resource, the team ensures that trust, confidence, and openness persist as the network evolves.

Example:
Every month, the team holds a retrospective, reflecting on how norms, interactions, and feedback loops are functioning. One member notes that quieter voices aren't being heard, and the group collectively experiments with structured "round-robin" speaking to improve inclusion. The culture adapts, reinforcing trust and safety as emergent properties.

IT'S THE LITTLE THINGS

Ultimately, distributed psychological safety is woven from small, everyday acts rather than grand gestures or formal edicts. It lives in micro-moments: a nod to a colleague's idea, the candid admission of a misstep, the quiet clarification of a decision. These are the threads that, over time, form a resilient social fabric.

Just as in personal relationships, it is not the spectacular acts that create lasting trust. It's not the bouquet on Valentine's Day or the theatre tickets for a birthday. It's the cumulative hum of attention: noticing, acknowledging, responding, celebrating, supporting. The shared rhythms and cues, the inside jokes and mutual rituals, the ways each person amplifies the other. These are the signals that say, "I've got your back." It's invisible yet palpable, and it grows because humans are wired to sense it.

In a Constellation Leadership environment, these relational threads hold the network together and allow autonomous teams to move with fluidity, step into leadership where needed, and maintain cohesion without a central figure. Trust, participation, and experimentation emerge naturally, not because someone declared them sacred, but because the team tends them day by day.

We make a big deal about those little things, before those little things become a big deal.

The next section shifts from observation to design. It explores how to create environments where culture leads, purpose anchors, and constellations of autonomous contributors form intentionally, rather than by chance.

Part Three:
Making the journey

07

THE REAL WORLD:
Applying the constellation

*"Leadership is not about making decisions on behalf of others.
It's about creating the conditions that
enable others to face their challenges."*

Ronald Heifetz
Leadership Without Easy Answers (1994)

The stars do not arrive pre-arranged. We look up and see scattered pinpricks of light against a black sky. It is the human mind – not the universe – that connects them. We draw lines between stars and call them stories. Orion. Cassiopeia. The Great Bear.

No star belongs to a single pattern; no pattern is fixed. One culture sees a hunter; another sees a plough. The constellation is not what is, but what we choose to see.

The same is true in organisations. Teams, departments, partnerships. These need not be fixed, immovable formations in an organisational hierarchy. Like our interpretations of constellations, these can be flexible groupings shaped by need, purpose, and perspective. The people within them may shine brightly in one setting and quietly support in another. Leadership is not tied to rank, but to relevance. In one project, I lead. In another, I follow. In both, I contribute. Like people, stars might belong to more than one constellation; contributing their unique strengths to multiple teams simultaneously. Not every star needs to lead. But every star should be ready to, when the context calls for it.

The idea of Constellation Leadership rests on a simple but often overlooked principle: leadership is not a person, but a pattern. In traditional hierarchies, that pattern is predictable, and rooted in formal reporting lines, decision trees, and escalation pathways. But this is not the only way to lead; it's merely the way that leadership theory has been approached as it evolved alongside the hierarchies of industry.

To operate without rigid hierarchy is not to abandon structure. It is to become more intentional about how structure forms. In constellations, structure is shaped by purpose, reinforced by culture, and refined through iteration. These are not permanent teams but responsive formations that organise around a shared objective, contribute their best available thinking, and reconfigure when the need changes.

In this chapter, we begin to shift from research to application. We'll look at how constellations form, how they operate, and how they stay aligned without needing to be controlled. We'll explore how modern organisations are already embracing forms of Constellation Leadership, often without naming it as such. From vision-setting to strategy, from forming autonomous teams to maintaining coherence across them, the following sections offer a practical lens on what works, what fails, and what it takes to lead when no single person has all the answers.

DIVERSITY AS THE OUTPUT OF INCLUSION

At its heart, Constellation Leadership is about inclusion. By nurturing the conditions that allow every member to contribute meaningfully toward a shared objective, diversity is encouraged as an outcome of that inclusivity.

This might feel counterintuitive. Organisations that want a more diverse workforce often begin by focusing directly on diversity – through hiring targets, succession plans, quota commitments etc. These may include bold statements, such as: "We aim to increase the number of women in leadership roles to 50% within three years."

But this is not diversity. This is representation. Representation absolutely matters. We need to see ourselves in positions of influence and authority and much work remains across organisations to make this a reality. Organisations *should* reflect the communities they serve and the customers they support, and quotas can help correct historic imbalances and shift visible power dynamics.

But changing the nightclub's door policy to welcome a broader mix of people means little if the DJ keeps playing just one kind of music. The same crowd will keep dancing, while others stand at the edges, uninvited by the rhythm. The room might appear more representative, but it's not inclusive.

So how do we build truly inclusive teams capable of forming agile, purpose-led constellations?

BUILDING THE TEAM

In 1950, the Peruvian city of Cusco began to shake. Just before noon on 21st May, a 6.1 magnitude earthquake struck the former capital of the Inca Empire. Walls cracked. Churches crumbled. Colonial-era mansions collapsed into the streets, sending centuries of stone and dust into the air. What had once seemed solid turned to rubble in moments. But not everything fell.

Along certain streets, the old 15th-century Inca walls stood firm. Their stones – some the size of small cars – had been laid centuries earlier, long before the invention of concrete or the arrival of Spanish architects. There was no mortar between them. No binding agent. The Incas had not built for speed or symmetry. They built for strength. Each stone was selected by hand to fit the space beside it. Some were smooth, others jagged. No two were alike. But together, they held. When the earthquake came, the walls flexed with the earth and absorbed the shock.

By contrast, many of the newer Spanish buildings had been constructed with uniform bricks and lime mortar. Neat and orderly. Straight lines. Built quickly. But when the ground moved, those walls split apart. The bricks were all the same, and the glue that held them couldn't adapt to the strain. The structures were rebuilt. But when another earthquake struck in 2009 – this time, 4.9 on the Richter scale – it was the same story. The Inca stonework endured. The modern buildings fractured and failed once more.

Inca stonework was not just more beautiful. It was more resilient. Not because the stones were stronger, but because of how they were selected and placed. The genius of Inca design was not in the strength of individual stones, but in the way their differences were arranged. It was not uniformity that gave them resilience, but care. This is how you build something that lasts. Even when the ground shakes.

Now consider how teams are typically built inside organisations. Most recruitment begins with a specification or job description: a list of criteria that outlines the 'ideal' candidate for a given role. This could be to resource a new position or to replace someone leaving. Either way, the hiring process centres on alignment – who ticks the most boxes? If the list has ten items, success is often defined as "who meets or exceeds the greatest number of criteria?"

This reveals the first challenge. Multiple studies show that one of the strongest drivers of engagement and loyalty is the opportunity to grow within a role. Hiring someone who already meets every requirement may serve the short-term goal of getting someone productive fast (i.e., hit the ground running), but it can also undermine long-term motivation and retention. There's nowhere left to stretch. If the position is replacing a departing employee, an additional bias creeps in. We're often, even unconsciously[26], looking for a replica – a like-for-like replacement. Sarah's leaving, and it can feel like we have a "Sarah-shaped hole." So, we go searching for another Sarah.

---

[26] Confirmation bias is the tendency to search for, interpret, and favour information that confirms pre-existing beliefs or hypotheses, while ignoring information that contradicts them. Status Quo bias (unrelated to the British rock band) is defined as the tendency to prefer things to remain the way they are, even when better alternatives exist. Together, these can subtly influence and encourage our hiring and succession practises.

The second challenge is deeper. This form of hiring tends to flatten people into lists. It reduces the individual to a set of measurable traits, skills or experiences that match the specification. In doing so, it encourages homogeneity – like bricks – that stack quickly and neatly, held together by HR processes and predictable routines. Building with bricks is efficient. It brings order and repeatability to team construction. It allows teams, departments and functions to be created quickly, and to slot into existing organisational structures. But when pressure comes – when the ground shifts – will these structures flex and hold? Or will they crack?

Building a team like an Inca wall isn't quick or simple. It takes vision. It takes care. It means resisting the urge to standardise or reshape people to fit a pre-designed mould. The Inca builders didn't alter their stones to conform to one another. They studied each one, understood its contours, and placed it where it could serve its best purpose. Strength came not from uniformity, but from placement. In the same way, Constellation Leadership begins with the individual as they are. It's a model that builds around purpose, not position. Instead of hierarchy or homogeneity, it relies on intelligent assembly.

Many team-building approaches begin by selecting people with distinct capabilities and positioning them where they can contribute to a predefined goal. While this can be effective, it also carries the risk of becoming the metaphorical nightclub door policy – selecting only those who look the part or match previous models of success. The danger is not just exclusion but missed opportunity. Biases can filter out individuals whose skills, experiences or perspectives haven't yet been recognised but could be vital to the mission ahead.

Constellation Leadership takes a different route. It allows for self-assembly. Purpose orients both the team and its members. From there, the team determines how best to achieve the goal.

THE JOURNEY DEFINED

Before we explore how Constellation Leadership works in practice, it helps to clarify a few commonly misunderstood terms. Words such as purpose, vision, strategy, values and culture are often used interchangeably. In reality, they describe very different things. When one leader speaks of "purpose," another may be thinking of a goal, an ambition, or a guiding principle. To establish a shared language, let us turn to a single story: the voyage of the Mayflower.

The Mayflower left Plymouth on 06 or 16 September 1620[27], carrying 102 passengers and crew. After a hazardous journey across the Atlantic, it reached Cape Cod, Massachusetts, two months later. But the real question is why they made the journey at all – and what that decision reveals about leadership and culture.

The Pilgrims were English Separatists who had broken away from the Church of England. They wanted to practise their faith without pressure, punishment or persecution. That desire for freedom led them first to the Netherlands. But financial hardship, fears of war, and concerns about the influence of Dutch culture on their children caused them to return to England and then prepare for the New World.

---

[27] Different European countries moved from the Julian calendar to the Gregorian calendar at various points in history. Britain (and its colonies) adopted the new calendar in 1752, which removed 11 days in September and moved New Year's Day from 25 March to 01 January.

That deep motivation – the reason they chose to go at all – was their **purpose**. It explains their actions and motivation. Alongside that purpose, they also held a broader and more aspirational hope: that they might build a new life without interference or fear. This was their **vision**. Vision does not need to be realised to serve its purpose. It can be aspirational, and its job is to guide. It sets the direction. It is their north star.

But purpose and vision are not the end of the story. The Pilgrims did not simply want to reach a new land or live freely for their own sake. They hoped to build a different kind of society grounded in their beliefs and able to endure beyond their generation. That legacy was the difference they intended to make. This is **impact**. It is the broader consequence of the journey. Purpose explains why they left. Vision gave them direction. Impact tells us why it mattered.

Reaching the destination meant tackling real, tangible steps. How would they cross the ocean? What would progress look like along the way? These are **missions** – the specific, measurable goals that make the vision more achievable. A mission differs from a vision in one important way: it can be completed. That is why we say, "mission accomplished."

To complete those missions, someone had to decide how. What route would the captain take? How fast should the ship travel? When should the sails be raised or stowed? These are questions of **strategy**. Strategy is the method we choose to accomplish our missions.

While the ship's strategy provided how we work towards the missions, another layer governed how people treated one another. No alcohol was permitted on board. The passengers and crew were expected to follow behavioural codes and keep to their roles. These were their **values**. Values are the shared principles and conduct that make the mission more likely to succeed.

And then there was the current. Powerful but invisible, the current could either support the journey or work against it. When it moved in the same direction, sailing felt effortless. When it pushed the other way, everything became harder. This is **culture**. Its presence is felt through momentum or resistance. But even the strongest current is useless without a direction. Culture becomes meaningful only when purpose and vision give it something to push toward.

To make these terms useful beyond analogy, and to ensure a common understanding for what follows, the table summarises each concept, both in the context of the Mayflower and how it applies in organisational life. These definitions will form the foundation for how Constellation Leadership is applied throughout the rest of this chapter.

Term	Mayflower Analogy	Organisational Definition
Purpose	The Pilgrims' motivation to seek religious freedom and escape persecution.	The reason the organisation exists – its driving motivation or cause.
Vision	The hope of building a life free from interference in the New World.	The aspirational future the organisation aims to create. A guiding star, not always reached.
Mission	The practical goals: crossing the Atlantic, reaching land, surviving the voyage.	Achievable objectives that mark progress toward the vision.
Strategy	The ship's route, speed, sail management and tactical decisions made by the captain.	The plan of action or methods used to achieve the mission.

Values	Onboard conduct rules – no alcohol, no fraternisation, shared expectations.	Agreed behaviours and principles that guide how people act and work together.
Impact	The legacy they hoped to leave: a society built on their principles, enduring beyond their generation	The difference the organisation intends to make in the world. The lasting consequence of its actions.
Culture	The ocean current – sometimes helpful, sometimes a resistance to be navigated.	The invisible force of shared norms, habits and assumptions that shape daily experience.

With these definitions in mind, we can begin with the first and most vital of them: vision. In any distributed or autonomous system, clarity of direction is essential. Without it, even the most well-meaning teams can drift. And in Constellation Leadership, vision plays a unique role – not as corporate poetry on a poster, but as a shared and functional guide to coordinated effort.

The Mayflower journey shows us that vision is not a line in a document, but a direction that makes the hardship worthwhile. It names what we are trying to change in the world and why it matters. It gives shape to the effort and makes space for individual contributions to align.

But in modern organisations, especially those built on autonomy, vision needs to do more than inspire. It needs to orient. It must act as a shared reference point that enables decisions without constant direction. Just as early sailors looked to the stars, modern teams need something fixed in the sky – a north star to guide them through complexity.

A SHARED NORTH STAR

In a constellation, every star plays its part, but not every star leads the eye. Some anchor the shape (e.g., Alnitak, Alnilam, and

Mintaka forming Orion's Belt), while others shimmer quietly at the periphery (e.g., π^4 Orionis). The shape we recognise and the meaning we derive begins with one thing: orientation. In the night sky, we find our place not by tracing every star, but by knowing which ones matter most. We look for a constant: a north star.

In organisations, that same sense of orientation is crucial. Autonomy without alignment drifts into chaos. Paradoxically, that chaos can feel both purposeful and fun. It can feel like a great place to work. But even the most exciting, employee-centric and agreeable organisations can (and do) go out of business. Culture, it bears repeating, is not about creating a great place to work; it's about creating a place where great work is done. The two may coincide (they often do). But one is the by-product, not the goal.

Constellation Leadership does not simply advocate decentralisation for its own sake. It depends on a shared direction. This direction is not handed down from on high, but built together, seen in action, and used to steer decisions. This is not the vision statement framed on a boardroom wall. It is the living north star: a purpose that makes individual effort meaningful and enables coordinated action.

Organisations can be successful in the short to medium term without a vision. For example, in fast-growing industries, high demand can carry a company forward even without strategic direction.

In the mid-2000s, Research In Motion (RIM) – the Canadian company behind Blackberry mobile devices – reached nearly 80 million subscribers. Growth came easily, despite not having a defined, articulatable vision. But by 2010, when the mobile market shifted, the absence of a clear direction left them vulnerable, resulting in a rapid decline in operating profit and market share[28].

A clear, purposeful and well-communicated vision helps orientate each member of an organisation by asking why do we exist and what change are we trying to make in the world? It provides strategic clarity. In the absence of an intentional vision, the loudest voices or habits from the past shape your culture. Culture becomes accidental. And whilst it is possible to be successful without a shared vision, an organisation will struggle to thrive, scale or adapt for long without one.

Many leadership teams claim to operate with a strong vision. But when pressed, few employees can articulate it. Fewer still use it to make decisions. In one client workshop, a team of 12 mid-level leaders were asked to write down their organisation's vision, without looking it up. The results were instructive. Twelve leaders; twelve different answers. Some focused on revenue targets. Others cited customer satisfaction, or employee wellbeing, or growth. One person wrote simply, "I'm not sure anymore."

This is not a failure of memory. It's a failure of cultural embedding. A true north star doesn't need to be memorised verbatim. It needs to be felt, used, and seen in action. In distributed teams, especially those operating without constant supervision, the north star becomes a substitute for hierarchy. When everyone knows what we're moving towards, people don't need to be told what to do.

---

[28] Ironically, Apple – who launched the iPhone in 2007 and added to RIM's competition challenges – didn't have a formal vision statement in their early days. But, with a charismatic leader at the helm, everyone followed Steve Job's instinctive direction.

Organisations can struggle with articulating their north star, creating word salads of clichéd phrases: 'best customer value', 'market-leading', 'world's best', 'best-in-class', 'most successful' etc. Consider Volvo Group's 2007 vision statement:

"By creating value for our customers, we create value for our shareholders. We use our expertise to create transport-related products and services of superior quality, safety and environmental care for demanding customers in selected segments. We work with energy, passion and respect for the individual."

If you were an employee of Volvo, would you feel that your passion, purpose and productivity mattered? Probably not. Today, Volvo have a vision that inspires and allows all to contribute toward: "For life. We want to provide you with the freedom to move in a personal, sustainable and safe way."

A clear vision is rarely born in a boardroom. It's seldom the product of a brainstorming session or a polished line of corporate poetry. More often, it begins as something messier: a question, a frustration, a hope. And yet, in many organisations, vision work is treated as a branding exercise. Something to be written, printed, and forgotten. But vision is not a slogan. It is orientation. Without it, even the most talented teams lose momentum. With it, they self-organise, self-correct, and self-drive.

In one coaching engagement, a newly promoted CEO of a UK CIC[29] spoke about her plan to "refresh the vision." She shared a draft: twelve lines of lofty ambition, all carefully phrased. But when asked what her team was actually trying to build, she paused. Then she said: "Honestly? A place where kids don't fall through the cracks." That was the real vision. Short, human, and cogent enough to align every team in the organisation.

Creating a vision is not an act of writing. It's an act of clarity. It's not about what sounds good. It's about what pulls people forward. Will the CIC organisation succeed in preventing children from falling through the cracks in society? No organisation can fully prevent that. But it's a vision worth aspiring to – and one powerful enough to unite everyone who wants to try. The next question isn't how to write a vision. It's how to uncover one.

FINDING THE NORTH STAR

Vision isn't invented. It's revealed. Behind every compelling vision is a thread that runs through the frustrations, hopes, and moments of meaning that already exist in the organisation. The leader's task is not to write a single, perfect sentence. It's to name what matters. To surface what people already care about but haven't yet put into words.

Clarity doesn't come from branding, but from sensemaking. It requires listening, reflection, and sometimes difficult conversations. But when you find it – when the

---

[29] In the UK, a CIC is a Community Interest Company. It's a special type of not-for-profit limited company designed to benefit the community rather than private shareholders.

organisation can name what it's truly trying to do – something powerful happens: alignment emerges.

That discovery is not a solitary journey for the CEO or executive team. It requires collective sensemaking through inviting diverse voices, perspectives, and experiences into the conversation. This inclusivity doesn't dilute clarity; it enriches it, ensuring the vision resonates across the organisation's constellations.

To surface a shared vision, organisations need safe spaces for honest dialogue. This could be facilitated workshops, story-sharing sessions, or small-group interviews. The aim is to create an atmosphere where people feel heard, trusted, and empowered to speak beyond official talking points. The role of a leader here is not to dominate the conversation, but to create the conditions where others can speak freely. Sometimes that means asking the right questions; more often, it means listening without rushing to solve or summarise.

So how do you find your north star? You start not with answers, but with questions. They should be open-ended, practical, and shift thinking from operational to aspirational.

Questions to consider:
- What do you never want to compromise on?
- When does your work feel most meaningful?
- What frustrates you about your sector or competitors?
- What would the world lose if your organisation disappeared?
- What is the story you want to tell your future self?

These questions are more than conversation starters. They serve as mirrors, reflecting what already pulses beneath the surface. They challenge assumptions, expose conflicts, and reveal shared desires that might otherwise stay hidden.

Listening carefully to the answers (especially the contradictions and hesitations) can provide compass points to help leaders and group members understand where the true heart of the organisation lies. Encourage stories that reveal when the organisation feels most alive or aligned with its purpose. These moments highlight the values and aspirations that are already present but may not yet be fully understood or expressed. Use these stories to build a foundation for your vision.

Do not shy away from tension or disagreement. Conflicting perspectives often point to deeper issues that need attention. Creating a safe space to address these openly can strengthen the vision and foster genuine alignment.

Visual tools like a Visioning Canvas can help make the vision concrete. Mapping out purpose, values, and goals in a visual format turns abstract ideas into clear guides for decision-making and behaviour.

IN SEARCH OF LEGACY

Now the vision is established, why does it matter? What is the effect of working towards it? What legacy does the organisation hope to leave behind?

Impact is the difference the organisation seeks to make in the world. It's the lasting consequence of its vision. If vision is the star that guides us, impact is the footprint we leave behind. It includes both tangible and intangible outcomes: the people helped, the problems solved, the norms challenged. It's not just something that can be tallied in end-of-year reports. It's felt in stories, relationships, and change. It lingers when each mission is accomplished.

Too often, impact is mistaken for scale. But reach and resonance are not the same. A social enterprise that helps 100 local families thrive may have more meaningful impact than a multinational that grows profit while deepening inequality. The question is not "how many?" but "what difference did we make?"

This is where clarity matters most. When an organisation is aligned around a shared vision and rooted in purpose, impact becomes more than a side effect. It becomes the reason for choosing one path over another. It shapes priorities, sharpens decisions, and reminds people why their work matters.

Naming the intended impact also helps to show why the vision is worth pursuing. It brings aspiration back down to earth and offers something people can invest in. When people can see the difference they're making – even in small ways – they're more likely to act with intention, creativity, and care.

When leaders attempt to name the impact they hope to make, it's easy to default to obvious measures (e.g., profit, growth, market share, efficiency etc.). But impact is rarely one-dimensional, and describes intent and legacy, rather than specific objectives (which reside in the missions). It lives in different places and touches people in different ways. Understanding these dimensions can help sharpen and justify a vision, especially when the path ahead isn't purely commercial.

- **Social impact** includes the changes an organisation creates in people's lives, such as improving wellbeing and inclusion, reducing harm, or unlocking potential. It might show up in how a workplace supports its employees, how a product empowers its users, or how a service shifts outcomes for communities.

- **Cultural impact** is about shifting norms, expectations, or ways of thinking. It may involve challenging outdated assumptions, amplifying underrepresented voices, or helping to shape how a sector defines value. Sometimes the most powerful legacy an organisation leaves is the way it changed the conversation.

- **Emotional impact** is often overlooked but deeply important. It includes the way an organisation makes people feel (e.g., safe, inspired, respected, trusted, or proud). These feelings shape identity, loyalty, and behaviour. When people feel emotionally aligned with a vision, they don't just support it. They carry it forward.

- **Environmental impact** asks what the organisation takes, protects, or regenerates in its relationship with the planet. This could involve reducing harm, building resilience, or creating new systems of sustainability. Even organisations not directly linked to the natural world have choices that affect it.

- **Economic impact** includes the ripple effects an organisation has on livelihoods, local economies, or long-term value creation. This might mean supporting ethical supply chains, creating fair employment, or building lasting stability in fragile contexts. But it also involves recognising the limits of purely financial metrics.

Each of these areas may not be relevant for every organisation. But when leaders pause to consider which forms of impact they truly care about, the vision becomes more grounded. It becomes something others can connect to, defend, and believe in.

WHY DID WE BEGIN?

Identifying purpose is not always straightforward. For those who were part of the organisation's founding, purpose often emerges from memory. It's there in the story of what was missing, what needed fixing, or what could be better. It's the famous Simon Sinek 'why' behind the organisation. It's the fuel that powers the journey.

These founding intentions become a kind of origin myth; a myth that continues to shape culture, language, and decision-making, whether people realise it or not. But as organisations grow, mature, and evolve, purpose can become obscured. Mergers, market shifts, and leadership changes layer over the original intent. New employees arrive with little connection to the early mission. Over time, "why we began" may no longer feel relevant to "who we are now."

In established organisations, this can feel like a problem. But it doesn't have to be. Purpose isn't always inherited. Sometimes it's discovered, claimed, or created. In fact, many people join a workplace not because of its founding story, but because they see alignment between their own personal values and the organisation's current vision, values, and impact today.

For them, purpose is not handed down. It is discovered in practice.

Consider Microsoft. Under founder Bill Gates, the company's purpose was to democratise access to computing through *a belief in the empowering potential of technology*. This underlying purpose remained constant. But when Satya Nadella became CEO in 2014, the company's vision shifted. The original vision – "a computer on every desk and in every home" – had largely been achieved. A new vision was needed. Nadella reframed it as: *to empower every person and every organisation on the planet to achieve more.* The purpose hadn't changed, but the horizon had. Vision became a tool for renewal, allowing the organisation to orient toward the future while staying anchored in its core motivations.

This means an organisation's purpose can be both a statement and a container: a declaration of why it exists today, and an invitation for others to bring their own meaning to the work. When framed this way, purpose becomes a meeting point.

To explore this more deeply, organisations should reflect on questions like:

Questions to consider:
- What needs are we here to serve?
- What would be missing if we ceased to exist?
- What are we most proud to stand for?
- What kind of change do we exist to catalyse?
- What do our people, partners, or customers believe we're really about?

These questions help uncover a deeper sense of identity that isn't bound to a single product or time period. They also allow for diversity of motivations. Not everyone needs to be driven by the same fire, as long as the heat feels meaningful. When people see purpose in their work, motivation follows. But to understand how that motivation works (and how to support it) we need to look deeper.

Psychologists define motivation as the internal and external factors that initiate, sustain, and direct behaviour. It's the study of what gets us going and what keeps us going. Decades of research have produced countless models, from Maslow's hierarchy to Locke's goal-setting theory, and newer frameworks like Carol Dweck's growth mindset or McGregor's Theory X and Y – though a single, unified theory of motivation has eluded psychologists for decades (remember: psychologists never agree on anything!).

But one theme runs through almost all these theories: motivation cannot be done to someone. It has to come from within. That may sound counterintuitive. After all, we see rewards offered everywhere: bonuses for high performance, trophies for sports, loyalty points for shopping. Aren't these forms of motivation?

Each of these is a form of extrinsic motivation. This is the drive to engage in an activity or a behaviour to gain an external award or to avoid the negative consequence of not engaging. Examples might include praise, payment or performance, or avoiding punishment. Even within extrinsic motivation, psychologists describe three types:

- **External regulation:** acting to meet a demand (e.g., a contact centre adviser chasing call time targets to satisfy a manager).

- **Introjected regulation:** acting to avoid guilt or disapproval (e.g., staying late so as not to let the team down).

- **Identified regulation:** acting because it aligns with personal values (e.g., resolving a customer issue because it feels like the right thing to do).

The problem arises when external rewards start to displace internal meaning.

Consider a contact centre adviser who once took pride in helping frustrated customers find real solutions. Introduce a cash incentive for reducing average call times, and suddenly, speed matters more than problem-solving. Calls get rushed. Customers feel dismissed. Employee satisfaction declines. The adviser who used to find meaning in their work is now just chasing the incentive. The system has redirected their attention, and the behaviour has become transactional.

This phenomenon is not limited to contact centres. People often voluntarily donate blood out of a sense of altruism and social good. With blood stocks declining in the UK and USA in the sixties, financial incentives were introduced in some areas to increase donation rates. However, the donation rates actually decreased. Researchers found that people who had once donated out of a sense of moral duty began to see it as a transactional activity, and those who had been willing to give for free lost motivation when money was involved.

A separate study found that when children were paid to read books, their overall interest in reading declined once the rewards stopped. The external incentive – money – displaced their intrinsic love of reading, making the activity feel like work rather than a pleasurable pastime.

This doesn't mean extrinsic motivators are useless. They can increase short-term performance, particularly in competitive environments or for measurable goals. Once people see work as a means to an end rather than something inherently valuable, motivation diminishes.

Psychologists Edward Deci and Richard Ryan, in their Self-Determination Theory, identified three essential ingredients for human motivation: autonomy (feeling in control of your actions), mastery (developing skills and competence), and purpose (believing the work matters). A strong organisational purpose supports all three. It offers direction without dictation, it gives people a reason to grow, and it shows why their work matters.

A clear, living purpose helps people understand why their work matters. It gives shape to decisions, encourages the development of mastery, and supports a sense of autonomy. People aren't following instruction; they're following meaning. When personal and organisational purpose align, people don't just turn up. They show up with intent and are more willing to take initiative.

In decentralised teams, this clarity acts as a silent governor. Rather than needing detailed instruction or top-down oversight, individuals make choices aligned with shared intent. Consider an agile product team deciding whether to delay a release to fix a flaw that only a few users would notice. With a clearly held purpose and vision the team doesn't need permission to make the call. Purpose becomes the anchor that guides local judgement. It allows autonomy without chaos.

This is where autonomy becomes more than just a motivational tool. In Constellation Leadership, purpose and vision act as a decentralised decision-making framework. Teams don't need to escalate every choice or defer to hierarchy. Instead, they use them as a filter asking, "Does this move us closer to the kind of change we exist to create?"

In this way, purpose doesn't just inspire action; it coordinates it. It becomes the quiet logic behind thousands of small decisions made at the edges of the organisation. It informs culture.

HOW WE MOVE

By this point, we've established our north star (vision), understand why we started or joined the journey (purpose), and recognise the difference we want to make (impact). But a vision does not manifest because it is agreed upon. Purpose does not inspire simply because it is powerful. Neither creates change until they are translated into motion and people begin to act in ways that express, extend and embody them. Between intention and outcome lies something quieter, messier and more revealing: behaviour.

In Constellation Leadership, there is no permanent leader at the helm. Influence flows like a current, moving to where it is needed most. Any individual might step forward for a moment to guide, or step back to follow. In such a system, behaviour becomes our most consistent form of leadership. It shapes how decisions are made, how work gets done and how people relate to one another. When no one person is permanently in charge, behaviour becomes the culture's compass.

If purpose is the reason we exist and vision is the direction we travel, behaviour is the way we move. It is not just a set of tasks or habits. It is how we interpret values in context, how we respond under pressure, and how we build or break trust in each other. Values aren't just words on a wall. They're the relational glue of the constellation. They define the rules of engagement, express what matters most in the day-to-day, and help people make decisions when no one's watching. In this sense, behaviour is the gravitational force of a constellation. Without it, the system drifts.

To design for behaviour is not to write rules. In a self-organising group, we don't control others' actions. But we can create the conditions where shared behaviours become more likely. These patterns tend to fall into three categories: signature behaviours, friction behaviours, and decision behaviours.

Signature behaviours:

These are the distinct ways of working and relating that set one group apart from another. They might be small, but they are telling. A design studio might use daily "open sketch" sessions to invite critique and co-creation, while a care organisation might describe "pausing before speaking" as a behavioural norm that honours the stories of those they serve.

Signature behaviours are often symbolic. They say, "This is who we are." They are not copied from competitors or written into performance frameworks. They emerge from purpose and context. But once they're recognised, they can be named and nurtured. A constellation becomes defined only when the stars are connected. Signature behaviours are those connections. They make the pattern visible.

Questions to consider:
- What behaviours would others notice if they spent a week with your team?
- What do you hope they'd notice?
- What do you reward, even if informally?

Friction behaviours:

Not all behaviour helps us move forward. Sometimes, it pulls us apart.

These are the behaviours that emerge when values conflict, or when vision meets pressure. A team that values openness might begin to sugar-coat bad news when under scrutiny. A group that prizes initiative might slip into siloed action during busy periods. These tensions are not failures. They are natural, and often predictable. But they require conscious design.

Friction behaviours usually arise from competing commitments. A value like "transparency" may sit uncomfortably beside a desire to "protect morale." The organisation might not know which to prioritise, so individuals make the call in real time. Over time, these decisions accumulate. They shape the culture more than any formal declaration. Friction tells us where the culture needs conversation. It reveals the gap between what we say and what we do.

Questions to consider:

- What behaviours appear when the pressure is on?
- Which values are in conflict in those moments?
- What do people fear – and what does that tell you?

Decision behaviours:

In a distributed system, decision-making is everyone's job. Not just when the work is tactical, but when it is ethical, strategic or uncertain. In Constellation Leadership, we do not escalate decisions through hierarchy. We build the capability to make decisions through shared purpose, context and behavioural norms.

Decision behaviours are the informal guidelines people follow when no one else is watching. They are the difference between autonomy and chaos. In well-designed cultures, these decisions are guided by principles, rather than policies. In teams with high alignment, people may act with surprising boldness because they are confident it fits the mission, rather than because they were told to.

Consider an open-source software collective whose vision is to empower creators without barriers. A contributor notices that a new feature makes the interface harder for screen readers. No one has asked them to fix it. But they make the change anyway, knowing that inclusion is not just a technical detail but a core expression of the group's purpose. In the absence of hierarchy, behaviour becomes the map.

When behaviours are consistent with the organisation's vision and intended impact, trust grows. People are more likely to act independently when they trust that others will do the same.

This is how constellations move. Not in lockstep, but in synchrony.

Questions to consider:
- When people act without asking, what guides them?
- What do we encourage others to decide for themselves?
- When someone makes a wrong call, how do we respond?

When behaviours are consistent with the organisation's vision and intended impact, trust grows. People are more likely to act independently when they trust that others will do the same. This is how constellations move. Not in lockstep, but in synchrony.

FROM VALUES TO VELOCITY

Values give a constellation its movement, but without focus, that movement becomes drift. Shared behaviours keep the group connected, yet without something tangible to work towards, they risk travelling together without direction. A constellation needs more than a north star. It needs points along the journey where energy converges into defined objectives. It needs a mission.

A mission is a shared commitment to achieve a specific outcome within a set timeframe. It sits closer to the ground than the vision, which remains steady and enduring. Missions give direction to the here and now. They are both a reason to gather momentum and a way to measure progress. Purpose explains why the constellation exists. Vision describes where it is heading. Mission focuses on what must be achieved next to keep moving in that direction.

In Constellation Leadership, a mission is not assigned by a fixed leader. It emerges from the group's shared sense of direction and is owned collectively, with any member able to step forward to coordinate its delivery. These missions can form in two ways. They can be set from the outside (prescribed), or they can emerge from within (emergent).

Prescribed missions:

Some missions are set in advance and arrive as a directive from outside the constellation. A client may request a project delivered by a certain date. A parent organisation may set a target. A partner may ask for support in solving a pressing problem.

When these missions arrive, the group's task is to interpret them through the lens of their shared vision and behaviours. This is not a question of obedience but of alignment. If a prescribed mission supports the constellation's purpose, it can be accepted as a focal point. If it conflicts, the group must decide whether to adapt it, negotiate it, or decline it.

Example:

A partner organisation asks the constellation to design a new onboarding programme for a joint project. The deadline is eight weeks. The group interprets the request in line with its purpose, agreeing that the work supports their vision of improving user experiences. Members self-select into task groups, drawing on their established behaviours to share information, challenge weak ideas, and make decisions without delay.

Prescribed missions have the benefit of clarity. They create urgency and can channel energy quickly. But they carry a risk of detachment if the group does not feel ownership. Without alignment to the constellation's values, the mission risks becoming a transaction rather than a shared endeavour.

Emergent missions:

Other missions arise from within the group in response to unfolding events. These emergent missions are one of Constellation Leadership's greatest strengths. They allow the group to adapt rapidly without waiting for instruction.

They begin as ideas, concerns, or opportunities noticed by members. A new market trend sparks a proposal. A service gap reveals a chance to act. A shared frustration points to something that needs fixing.

Emergent missions tend to generate high engagement because they are owned from the outset. They reflect the group's interpretation of the vision in the present moment. They can be agile and creative, adapting quickly as circumstances change.

Example:

Several members notice that clients are struggling with a particular reporting tool. They propose creating a simplified guide. The idea is discussed openly, tested for value against the vision, and agreed. No one waits for permission because the behaviours and decision processes are already in place.

Emergent missions rely on members having the awareness to detect changes, the confidence to speak up, and the trust that others will respond constructively.

Yet these missions are not without risks. Without a clear connection to the shared vision, emergent missions can fragment the group's attention. Energy may be spread across too many directions, diluting the impact of each effort and leading to scope creep.

Questions to consider:

- What would make this mission worth committing to?
- How will we know when it is complete?
- Which of our behaviours will help us achieve it, and which might hold us back?

STAYING ON-TRACK

The behaviours established in the constellation shape how missions are pursued. Signature behaviours give each group a distinctive way of working and can help to differentiate their approach. Friction behaviours – when used constructively – create the space to test assumptions and strengthen ideas before committing. Decision behaviours provide the discipline to move from discussion to action.

In a constellation, where there is no fixed individual leadership position, these behaviours become the closest thing to a command structure. They enable members to act without waiting for permission, trusting that others will interpret the mission through the same shared patterns. Whether prescribed or emergent, a mission benefits from clear principles. It should consider:

- **Shared ownership**: Treating the mission as a collective responsibility

- **Active communication**: Keeping others informed and inviting input

- **Constructive challenge**: Questioning assumptions without undermining trust

- **Adaptive prioritisation**: Knowing when to pause one mission in favour of another

Missions are best introduced and refined in open conversation. In the absence of a fixed leader, it is the responsibility of all members to raise questions, offer perspectives, and test the mission's relevance before committing. Once agreed, the mission should be shared in simple, unambiguous terms so anyone in the group can restate it if needed. This requires an understanding of team psychological safety (note: This is a primary requirement in Constellation Leadership and a complex subject deserving of its own chapter.)

The group must also recognise that missions are temporary. They should not drift into becoming 'mini visions' that remain permanently unfinished. A completed mission clears space for the next, allowing the constellation to keep moving.

By treating missions as shared endeavours rather than orders, Constellation Leadership turns movement into momentum. Every member can step forward to lead when the moment demands it, and step back when others are better placed to guide. This fluid exchange keeps the constellation responsive, focused, and moving together.

Questions to consider:
- Does this mission still serve our purpose?
- Are we aligned on the intended outcome?
- Do we have the right people and resources in place?
- What new information might affect our course?
- How will we know when the mission is complete?

COORDINATION AND SELF-ORGANISATION IN ACTION

Each spring, the swallows of San Juan Capistrano return from their wintering grounds in South America, covering thousands of miles in small, shifting formations. No one bird dictates the route. Instead, the flock navigates through a combination of inherited instinct, collective memory, and moment-by-moment adjustments to wind, weather and predators.

The bird at the front does not hold the position for long. As the air resistance takes its toll, it slips back, and another moves forward. Those at the rear keep watch for danger. Others adjust the formation to keep the group's energy in balance. In this way, the swallows move as a coordinated whole without needing a single permanent leader. The murmuration[30] is mesmerising.

Constellation Leadership mirrors this fluid exchange. Any member can take the lead when conditions require it, stepping

---

[30] A murmuration of swallows is a mesmerising aerial display where large flocks of swallows fly in synchronised, swirling patterns, often forming shapes and vortices in the sky. This behaviour is not unique to swallows; starlings are also known for their spectacular murmuration, but swallows' displays are unique and beautiful in their own right.

forward with clarity and direction, then returning to the group when the moment no longer requires it. The shared vision – like the swallows' innate pull toward Capistrano – provides the alignment that keeps the group moving together, even when the journey is long and the terrain unseen. Just as the birds adjust their course mid-flight to respond to shifting winds, so too do constellations recalibrate their missions based on new information or obstacles.

What's most impressive is that the swallows return to California, arriving almost precisely on 19 March every year. The birds navigate thousands of miles, relying on a shared sense of timing, direction, and constant adjustment, yet always arrive together as a community.

The swirling, shifting flight of the swallows shows us that coordinated action does not require a fixed leader issuing commands at every turn. Instead, it depends on each member's awareness, responsiveness, and trust in the group. Coordination emerges through continuous, local interactions – small adjustments made by individuals who share a clear sense of purpose and an understanding of the group's behaviours.

Constellations rely on vision, friction, and decision behaviours to maintain alignment and adapt rapidly. These behaviours act as invisible currents that keep the group moving in synchrony, even when the path is uncertain. Each person senses when to lead and when to follow, when to push forward or hold back, responding to both the evolving external environment and the internal dynamics of the constellation.

This fluid self-organisation allows the constellation to navigate complexity with agility. It supports distributed leadership – the ability for anyone to step into a leadership role as needed – while sustaining cohesion and shared commitment to the mission.

The swallows' migration also highlights the importance of synchrony and shared rhythm. Their timing ensures that the group benefits from safety in numbers and the energy of collective movement. Similarly, in a constellation, aligned timing and coordinated effort ensure that momentum builds, trust deepens, and the mission is achieved efficiently.

This metaphor invites us to think about timing not as a fixed deadline imposed from above, but as a living rhythm co-created by the group. It encourages flexibility within discipline, responsiveness within commitment, and shared responsibility for when and how the mission unfolds.

Just as the swallows rely on shared timing and mutual adjustment to navigate their journey, so too must constellations develop a collective sense of rhythm and pace to manage their work. Through a shared understanding of key moments for decision, review, adaptation, and action, constellations can perform exceptionally. Teams can create this by:

- **Setting regular touchpoints** that provide natural pauses to reflect, recalibrate, and realign on mission progress without micromanaging day-to-day activity

- **Agreeing on flexible "windows" for delivery** rather than fixed deadlines, allowing for responsiveness to new information or obstacles while maintaining momentum

- **Encouraging individuals to listen actively** for signals that leadership or focus needs to shift—when someone steps forward to guide or when it's time to follow and support

- **Balancing autonomy with collective rhythm** through transparent communication and shared norms about when and how to escalate issues or pivot course

By approaching timing as a living, emergent rhythm felt and co-created by the group, constellations can maintain focus and momentum even amid uncertainty and complexity. This shared temporal awareness deepens trust and builds resilience, enabling the group to move confidently together towards their mission.

Questions to consider:
- Does our mission align with our vision and shared purpose?
- Who is best placed to lead right now, and who needs to support or follow?
- Are our behaviours helping or hindering progress?
- How are we managing tensions and maintaining trust?
- Is our timing flexible and responsive to new information?
- Do members feel safe and encouraged to speak up?
- When do we know a mission is truly complete?

PUTTING CONSTELLATIONS INTO PRACTICE

To bring Constellation Leadership to life, groups must begin with a shared clarity around their vision and purpose. This foundational understanding serves as a compass that guides decisions, behaviours, and energy throughout the journey. Without it, even the most well-intentioned efforts risk drifting without alignment or meaning.

Missions, the tangible objectives that propel a constellation forward, must be defined collaboratively. Whether these missions are prescribed by external demands or emerge organically from within, their relevance and scope require open conversation and collective agreement. This ensures the group owns the mission fully and remains committed to achieving it.

The behaviours within the constellation act as the invisible currents shaping how the group moves together. Signature behaviours distinguish one constellation from another, expressing its unique culture and values. Friction behaviours, when managed constructively, provide necessary space for challenge and refinement. Decision behaviours guide the group from discussion to action, sustaining momentum without rigid hierarchy.

Leadership in a constellation is fluid and distributed. Any member can step forward to lead when circumstances call for it, and step back to support or follow when others are better placed. This dynamic requires deep trust in one another's judgment and responsiveness, as well as confidence that the group shares a common purpose.

Timing and coordination are equally vital. Rather than relying on fixed deadlines or top-down scheduling, constellations cultivate a shared rhythm – a living, emergent tempo that balances flexibility and discipline. Regular check-ins, flexible delivery windows, and transparent communication allow the group to sense when to accelerate, pause, or pivot. This temporal awareness builds resilience and keeps momentum alive amid complexity.

Psychological safety underpins all of this. Members must feel safe to raise questions, offer constructive challenge, and admit mistakes without fear of blame or retribution. Only then can honest dialogue thrive, strengthening trust and enabling the constellation to adapt and grow.

Finally, missions should be recognised as temporary and iterative. Completing a mission fully before moving on prevents drift into endless 'mini visions' and keeps the constellation dynamic and focused. Each mission is a stepping stone, clearing the way for the next phase of collective movement.

In summary, putting Constellation Leadership into practice means nurturing shared clarity, embracing collective ownership of missions, cultivating adaptive behaviours, practising fluid leadership, fostering a shared rhythm of timing, prioritising psychological safety, and treating missions as temporary yet purposeful endeavours. These interconnected elements create the conditions for a constellation to navigate complexity with agility and cohesion.

With these practical considerations, we have laid the groundwork for intentionally nurturing Constellation Leadership. Understanding the interplay of shared purpose, adaptive behaviours, fluid leadership, and collective rhythm equips groups to navigate complexity with confidence. But principles alone can only take us so far. To see how this approach unfolds in reality, we will explore organisations already living these dynamics –

often without explicitly naming them as Constellation Leadership.

The next chapter reveals the constellation in action through real-world cases of distributed leadership, self-organisation, and shared mission driving meaningful impact.

08

IN PRACTICE:
Utilising constellations

*"For the things we have to learn before we can do them,
we learn by doing them."*

Aristotle
Nicomachean Ethics (340 BCE)

When the idea of a Constellation Leadership model was first
proposed for research, it was surprising to discover that this
approach had not yet been studied in any formal academic
context.

While many leadership theories and frameworks have been
explored extensively, this fluid, distributed model of leadership –
where purpose, behaviours, and collective rhythm replace fixed
hierarchy – had remained largely invisible in scholarly literature.

Yet, this does not mean that Constellation Leadership is
purely theoretical or untested. On the contrary, there is abundant

evidence that organisations and teams across diverse industries have been embodying these principles for years, often without explicitly naming or conceptualising them as such. Whether in agile teams, innovative startups, or purpose-driven communities, the dynamics of shared vision, emergent missions, adaptive behaviours, and distributed leadership are alive and thriving.

This chapter aims to uncover these real-world examples, revealing how Constellation Leadership naturally emerges in practice. By examining organisations that successfully harness self-organisation, collective ownership, and shared purpose, we can see the model's practical power to navigate complexity and accelerate impact. Through these case studies, the often intangible dynamics of Constellation Leadership become visible, demonstrating that while the academic lens is catching up, the practice has already taken root.

STUDY 1: DISCIPLINED FREEDOM

"A favourable situation will never be exploited if commanders wait for orders", wrote Helmuth Karl Bernhard Graf von Moltke.

The 19th century Prussian field marshal recognised that the expansion of army personnel numbers since 1820 onwards had made it impossible to maintain control solely through detailed military orders. In the dense fog of battle, those rigid orders could be fatal. A commander who insists on dictating every movement soon finds that their plans collapse at first contact with the enemy. Commanders of distant attachments would have to exercise initiative for their forces to be effective in battle.

Moltke termed this *Auftragstaktik* or *mission tactics*. Rather than detailing orders, commanders could share their intention and the objective and allow deviations to the directive providing those deviations were still aligned with the overall mission. This became a fundamental philosophy of all German military theory and, later, was adopted across many other nation's military services.

The British Army, hardened by two world wars and shaped by the complex conflicts that followed, adapted the approach and birthed what is now called *Mission Command*: a philosophy that combines clear intent with decentralised execution. Instead of instructing subordinates on what to do step by step, leaders articulate the why and the what – the purpose, the objective, the boundaries – and then leave the how to those closest to the action.

There is, of course, much more nuance to the real-world approach taken, and the philosophy is not only used in combat situations. Even in peacetime, a plan might not survive contact with the enemy.

The principle is not confined to combat. Operation Rescript, the UK's military response to the COVID-19 pandemic, showed how Mission Command plays out in peacetime. Between 2020 and 2022, over 23,000 personnel were mobilised in the COVID Support Force, the largest domestic operation in British military history. Soldiers airlifted patients, designed and staffed temporary hospitals, distributed PPE, manned mobile testing units, and even helped counter misinformation. The scope was vast, the environment unpredictable, and yet coordination held.

Lieutenant Colonel Samantha Brettell DL, who oversaw operational stress management for service personnel during Rescript, describes the delicate balance between prescription and autonomy. "Even though we talk about mission command, we are still very prescriptive. Having that confidence that my right-hand person and my left-hand person knows what they're doing;

everybody has to have that same level of understanding and education."

That shared understanding is what makes freedom possible. Mission Command is not a licence for improvisation in the dark; it rests on a foundation of exhaustive preparation. Before a mission begins, every variable is interrogated, every contingency mapped, every fallback rehearsed. Ideally, the Army would anticipate every eventuality so that initiative need not be exercised. But real life rarely grants such perfection. And it is in the gaps between plan and reality that Mission Command reveals its worth.

The British Army codifies this philosophy in the *Combat Estimate,* a structured set of seven questions used by commanders to frame decisions:

- What is the situation and how does it affect me?
- What have I been told to do and why?
- What effects do I need to achieve and what direction must I give to develop my plan?
- Where can I best accomplish each action or effect?
- What resources do I need to accomplish each action or effect?
- When and where do these actions take place in relation to each other?
- What control measures do I need to impose?

This process accelerates decision-making and ensures that, even when decentralised, actions remain coherent. Yet freedom has limits. Orders must still align with the Geneva Conventions, with Army values, and with ethical codes embedded in regimental culture. As Lt Col Brettell cautions, "Every bullet is accounted for. Everybody is accounted for. And there will be an after-action review on everything. Mission command isn't where we're doing what we want and 'isn't this great?' The mission will always be within the realms of the law. It's about my intent, my commander's intent and my commander's commander's intent. Even the nation's intent."

This framework echoes Constellation Leadership. The intent can be considered as "What are we here to achieve?" It's the mission that guides the model. Freedom of action is possible only because this north star has already been made clear.

The cultural framework is replaced by a combination of explicit protocols (i.e., laws, regulations, and pre-mission planned approaches) and by implicit culture (shared behaviours, values and trust within the company).

MILITARY'S MECHANICS OF DISCIPLINED FREEDOM

What Mission Command demonstrates is that leadership need not mean micromanagement, even in environments where lives are at stake. It shows that trust is not a luxury but a necessity, and that purpose-driven autonomy creates agility under fire. Quite literally.

But this flexibility takes planning – diligent, punctilious, precise planning – so that when the plan needs adapting, the team understand intent and effect.

- **Clear Commander's Intent**: Every operation begins with a statement of purpose – what must be achieved and why it matters. This anchors all subsequent decisions.

- **Decentralised Execution**: Authority is deliberately pushed downwards. Junior officers and even NCOs have the discretion to act in ways that suit the moment, so long as they remain true to intent.

- **Mutual Trust**: Leaders trust subordinates to act with initiative; subordinates trust that their actions will be backed, even if they diverge from the plan.

- **Tolerance for Adaptation**: Failure to follow orders to the letter is not punished if the deviation serves the intent and is within legal, ethical and regulatory frameworks. Initiative is prized above blind obedience.

- **Shared Training and Doctrine**: Freedom works only when underpinned by common language and shared standards. Soldiers are steeped in doctrine, drills, and values so that decentralisation does not mean chaos.

Mission Command thrives on a paradox: freedom within boundaries. This freedom is carefully bounded by law, doctrine, and shared culture. Its genius is to acknowledge that uncertainty is inevitable, and that resilience lies not in clinging tighter to control, but in preparing people so thoroughly that when control must be loosened, they act with confidence.

As a philosophy, it transforms autonomy from a risk into a resource. The result is not anarchy but coordinated adaptability, a reactive system that outpaces rigid hierarchies precisely because it allows leadership to emerge where it is most needed: at the edge.

STUDY 2: FROM NASA TO NEIGHBOURHOODS

Few leadership thinkers can claim a résumé that spans rocket launches, refugee schools, and retail empires. Dr. Ted Anders can.

In the 1980s, Anders worked inside NASA's Astronaut Training Office, helping prepare crews for space shuttle missions during one of the agency's most challenging chapters. When the Challenger exploded in 1986, killing all seven astronauts on board, Anders was close enough to see how command-and-control cultures can amplify risk rather than reduce it. Later, he would guide the Dalai Lama on revitalising schools for Tibetan children in exile throughout India, installing learning systems rooted in autonomy and dignity rather than outdated and instructional hierarchy. In between, he partnered with Baroness Michelle Mone as she scaled Ultimo into a global lingerie brand and with Sir Tom Hunter as he grew Sports Division into one of the UK's largest sports retailers. He has provided government leadership development, proposed recommendations for resolving Middle East conflicts. As a child entrepreneur in Florida, he took his first self-funded international flight at age 10, funding it by selling crabs as bait to local fishermen.

This diverse journey might appear unconnected. But for Anders, each episode pointed toward a single conclusion: top-down control limits true leadership potential and team performance. The best systems empower people closest to the work and the customer to take ownership of decisions. From this conviction, Anders co-created a methodology that would become Customer Driven Leadership (CDL).

This framework for distributing authority, embedding accountability, and aligning everyone around customer need, offers organisations a way to flip the traditional hierarchy. Its premise was deceptively simple: invert the pyramid, put the customer at the top, and let leadership flow upward from there.

The model avoided abstract rhetoric because CDL was designed to be applied. Its mechanics hardwired autonomy into everyday routines:

- **Intent as compass:** mission and values set the destination, visible and explicit

- **Decentralised execution:** teams act without waiting for orders, guided by customer need within a clearly allocated "playing field" of authority

- **Trust as atmosphere:** autonomy is only possible when leaders create the conditions for it

- **Adaptation as rhythm:** performance feedback and customer signals are turned into learning loops.

CDL is not a loose philosophy but an operating system: a structure that shapes behaviours, incentives, and culture. Few examples capture this more vividly than the long-running story of Automation Direct.

CDL'S MECHANICS OF SHARED INTENT

In 1995, PLC Direct was a small mail-order distributor of programmable logic controllers. Competing with much larger industrial suppliers, it faced a choice: grow by replicating traditional hierarchies or grow differently. Guided by Anders' CDL framework, it chose the latter.

Rebranded as Automation Direct, the company built its organisation around the customer rather than the boss's office. The strategy paid off. Over the following decades, Automation Direct expanded its catalogue to tens of thousands of industrial automation products, pioneered direct online sales in its sector, and became known for industry-leading shipping accuracy and service. The culture that enabled this success was CDL in practice:

- **Upside-down accountability:** Teams are organised around serving both external and internal customers. Instead of managers holding authority, teams hold one another accountable through transparent performance systems.

- **Report cards, not reports:** Every team's metrics are published on visible report cards. These include customer-critical outcomes such as shipping accuracy (measured at 99.98%), phone and email response times, and satisfaction ratings. Results are shared openly, reinforcing ownership rather than hiding problems.

- **Peer review of leaders:** Leaders are not immune to evaluation. Team members anonymously assess their supervisors, and these scores influence pay and continuation in leadership roles. Authority is earned through trust and credibility, not titles.

- **Customer outcomes embedded in pay:** Bonuses and incentives are directly linked to customer measures, aligning everyone's financial interest with the quality of service. Performance conversations are not about pleasing a manager but about serving the customer better.

- **Culture of recognition:** The company has been repeatedly recognised as a "Top Workplace," not because of perks or slogans, but because employees feel genuine ownership of decisions and results.

- **Technology as an amplifier:** Automation Direct invested early in e-commerce and logistics systems, allowing a small organisation to compete with giants. But technology never replaced human judgement; it freed employees to act with more autonomy.

This is CDL made tangible: transparency, distributed accountability, and alignment around customer values and expectations. The model helped Automation Direct retain the agility of a start-up while building the resilience of a large enterprise.

Automation Direct's application of CDL is significant because it demonstrates its durability. Many management approaches enjoy a burst of attention before fading. CDL has quietly underpinned nearly three decades of consistent performance in a highly competitive sector. Its lessons resonate beyond industrial distribution:

- **Autonomy scales when trust is systemic.** Empowerment cannot rest on inspirational speeches; it requires visible structures that reward ownership.

- **Customers are the ultimate anchor.** By linking pay, recognition, and decision-making to customer metrics, Automation Direct avoided the drift toward internal politics.

- **Transparency fuels accountability.** Performance summaries are published for all to see replace whispered reviews and hidden scorecards. Problems are surfaced, not buried.

- **Leadership is earned, not inherited.** By subjecting leaders to peer review, CDL embeds humility and responsiveness into the system.

For Anders, these features echo lessons from NASA and the Dalai Lama alike: when systems concentrate power at the top, they become brittle; when systems distribute leadership, they become adaptive. CDL is more than a set of organisational mechanics. It is Anders' answer to a lifelong question: how can human systems – whether schools, companies, or communities – create both freedom and responsibility?

The question runs like a thread through his biography. From entrepreneurial childhood ventures (selling lemonade, mowing lawns, gathering bait crabs), to pioneering Montessori education with his wife, to building nursing schools in Honduras and respiratory medicine initiatives for 9/11 responders, Anders has consistently applied CDL's principles: autonomy, accountability, and intent.

"I've always had an entrepreneurial approach", Dr. Anders shares. "When we create abundant societies everywhere that work well for everyone, the world is will be a better place."

His current projects – creating a Centre for Thriving Children in Florida, developing AI-driven investment platforms for low-income communities to reduce the barrier of entry for wealth generation, and his family-founded NGO: LoveLight SOULutions – show that the model is not finished but evolving, and applicable across industries and contexts.

For Constellation Leadership, CDL offers an instructive metaphor. Leadership is not the light of a single star but the pattern that emerges when many points of light are connected. Automation Direct's experience illustrates how this can work in practice.

STUDY 3: THE HEAT OF PLAY

The lights of Rogers Arena in Vancouver cut through the dark. On stage sit ten young men, hunched over keyboards, headsets pressed tight, each monitor a window into a shared battlefield. The International 2018 – the most prestigious tournament in esports – is at its climax. Millions of dollars hang on the outcome of a game that will be decided in less than an hour.

One of the teams, OG, is an anomaly. They are not the best-funded, nor the most star-studded. Just weeks earlier, bookmakers had written them off. Their opponents, PSG.LGD, boast sponsorship muscle and a reputation for ruthless tactical discipline. Yet, against all predictions, OG go on to lift the trophy. And a year later, they do it again, becoming the first team ever to win back-to-back Internationals. How did they manage this improbable feat? The answer lies in a kind of constellation leadership that thrives not in boardrooms but in high-pressure digital arenas.

Unlike traditional sports, esports lacks a fixed coach calling plays from the sidelines. In games like DOTA2[31] (a multiplayer online battle arena game), leadership is distributed. One player might call the early-game strategy, another mid-game rotations, a third might orchestrate late-game team fights. The role of "captain" exists, but the team's survival depends on an elastic leadership model. Whoever has the clearest vantage point in the moment takes the lead, while others fall into supporting roles.

This requires an extraordinary degree of trust. In interviews, OG players describe their bond less as teammates and more as family. The team was forged through hardship: a last-

---

[31] DOTA2 (Defense of the Ancients) is played between two teams of five players, with each team occupying and defending their own separate base on the map.

minute roster collapse forced them to rebuild weeks before the 2018 tournament. What looked like fragility instead produced resilience. Shared struggle created a culture of psychological safety. In the crucible of competition, no one feared speaking up or improvising; they trusted each other to adapt.

OG'S MECHANICS OF ADAPTIVE PLAY

Sports psychologists might call this a *shared mental model*. Each player holds in mind not only their own objectives but the collective picture. Because the model is shared, leadership can rotate fluidly without chaos. Cognitive load is distributed, freeing players to enter flow.

The constellation is clearest in OG's captain, Johan "N0tail" Sundstein. Rather than dictating every move, he acts as a stabilising star, keeping the team's purpose aligned, encouraging bold plays, and diffusing pressure. Whilst leadership is less command than context, there are shared mechanics and behaviours across the team:

- **Rotating shot-calling protocols**. The group establishes clear norms for who leads when: early-game lane leaders, mid-game map control, late-game team fight callers. The baton passes explicitly in-match through verbal instruction to prevent cross-talk and decision lag.

- **Shared language and compressed comms**. Pre-agreed shorthand reduces cognitive load. In fights, only one or two voices speak; others supply micro-info ("BKB 10s," "no buyback") in one-beat phrases.

- **Deliberate role flexibility**. Players practice with secondary heroes and swap playstyles, so leadership can rotate to whoever's hero's powerspike (a temporary increase in an attribute) is live. Scheduled timed practices (called scrim blocks) include off-role or off-meta drafts to increase the team's flexibility of experience.

- **Replay rituals and post-mortems**. Daily video-on-demand reviews analyse the performance with two lenses: mechanics (micro errors) and model (was our read of the map right?). The second lens builds a shared mental model, so future leadership handoffs are smoother.

- **Pressure training & tilt resets**. Just as the military practice war games, simulated high-stakes scenarios make comeback calls psychologically "normal." Between maps, scripted reset routines – breathing, cue words, two-minute silence etc. – are used to re-centre individuals.

- **Psychological safety on the clock**. During matches, a norm of instant, zero blame debrief occurs. Errors are named factually ("missed glyph call"), mined for signal, and released. This keeps comms clean and preserves confidence for the next call.

- **Leadership visibility rules**. When the leader is in a high-mechanics moment requiring more input and concentration from the player, a second voice is designated to protect bandwidth. Leadership is treated as a resource to be allocated, not a personality to be asserted.

This kind of distributed, in-the-moment leadership is not unique to OG. A similar approach can be seen in the UK-based Rocket League team Endpoint, supported by Chartered Sport & Exercise Psychologist Callum Abbott. His work mirrors that of psychologists in traditional sports: helping players build psychological scaffolding to manage stress, regulate reactions, and recover from setbacks. But in Rocket League, where three players compete at blistering pace without a coach in their ear, autonomy during play is absolute. Leadership before and after matches may be vertical (choosing line-ups, setting tactics, analysing replays), but during competition the team must lead itself.

Abbott describes his role as preparing players to thrive in those autonomous moments. That means building emotional regulation, resilience, and clarity under pressure, so each individual can step forward when the constellation requires it.

"Even though there tends to be three separate 'roles' within the [Rocket League] match – the first player goes in for a challenge; second player is ready for wherever that challenge pings off to; and that third player is then either in defence or, if they have the time, they may go up and make a [quite complex and mechanical] play. At the top level, those three positions are very fluid", Abbott explains. "At the semi-pro and amateur levels, they tend to have one player who's more about the mechanical stuff and the other two tend to…facilitate that star player."

Communication is also different. At the elite-level in-game discussion is purposeful and succinct. Abbott emphasises that effective comms in Rocket League hinge on clarity without emotion. "They're saying, 'Here's what I'm seeing', 'Here's what we need to do', and 'I'm going to let you know what I'm doing, so you can adjust' etc."

He notes that while players can train and compete remotely, performance measurably improves when they are physically co-located. Within esports this phenomenon is known as the "bootcamp buff" – a temporary performance lift when players are together in one place, sharing subtle cues, non-verbal rhythms, and a stronger sense of cohesion.

Like OG, Endpoint have developed explicit systems that allow autonomy without chaos:

- **Autonomous match play.** Once a Rocket League game begins, leadership belongs entirely to the players. Pre-agreed tactics provide a baseline, but in the speed of play, each member must take initiative and switch seamlessly between attack, defence, and support roles.

- **Psychological scaffolding.** Abbott equips players with stress-management routines, trigger awareness, and reset cues to prevent tilt (a spiral of frustration) from derailing decision-making. These routines act like an invisible coach in the room, carried by each player.

- **Vertical–horizontal blend.** Leadership shifts across phases: pre-match preparation and post-match debriefs use traditional hierarchies (coach, analyst, psychologist), but mid-match dynamics are wholly distributed. This reinforces autonomy as the default under pressure.

- **The "bootcamp buff."** When players train in the same physical space, trust and synchrony increase. Subtle cues – a sigh, a grin, a posture shift – create micro-feedback loops impossible to replicate online. The temporary "buff" becomes a reminder that leadership is not only cognitive but embodied.

- **Post-match rituals.** Endpoint players engage in debriefs that separate mechanics ("was my rotation too slow?") from mindset ("what was I feeling when I missed that shot?"). This dual lens strengthens both tactical cohesion and emotional resilience.

Together, these practices show how autonomy in esports is not simply a lack of formal leadership, but a deliberately prepared system in which leadership rotates, emerges, and dissolves in response to the moment. Just as OG demonstrated at the highest stage, Endpoint show that distributed leadership is trainable, sustainable, and measurable.

The results speak for themselves. Against wealthier, more rigidly structured and more practiced teams, OG thrived by being adaptable. Their victories rewrote what success in esports could look like: not the dominance of a single genius, but the collective intelligence of a rotating constellation.

What made OG's run remarkable was not just their technical execution but their capacity to lead without a fixed leader. Theirs was a form of leadership that bent and flexed with the rhythm of the game. At times it was tactical, at times emotional, at times silent. Each player had the capacity to step forward and then step back, contributing not as cogs but as stars in the constellation.

In traditional sports, the coach or captain tends to be the centre of gravity. In OG, the centre moved. Whomever saw furthest in that moment became the anchor around which the others orbited. This fluidity created resilience under extreme pressure. When setbacks came, no single point of failure existed, responsibility was diffused, and belief was shared.

OG's victory at The International was one proof point: five individuals trusting each other enough to lead and follow in fluid, shifting patterns. But they are not an outlier. Endpoint show that the same principles can be trained, nurtured, and applied in a different esport altogether. In both cases, leadership is not a role but a relationship that emerges in the spaces between players, sustained by trust, safety, and shared vision. Together, these teams reveal that Constellation Leadership in gaming is not a one-off miracle, but a repeatable pattern where clarity, trust, and autonomy can turn high-pressure competition into collective mastery.

STUDY 4: COOPERATIVE CONSTELLATIONS

The Basque country in the 1950s was a place of ruin. Civil war and dictatorship had gutted industry, leaving communities impoverished and uncertain. Amidst this landscape walked José María Arizmendiarrieta, a young priest with a vision. He believed that dignity could be restored not by waiting for employers to arrive but by building enterprises where workers owned their own future.

In 1956, five of his protégés pooled their resources to start a small cooperative producing paraffin heaters. This modest workshop, ULGOR, would grow into the Mondragon Corporation. Today, it is one of the largest cooperative federations in the world, employing over 80,000 people across industries from manufacturing to finance.

At the heart of Mondragon is a radical departure from hierarchy. Workers are not employees; they are members and owners. Each cooperative elects its own leaders and governs itself democratically. Pay ratios are tightly controlled – often 6:1 or lower between executives and shop-floor workers – and profits are reinvested into the business or distributed equitably. But what makes Mondragon more than a cluster of co-ops is its federated model. Each cooperative is autonomous, yet they align around shared institutions: a cooperative bank, a university, social welfare systems, and research centres. This constellation of enterprises is bound together by purpose and mutual support rather than by command.

The system has proven remarkably resilient. When Spain's economy collapsed in the 1980s and again during the global financial crisis of 2008, Mondragon weathered the storm better than many conventional corporations. Rather than mass layoffs, workers were redeployed to other co-ops within the federation. Stability came not from rigid hierarchy but from the flexibility of distributed solidarity.

The psychology of Mondragon's success is rooted in identity and fairness. Social identity theory tells us that people derive motivation from belonging to a meaningful group. At Mondragon, workers do not identify as "labour" opposed to "management." They are both. Equity theory suggests that perceptions of fairness drive satisfaction and performance, and Mondragon's tight pay ratios and democratic voice ensure that fairness is embedded structurally, not left to rhetoric.

MONDRAGON'S MECHANICS OF RESILIENCE

This equity approach is woven throughout the fabric of Mondragon. Many approaches are systemised before they are ever needed, to promote transparency, certainty and clarify the constellation's roles.

- **One member, one vote – with role clarity.** General Assemblies elect Governing Councils; Social Councils represent worker voice day-to-day. This ensures that strategic choices are democratic, and operational decisions stay close to teams to keep speed and momentum.

- **Pay-ratio caps & internal capital accounts.** Tight wage solidarity and personal capital accounts align incentives with strategic direction for the long-term. Members build equity in their co-op and fairness is baked into the math.

- **Inter-cooperative solidarity & redeployment.** When one co-op hits a shock, surplus labour and capital flow to others via the federation (and the cooperative bank, historically Caja Laboral). Roles are moved before they're removed.

- **Education as infrastructure.** Leadership is treated as a teachable craft, not a title. Mondragon University and in-house training socialise members into cooperative governance, finance, and operations.

- **Transparent performance dashboards.** Members see financials, productivity, and market data routinely. This transparency supports adult-to-adult conversations about trade-offs (dividends vs. reinvestment vs. wage adjustments).

- **Crisis playbooks.** Agreed mechanisms (temporary wage moderation, hour flexibility, redeployment) activate automatically in downturns. Because the rules are pre-decided, response is quick and legitimacy is high.

Mondragon's story shows that constellation leadership can scale beyond teams and companies to entire societies. What began as one workshop became a federation of enterprises linked by mutual commitment. The model proves that resilience can be engineered not through control but through solidarity.

In a conventional corporation, downturns lead to layoffs, morale loss, and often collapse. In Mondragon, downturns activate a choreography of redistribution. Labour and capital flow across the network so the whole constellation endures. What might seem inefficient in the short term becomes a foundation of long-term stability.

The lesson is not that every business should become a cooperative, but that designing organisations around fairness, transparency, and solidarity creates the conditions for distributed leadership. Constellation leadership here is not metaphorical; it is constitutional. Members act not just as workers but as owners, decision-makers, and guardians of purpose.

STUDY 5: THE OPERATING SYSTEM WITHOUT A BOSS

In 1991, a Finnish computer science student named Linus Torvalds typed a message onto an online bulletin board:

"I'm doing a free operating system (just a hobby, won't be big or professional like GNU) for 386(486) AT clones…"

What began as a hobby project is today the beating heart of the digital world. Linux, the open-source operating system Torvalds initiated, runs most of the internet's servers, powers Android smartphones, dominates supercomputers, and underpins critical infrastructure from stock exchanges to spacecraft.

Yet Linux did not grow through the command of CEOs or the funding of corporations. It grew through a structure that barely resembles traditional organisation at all. Contributors from around the world self-select tasks. Authority emerges not from titles but from the reputation of individuals whose code proves reliable and innovative earn influence. Disagreements are not crushed but forked: if consensus cannot be reached, developers split the project and pursue parallel visions.

In this sense, Linux is perhaps the clearest example of constellation leadership. There is no single leader, only shifting centres of gravity. Linus Torvalds remains a symbolic figure, but even his authority is bounded; his role is more coordinator than commander.

The open-source model works because it aligns with deep psychological drivers. Self-determination theory holds that humans thrive when autonomy, competence, and relatedness are satisfied. Open-source contributors choose their projects (autonomy), hone their technical mastery (competence), and build reputations within a global community (relatedness). Rather than financial incentives, the economy of open source is reputational. Recognition by peers and the visibility of one's contributions provide powerful non-hierarchical motivation.

The outcome has been staggering. While proprietary operating systems like Microsoft's Windows or Apple's macOS are carefully guarded and top-down managed, Linux has evolved faster and more flexibly because anyone can contribute.

LINUX'S MECHANICS OF LEADERLESS SCALE

The result is software of remarkable stability and adaptability that's good enough to dominate domains where reliability is paramount. The approach has also allowed Linux to scale at speed and maintain quality by providing clear guiderails for system releases, quality protocols and modular design.

- **Licensing as a governance lever.** Copyleft (e.g., GPL) and permissive licenses define contribution rights and obligations. The license is a constitution providing clarity and reducing negotiation overhead to ensure that the commons agreement stays healthy.

- **Meritocratic maintainership.** Influence accrues through sustained, high-quality contributions from group members. Maintainers files make ownership of subsystems explicit, with maintainers reviewing and merging, while contributors propose and iterate changes.

- **Patch pipelines & code review.** Standardised submission, automated builds, and CI test suites create predictable gates in code releases. Quality becomes enforced by the process, rather than by a leader/manager.

- **Modular architecture.** The kernel and surrounding ecosystem are decomposed into subsystems with clear interfaces. This modularity localises decision rights and failure blast radius, enabling parallel work at scale on separate modules.

- **Forking as a safety valve.** If consensus stalls, projects can fork into different working groups. The possibility of forking disciplines incumbents and keeps governance responsive without central coercion, whilst providing an option to investigate the value in the deviation of consensus.

- **Open roadmaps & release cadence.** Time-boxed release cycles and transparent roadmaps provide rhythm to the missions. Contributors can self-select to the next window and users can plan against predictable drops.

Linux illustrates how constellation leadership can succeed at planetary scale. Millions of contributors, spread across continents and cultures, cohere around a shared vision without ever gathering in a boardroom. What holds them together is not managerial control but a lattice of norms, licenses, and rituals that channel individual autonomy into collective achievement.

Traditional software companies often rely on centralised strategy and command structures. Linux relies on voluntary alignment. The gravitational pull is not pay or positional power but reputation, mastery, and contribution to a shared good. Out of this emerges a paradox: a system with no leader, yet astonishing coordination.

For those studying leadership, Linux is a reminder that influence does not need to be concentrated. When culture and purpose are clear, and when mechanisms protect fairness and transparency, leadership can emerge from anywhere and still hold coherence. Linux has no boss, but it has a direction. And that direction has redefined the digital world.

STUDY 6: A HEAD OF STEAM

In most organisations, leadership is visible in titles, reporting lines, and corner offices. At Valve Corporation, the American video game developer behind Half-Life, Portal, and the digital distribution platform Steam, leadership is nowhere to be seen – at least in its formal sense.

The company has no managers, no official hierarchy, and no fixed teams. Instead, it runs on a radical principle: that the best work emerges when individuals are free to choose what they do, who they do it with, and how they pursue it. From day one, the employee handbook makes clear why hierarchy won't be found:

"…when you're an entertainment company that's spent the last decade going out of its way to recruit the most intelligent, innovative, talented people on Earth, telling them to sit at a desk and do what they're told obliterates 99 percent of their value. We want innovators, and that means maintaining an environment where they'll flourish."

In an industry defined by rapid innovation and fierce competition, Valve's unorthodox structure achieved something extraordinary. By 2011, Steam controlled over half of all digital PC game sales worldwide: an estimated 70% of the market by some accounts. By 2017, the platform had grown to 67 million monthly active users, dwarfing competitors and reshaping an entire industry.

What makes this remarkable is not just the commercial success, but how it was accomplished: through a constellation of talent aligned by culture rather than hierarchy. Valve's approach is often described as "flat," but this undersells its radicalism. Most flat organisations still retain implicit leaders or project managers who coordinate. At Valve, the absence of hierarchy is total. New employees famously receive a handbook explaining that desks are on wheels so they can roll themselves into whichever project excites them. The message is clear: mobility is not just physical but organisational. You belong where your passion and skill are most useful.

This freedom is underpinned by a cultural contract. Employees are expected to act as both producers and entrepreneurs to identify opportunities, gather collaborators, and bring ideas to life. Instead of waiting for strategic direction from above, strategy emerges bottom-up, as clusters of employees converge on promising concepts. Valve calls these "self-organising cabals": temporary constellations of expertise that form, shine brightly, and then disperse.

The clearest proof is Steam itself. Launched in 2003 to streamline updates for Half-Life, it soon evolved into a full distribution platform. Crucially, Steam was not the brainchild of a single leader issuing orders. Instead, it emerged from teams who saw a fragmented marketplace of physical discs, piracy, and inefficient patching, and believed they could solve it. In a hierarchical company, a project of this scope would have required executive approval, budget allocations, and steering committees. At Valve, it gained momentum simply because enough talented people believed in it and acted quickly on both feedback and ideas. As Valve's President and Co-founder, Gabe Newall, explained, "We have approached the development of Steam the same way we treat our online games; we release something we've tested, we internalise the feedback, and then we release new features and functionality based upon the feedback received."

Steam grew organically, iterated rapidly, and by the 2010s commanded a market position stronger than many console manufacturers. Valve had quietly become the most powerful distributor in PC gaming, without ever drafting a strategy document or announcing a corporate pivot.

This illustrates a principle at the heart of Constellation Leadership: when vision and culture are shared, alignment does not require top-down control. Instead, collective energy flows toward opportunities that fit the larger purpose. Steam succeeded not despite the absence of leadership, but because leadership was distributed.

VALVE'S MECHANICS OF FREEDOM

The absence of hierarchy does not mean the absence of leadership. At Valve, leadership is situational, emergent, and tied to expertise. Whoever has the best idea or clearest path forward becomes a gravitational centre, drawing others into orbit until the project is complete. When the work ends, so does the leadership.

This is autonomy in action, but it is carefully engineered. Several mechanics make it viable:

- **Recruitment as cultural filter**. Valve hires slowly, prioritising those who thrive in ambiguity, take initiative, and collaborate well. Skill matters, but so does self-direction.

- **Transparency of work**. With no managers assigning tasks, visibility becomes the coordination mechanism. Progress, blockers, and opportunities are shared openly so others can decide where to contribute.

- **Peer review and compensation**. Salaries are tied to peer evaluations, incentivising meaningful contribution and discouraging free-riding.

- **Purpose-driven storytelling**. Though Valve avoids grandiose mission statements, it consistently frames its purpose as empowering players and developers. This loose but guiding vision ensures projects orbit a shared North Star.

Together, these mechanics echo the psychological needs described in Self-Determination Theory: autonomy (choosing one's work), competence (mastery visible through peer recognition), and relatedness (connection through collaboration). Valve didn't just flatten hierarchy. It built a system that sustains intrinsic motivation at scale.

Valve's model is not without tension. Critics note that new hires can struggle without clear guidance, and informal hierarchies sometimes emerge, privileging veterans. Large projects may drift without sustained oversight. Yet these limitations do not obscure its achievements. Steam's dominance, combined with the enduring success of Valve's games, demonstrates that leaderless structures can compete at the highest levels of global industry.

Part of the story lies in scale. Valve was large enough (around 400 employees during its peak market control) to wield global influence, yet small enough for culture to replace bureaucracy.

Viewed through the lens of Constellation Leadership, Valve shows how leadership can be distributed across culture, purpose, and context rather than concentrated in individuals. Employees are stars, not satellites: they shine in their own right, but align into constellations that give shape and meaning to the organisation's work.

But Valve is not a blueprint. Most companies cannot simply remove managers and expect brilliance to erupt. The lesson is subtler: design systems where leadership is situational, emergent, and collective. Valve's desks on wheels are more than quirky furniture – they are a symbol of what happens when people are free to move toward where they can make the biggest difference.

When culture is strong and vision is shared, hierarchy becomes optional. Leadership, like starlight, can be distributed. And when the constellation forms, it can outshine even the brightest of centralised commands.

STUDY 7: THE AGILE ADVANTAGE

Ben Booth has a disarming smile. The CEO and co-founder of MaxContact, a Manchester-based company specialising in cloud-based contact centre software, is a former powerlifter who was named one of the UK's Top 50 Most Ambitious Business Leaders by LDC, in partnership with The Times, in 2024.

That might suggest someone intense, driven, competitive, and decisive – but that's not the full picture. Instead, Booth exudes a deep curiosity about people, a voracious appetite for learning, and a quiet awareness of when to let others take the lead.

Under his leadership, MaxContact has grown rapidly, featuring in the top 50 fastest growing technology companies in the North three years in a row, and handling over 100 million interactions each month for clients such as Utilita, Papyrus UK, and Whistl. The company has expanded its product offerings, including AI-driven analytics tools, and has ambitious plans for international growth.

Booth also recognises the importance of innovation and service in a competitive market. He believes that staying at the forefront of technology and providing exceptional service are key, and that part of this success comes from a unique approach to technology innovation.

Most software companies talk about agility. MaxContact lives it. At the heart of their innovation engine lies an unusual rhythm: a dual-sprint system that runs two parallel tracks at once.

The first, the discovery sprint, never stops. Its purpose is not coding or release, but sensemaking. Product managers, UX specialists, and researchers work with customers and study the external market to identify emerging needs. What do clients struggle with? Where is the industry shifting? Which features would add the most value to customers' lives? This is the listening post, the scout team, the bridge to the outside world.

From there, the findings are channelled into the second track: the production sprint. Running on a strict two-week cycle, these sprints are deliberately shorter than most Agile rhythms. They have no scrum master. Instead, teams of seven or eight people self-organise around specific goals, known internally as story points. Each story point is a tangible deliverable, tied not only to customer requests but also to MaxContact's strategic direction. The result is an engine that can release features and improvements fortnightly – far faster than many competitors in the cloud contact centre market.

The absence of a scrum master in the production sprint is deliberate. MaxContact's teams are trusted to distribute responsibility, rather than rely on a single point of control. Leadership shifts depending on the nature of the sprint. A front-end developer might step forward during a UI redesign. An infrastructure engineer might anchor a sprint focused on scalability. Booth and his senior team resist the urge to insert themselves. Instead, they focus on context, ensuring teams know the "why" and the "what," while leaving the "how" to those closest to the work.

MAXCONTACT'S MECHANICS OF AGILITY

MaxContact's approach embodies the principles of constellation leadership. Instead of fixed hierarchies or single points of control, leadership emerges fluidly within teams and across sprints. This manifests in several practical ways:

- **Continuous discovery:** By running a parallel sprint dedicated to research and customer voice, MaxContact ensures that development is not reactive but anticipatory.

- **Shorter cycles, faster releases:** Two-week production sprints give the company a competitive edge in a crowded SaaS market. Customers see improvements in almost real time, rather than waiting months for updates and feature releases.

- **No scrum master, no bottleneck:** Leadership is situational. Whoever holds the most relevant expertise takes point, ensuring flexibility and resilience.

- **Story points as shared currency:** Instead of long lists of deliverables that might roll over unfinished, each sprint is anchored in story points. This sharpens focus and gives teams shared clarity on value creation.

- **Retrospectives as non-negotiable:** Every sprint ends with a review. Lessons learned are captured, shared, and applied, ensuring improvement compounds rather than stalls.

- **Dynamic team composition:** Sprint teams are built around the work, not the other way around. A front-end heavy sprint looks different from a back-end one, with no fixed "right" team shape.

- **Freedom within a framework:** As Booth puts it, "success leaves evidence." Frameworks make agility repeatable. Teams can move quickly precisely because there are guardrails: planning rituals, visibility of all change, and clarity about the company's north star direction.

- **Trust over supervision:** Senior leaders create context and guardrails but resist micromanagement. Teams own delivery, learning, and accountability.

The result is more than just faster code. By shortening the feedback loop between customers, discovery, and development, MaxContact has built an organisation that learns in real time. Clients benefit from fortnightly improvements, often co-created with them. Internally, the rhythm builds momentum. Teams see the tangible impact of their work every two weeks, which fuels motivation and pride.

Yet Booth is quick to stress that agility does not mean an absence of discipline. Communicating this volume of updates so frequently with customers and employees risks overwhelming them unless change is made visible and coherent across the business. Training, awareness, and consistent rituals ensure the system doesn't collapse under its own speed. In this way, MaxContact has normalised iteration – "little and often," Booth advises – until it feels like the natural way of working, not an exception.

The temptation in many organisations is to release updates in larger, less frequent drops. Booth has seen first-hand why that approach backfires. "Even though you might release the same amount of changes [using a less frequent, but larger update drop], and the overheads – in terms of training our people on the updates, updating customers on new features – are higher, the benefits of shorter sprint cycles outweigh the costs," he says.

This way of working also gives MaxContact room to manoeuvre when priorities suddenly change. "We can very quickly change what we do and it doesn't affect anything, because we're only ever two weeks away from a release. When a release goes out, we can completely pivot if we want to – and we have," Booth explains. One example of this agility was the recent acquisition of Curious Thing AI, an intelligent conversational platform that was rapidly folded into MaxContact's development cycle.

The advantage is not just operational, but competitive. Many contact centre software providers still work on quarterly release cycles, a pace that leaves them lagging in a sector where customer expectations evolve rapidly – whether driven by AI, omnichannel communication, or regulatory change. By contrast, MaxContact can pivot and deliver at speed.

Booth's role in all this is striking. He doesn't sit in production sprint reviews dictating direction, nor does he act as product visionary in the traditional mould. Instead, his focus is on building the conditions for distributed leadership to thrive: clarity of purpose, psychological safety, and a culture that celebrates learning as much as delivery.

MaxContact's story shows that constellation leadership is not confined to elite sports teams or high-stakes military units. Their model reminds us that innovation does not come from speed alone, nor from vision alone, but from a system where listening, learning, and leading are shared responsibilities. In a world where technology shifts daily, that may be the greatest competitive advantage of all.

THEORY IN THE REAL WORLD

These case studies remind us that Constellation Leadership is not a leap into the unknown. It is not an abstract design drawn only on whiteboards or in seminar rooms. Whether in the disciplined autonomy of Mission Command, the fluid strategies of esports teams, or the cooperative resolve of Mondragón, the same principles are already visible. Vision as a guiding north star; culture as the binding tissue; freedom of action within shared boundaries. None of these examples called their practice "Constellation Leadership," yet each shows its spirit at work.

This is why the preceding chapters have not been an exercise in academic vanity. The theory matters because it gives language, structure and clarity to patterns that already succeed in the world. Constellation Leadership is not invention so much as recognition: pulling together the threads of trust, autonomy, and shared intent into a coherent model that others can consciously adopt.

The question, then, is not 'does it work?' – the evidence shows it already does. The question is 'how might we use it deliberately?' How can leaders in organisations of every size and sector learn from these constellations and draw their own?

09

NEW HORIZONS:
An invitation to the future

*"And suddenly you know: It's time to start something new
and trust the magic of beginnings."*

Meister Eckhart
Attributed (14th Century)

When we look up at the night sky, the stars appear timeless and fixed, scattered across a velvet canvas. Yet constellations are not natural phenomena. They are human constructions: lines of meaning drawn between points of light. One culture sees a hunter, another a plough, another a lion. The stars are the same, but the stories we tell about them vary, shaped by context, imagination, and need.

Constellation Leadership is much the same. What you have read in this book is not a finished map, but the beginnings of a sketch. The research so far has traced some of the stars: the role of culture in guiding behaviour, the mechanics of psychological safety, the dynamics of distributed leadership. The case studies have shown what can happen when these stars are linked into patterns that help teams navigate complexity. But no constellation is permanent. The picture you have encountered here is one possible arrangement, drawn from current knowledge and early practice.

The truth is, Constellation Leadership is still in its infancy. Its foundations rest on a relatively small body of academic work, most of it conducted in specific contexts: agile technology teams, creative projects, and short-term collaborations. Its applied use in organisations remains rare and fragmented, often appearing as isolated experiments rather than a coherent system. The ideas are promising, the metaphors evocative, and the evidence encouraging. But the constellation is far from complete.

This is not a weakness. It is an invitation. Constellations exist because someone once dared to look at the stars and imagine new shapes. The task before us is similar: to imagine, to test, and to refine. Constellation Leadership will only mature if it is applied beyond theory. If leaders, teams, and organisations experiment with its principles and share what works, what fails, and what transforms, this will write the next chapter of the story.

Looking back over this book, you have already journeyed through its core terrain. We have explored how trust, culture, and shared purpose can function as a leader when no single figurehead exists. We have seen how psychological safety, carefully nurtured, allows distributed teams to step into leadership fluidly and return responsibility gracefully. We examined the zebra herd, which showed us how groupthink can protect and constrain.

The scaffolding of Constellation Leadership rests not on structure, but on trust. A team may draw the most intricate constellation map, but without safety it is a picture that few dare to follow. The foundation here is psychological safety: the belief that one can speak up, take risks, or admit mistakes without fear of ridicule or punishment.

Amy Edmondson's research at Harvard Business School remains the touchstone. In her studies of medical teams, she found that units with higher error-reporting rates were not more careless, but more honest. Nurses and junior doctors spoke up when mistakes occurred, allowing the system to learn and adapt. By contrast, teams with low safety appeared more "competent" on the surface, but only because their errors remained hidden. What looked efficient was, in fact, fragile.

Safety is not the absence of fear, but the presence of voice. Fear suppresses novelty: the new idea left unspoken in a meeting, the emerging risk ignored in a project review. Safety enables contribution: the shy analyst who points out the overlooked flaw, the frontline worker whose insight sparks an innovation. In this sense, silence is the tax organisations pay when safety is absent. The currency is creativity, and the loss compounds over time.

The psychology is straightforward. Humans are finely attuned to social threat. A raised eyebrow, a sarcastic aside, a manager's visible irritation – each cues the amygdala to retreat into self-protection. Even small signals are amplified in group contexts. When a team normalises caution over candour, homogeneity follows. Ideas flatten into platitudes. Language fills with corporate clichés and safe buzzwords. This is the comfort of groupthink: sameness mistaken for unity.

The paradox is that true safety does not banish conflict; it transforms it. When trust is high, dissent strengthens bonds rather than fraying them. Disagreement becomes a contribution to the whole, not a fracture of belonging. In such groups, conflict is not corrosive but catalytic: the spark that generates energy rather than the flame that consumes it.

Constellation Leadership depends on this paradox. Without safety, distributed leadership reverts to silence or factionalism. With it, teams can self-correct, self-organise, and self-renew. The stars only form a constellation when each light is visible.

We considered the invisible structures that support collaboration without confining it. And we saw how culture itself, not hierarchy, can coordinate effort across boundaries. These were not abstract lessons but lived examples, drawn from organisations grappling with the tension between structure and freedom. Together, they form the system of Constellation Leadership – not as a fixed doctrine, but as a living framework.

This framework is organic. Every individual is a star in their own right; an expert. But today's approaches of fixed job roles and stay-in-your-lane social norms can prevent them from using all of their toolkit. Those stars bring with them their own personalities and individual differences, which shape their reality and mould their relationships. Creating inclusive environments based on self-knowledge and valuing the diversity others bring is where the power of Constellation Leadership can be liberated.

THE GHOST OF INDUSTRY

The models we rely on today are still shaped by the industrial age. They were designed for the rhythms of the factory floor and the discipline of the production line, where efficiency was paramount, tasks were repetitive, and control was exercised through hierarchy. Frederick Taylor's time-and-motion studies, designed to shave seconds from each gesture, gave us scientific management. In the mills and workshops of the nineteenth century, these pyramids of control offered stability and predictability. The pyramid became our dominant symbol of leadership: layers of authority narrowing to a single point at the top.

For a time, this structure served us well. It enabled railways, steelworks, and shipping companies to coordinate vast enterprises at scale. It allowed armies and bureaucracies to function with order and consistency. But in today's world, where organisations are complex, fluid, and matrixed, the pyramid has become a trap. Hierarchical models struggle to cope with rapid change, cross-boundary collaboration, and the need for innovation that cuts across silos. They reward caution over creativity and compliance over curiosity. What was once a strength now constrains us.

In an age of networks, ecosystems, and rapid technological change, pyramids feel increasingly out of step with reality. We need models that reflect the messiness of complexity. We need leadership that can flex, distribute, and adapt rather than command, control, and confine.

Yet this does not mean Constellation Leadership is always the answer. There remain contexts where hierarchy provides clarity, safety, and speed. In fact, effective use often depends on structure: Mission Command, the armed services' dynamic leadership approach, works only because of the exhaustive planning and debriefing that bookend each mission.

Constellation Leadership is not a call to abolish leaders altogether, but an invitation to notice where leadership can be shared – and where unleashing collective intelligence can outperform traditional models. The challenge is not choosing one system over another, but knowing when to sketch constellations and when to lean on structure.

Constellation Leadership is one response to this need, but it is not the only one. Other models have sought to challenge the dominance of hierarchy: shared leadership, servant leadership, adaptive leadership, and more. What distinguishes Constellation Leadership is the emphasis on culture and vision as coordinating forces. This is the idea that what binds people together is not a single authority, but a shared north star, reinforced by trust and the lived experience of psychological safety. It is a model not just for organisations, but for communities, movements, and networks.

THE FUTURE

What, then, comes next? Where does this framework travel from here? The answers will differ depending on who holds the map.

For academics, the future may lie in large-scale, longitudinal studies across industries and cultures, testing whether distributed safety and cultural scaffolding can consistently outperform traditional hierarchies. We need to know not just that it works in software teams or military operations, but whether it scales across healthcare, manufacturing, education, or government. The constellation will only become clearer when traced in many different skies.

For practitioners, the next step may be experimentation. Not wholesale organisational redesign, but small, deliberate trials: replacing reporting structures with rituals that reinforce purpose; redesigning meetings so that culture speaks louder than status; creating cross-functional teams where accountability flows through trust rather than job titles. These are not abstract aspirations but practical design choices that leaders can test in the everyday flow of work. Over time, small constellations can connect into larger patterns.

For you as a reader, the challenge may be simpler and more personal. It might mean noticing the small stars that are already present in your work: the fragments of trust, purpose, and collaboration that could be connected into a larger pattern. It might mean inviting dissent rather than smoothing it over, or treating culture as a leader in the room rather than an afterthought. The first constellation you draw may be modest, but if it helps you and your colleagues navigate better, it will matter.

The work is unfinished, and perhaps it always will be. That is part of its strength. Constellations are living creations: they shift with perspective, expand with imagination, and endure only if they remain useful for navigation. Constellation Leadership should be no different. The stars – individual expertise, trust, safety, culture, vision – are constants. But the lines we draw between them are ours to imagine and reimagine.

The stakes are not small. The challenges that organisations face in the twenty-first century – climate change, technological disruption, global interdependence, demographic shifts – cannot be solved by pyramids alone. They demand collaboration across boundaries, the courage to innovate, and the humility to distribute leadership widely. In this sense, the promise of Constellation Leadership is not only organisational but societal. The way we lead together will shape how we meet the great problems of our time.

FUTURE CHALLENGES

If safety provides the conditions, complexity provides the necessity. The world pressing in on organisations today is not one that pyramids were designed to navigate.

Climate change demands cross-boundary coordination. No single government, corporation, or NGO can address the problem in isolation. The very nature of the challenge – dispersed causes, distributed consequences, deep uncertainty – requires leadership that flows across sectors and geographies. Constellation Leadership offers a frame: alignment not through command, but through a shared north star of sustainability and stewardship.

Artificial intelligence and automation present a second frontier. Decisions about algorithmic bias, workforce displacement, and ethical application cannot be left to technical elites alone, nor managed through rigid hierarchies. They demand inclusive dialogue, distributed accountability, and the courage to balance efficiency with human values. A culture that silences dissent risks building systems that encode its own blind spots.

Geopolitical instability adds further weight. The fragility of global supply chains, the re-emergence of populist politics, and the unpredictability of international crises highlight the weakness of single-point-of-failure leadership. In networks where disruption is inevitable, resilience comes not from the strength of the pyramid's apex but from the connectivity of its base. Constellation Leadership reframes power: redundancy is not waste, but resilience; distribution is not dilution, but durability.

Finally, demographic shifts and generational expectations are redrawing the social contract of work. Younger employees seek meaning, inclusion, and autonomy. They are less tolerant of top-down dictates and more motivated by shared purpose. Cultures that cling to rigid hierarchies risk not only disengagement but exit. Talent gravitates towards organisations where leadership is less about positional authority and more about collective contribution.

In addition to these complex, specific examples, what pressures will test this leadership in the years ahead? Three key areas stand out:

- First, **the velocity of change**. Disruption is no longer episodic but continuous. Organisations that cling to fixed structures will struggle to adapt. Constellation Leadership must prove itself capable of flexing as contexts shift.

- Second, **diversity and identity**. The workforce is more diverse than ever, across generations, geographies, and values. Constellations will need to draw coherence not from uniformity, but from the capacity to hold difference without fragmentation.

- Third, **technology**. AI and digital platforms are redrawing the boundaries of collaboration. They can flatten hierarchies and connect distant stars, but they can also create new forms of surveillance and control. Leadership will need to decide whether technology enables trust or erodes it.

Taken together, these challenges sketch a world where the failure of imagination becomes a strategic liability. Pyramids produce efficiency but at the cost of adaptability. Constellations, though less tidy, mirror the messiness of reality. They allow organisations to sense, learn, and respond in ways that pyramids cannot.

The task, then, is not simply to admire the metaphor, but to practice it. And here the question arises: what does Constellation Leadership look like in action?

PRACTICING THE PRINCIPLES

Constellation Leadership does not emerge by accident. It requires intentional design: choices about culture, process, and practice that enable leadership to be shared without dissolving into chaos. The principles are simple in form, but demanding in discipline.

1. Start with vision.

Constellations form around a north star. Without it, the map is noise. The role of leaders – whether formal or distributed – is to hold this star visible. Ask: What is the question this organisation exists to answer? What contribution do we seek to make together? When articulated clearly and revisited often, vision becomes the axis around which autonomy can turn.

2. Create scaffolds for voice.

Safety does not mean every meeting descends into debate. It means designing mechanisms so all voices can shape outcomes. Rotate facilitators. Use structured rounds where each person contributes. Employ "red team/blue team" methods to test assumptions. Normalise debriefs where mistakes are surfaced without blame. These small rituals accumulate into cultural muscle.

3. Gather diverse perspectives.

No single viewpoint can illuminate the full sky. By actively seeking input from every member, the constellation gains depth and resilience. Differences in experience, background, and thinking style challenge assumptions and surface blind spots. Encouraging contributions from all corners prevents decisions from defaulting to the loudest or most senior voice. Diversity of thought becomes both a compass and a safeguard: it helps the organisation navigate complexity while strengthening the cultural norm that every voice matters. None of us are as bright as all of us.

4. Balance freedom with frame.

Shared leadership does not abolish hierarchy; it reconfigures it. Teams need clarity on boundaries: where autonomy begins, where alignment is required, and who holds ultimate accountability before the constellation is formed. Freedom without frame breeds confusion; frame without freedom breeds compliance. The art lies in tensioning the two.

5. Watch the language.

Groupthink often reveals itself in speech before it appears in decisions. Corporate clichés, cult-like slogans, or jargon-laden mission statements can mask a lack of genuine dialogue. Leaders should listen not only for what is said but for what is absent: the awkward question unasked, the insight that trails into silence. Language is an early-warning system for conformity.

6. Honour the edge cases.
Constellations are shaped as much by their outer points as by their core. Invite perspectives from the margins: the junior employee, the customer on the frontline, the partner outside the walls. The edges often see what the centre overlooks. Innovation tends to come not from the chorus, but from the unexpected solo.

7. Debrief, learn, and adapt.
Constellation Leadership is iterative. Just as astronomers redraw maps with each new discovery, organisations must continually revisit their practices. After each project, ask: Where did leadership flow? Where was it blocked? What did we learn about our constellation? Learning is not an add-on but the rhythm of the system. What stars compliment the next constellation?

Pitfalls abound. Shared leadership is not consensus. It is not the endless pursuit of harmony, nor the abdication of responsibility. It requires courage: to dissent, to decide, to be accountable. The risk is not chaos, but complacency. Without vigilance, constellations can collapse into pyramids of habit or into the vacuum of leaderless drift.

Yet when practised with intent, the rewards are profound. Teams become more resilient, organisations more adaptive, and leadership more human. What emerges is less a model to be implemented than a pattern to be recognised – a way of seeing leadership not as a scarce resource at the top, but as a capacity distributed throughout the whole.

This book, then, is less a conclusion than a beginning. It sketches the edges of what we know, highlights the gaps yet to be explored, and invites you into the role of co-creator. Constellation Leadership is not something to be received passively. It is something to be tested, shaped, and extended. The stars are already in place. The constellation we draw together will depend on how boldly we choose to connect them.

So perhaps the most important lesson is the simplest: when we look up at the stars, the shapes we see are never fixed. They are stories we choose to tell, connections we decide to draw. The same is true of leadership.

We can cling to pyramids built for a vanished age, or we can choose to sketch new constellations that reflect the world as it is – fluid, complex, alive with possibility. The sky is wide, the stars are waiting, and the patterns we draw next are ours to make.

EPILOGUE

Who is the leader in a beehive? It's not a trick question, though it might seem so on the surface.

The trap – if you've spotted it already – is that it's the queen. After all, we use "queen bee" as an informal description of someone (usually female) with a dominant or controlling position within a particular group or sphere. But, in the world of apiaries and bee culture, the queen is not the leader. The hive has no individual leader.

Instead, the hive has a mission: the survival of the colony. Every individual member is oriented towards that objective and each contributes specific skills and approaches in its achievement. The queen's skill is in laying eggs. She's exceptionally skilled at this, laying up to 2,000 eggs a day. This extraordinary feat is even more impressive when we consider that she is the only sexually developed female in the colony.

Other bees have equally specific roles. The drones' sole role is to fertilise the queen. Worker bees are divided by duties: younger bees are janitors; comb builders are the architects of the hive; guards protect the entrances; foragers fetch food. There are even undertakers, nurses and attendants to the queen. Each has a defined task, and when that task is no longer needed, they become surplus to requirements. Drones are evicted (often forcibly) from the hive in late summer and autumn, when mating is finished[32].

Herein lies a truth of bee leadership: it is the hive's mission – not a specific individual bee – that is the leader. Each group

---

[32] Note: I am not suggesting that when a member is surplus to requirements that they are evicted from the group. Our organisations are far more complex and (hopefully) less gruesome than insect colonies.

member contributes towards that sole endeavour. The queen will never be tasked with fetching food; the drones are not asked to remove dead bees from the apiary. Each has a strength, which is exercised in service of the hive's shared objective.

A stable hive temperature is important for the development of pupae and bee larvae. When the weather is extremely hot, honeybee foragers will stop collecting food and focus on fetching water, placing it just inside the hive. Then, together, they will fan their wings, creating a current of cooling air, evaporating the water (which absorbs heat) and reducing the hive's temperature to promote a healthy brood.

This central mission – to ensure the survival of the hive – means that these foragers can utilise their skills when contexts change. In that moment, they can flex their approach for the benefit of that mission. This wasn't "ordered" by the queen. There was no instruction passed along a chain of command or from a single manager. There was no referring back to an employee (employbee?) handbook or a slide deck on strategy.

And so the hive thrives not because of a commanding figurehead, but because every bee orients itself to a shared purpose. Leadership, in this sense, is not a role but a rhythm. It emerges from alignment to the collective goal, not the authority of a single voice. **This is Constellation Leadership.**

When I began the academic research into this area of leadership, I was surprised at the paucity of studies available on distributed models. I was even more surprised that the topic of a leaderless leadership model hadn't been considered, despite there being evidence all around us of this phenomenon being applied in real-world organisations.

In hindsight, I might have been somewhat biased (and/or naïve). My belief is that, in the right environment, distribution of responsibility and accountability can be incredibly powerful and fulfilling for all group members. We can be, I believe, greater than the sum of our parts.

Our traditional, hierarchical leadership models have a place. Where environments are predictable, structured and routine, they provide scaffolding. But when unexpected change is encountered, that same structure and scaffold can hold us behind bars, shackled to process, protocol and preconceived approaches, awaiting instruction, decision and direction. Procedure manuals become shields, sign-off processes turn into barricades, and agility dissolves into bureaucracy.

At an individual level, change – particularly unanticipated change – can be interpreted as a threat; a threat to our control. And when we feel that our locus of control has moved, many individuals may double down on what they can control. Gatekeeping, decision avoidance and obsession with adhering to existing processes become normalised. Office politics are often rooted in a perceived lack of overall control, and an individual desire to regain some semblance of local control. "I'm not comfortable with what's going on with the rest of the boat, but I'll just make sure my bit is shipshape."

Yet change is the playground of leadership. Management aims to save today: to improve what we do, incrementally innovate, and deliver efficiency and effectiveness. But leadership is about tomorrow; and tomorrow is uncertain. Navigating change is, ultimately, what we look to leadership to achieve.

The pace of change today has accelerated. Technology – particularly AI tools that can replicate once-complex human tasks

– have lowered the barrier of entry to many markets, introducing new challengers and challenges. Geo-political unrest, climate change, interest and inflation rates, and the rise of global populism all add to the wider macroenvironmental pressures facing leadership. Our organisations have weathered change before, but not at this volume, variety or velocity. Just as an unexpected change in temperature can demand a new approach from the bees without the need for hierarchy, so too can contemporary leadership manifest outside of structure.

In the first section of the book, we established our current thinking. What are leadership and culture, and how have the relationships between historical figures, evolving organisations, and academic research shaped our views today?

The second section proposes a theory of leadership that isn't centred on individuals, but on culture and shared direction. This conceptual model has heritage (though largely forgotten or ignored), but has not previously been researched academically.

Our third section demonstrates how that conceptual model is already being applied across multiple industries and contexts. The case study organisations have shown that this is not blind naivety. Through interviews with leaders on the edge of traditional models, they have demonstrated that through applying clarity of vision, alignment of culture, and high-trust environments, groups can self-organise and outperform traditionally-led teams.

These cultures, of course, are not abstractions: they are built of people. Each individual brings their own history, personality, and perspective into the collective endeavour. The strength of a distributed model depends on recognising these differences not as obstacles, but as assets. As Amy Edmondson's research on psychological safety shows, people are most likely to contribute meaningfully when they feel safe to speak up without fear of ridicule or reprimand. By fostering environments that are inclusive, diverse, and psychologically safe, organisations can unlock the full spectrum of their members' strengths. In such spaces, individuality is not diluted but directed, aligned with a shared mission.

It is this integration of individual uniqueness into collective purpose that gives Constellation Leadership its resilience and creative power. But more research and practice are required to build on this foundation. The purpose of this book, then, is threefold:

- Introduce the academic research into Constellation Leadership in an accessible and practicable manner;

- Identify real-world scenarios where the model is being utilised today; and

- Provide a bedrock for practitioners and academic researchers to critique, challenge and develop future research and approaches upon

Leadership theory has always been a mirror of its age: the heroic great men of industrial empires, the scientific managers of mechanised workforces, the transactional leaders of neoliberal economies, the transformational leaders of a more individualised world. Constellation Leadership is not the next management fad, but a recognition of the world we now inhabit – one of interdependence, unpredictability, and accelerating change. Just as the hive thrives through distributed responsibility and alignment to a shared mission, so too must our organisations if they are to meet the challenges of this century.

The final word is not mine, but yours. Leadership has never belonged solely to the few who sit at the top of charts and structures; it has always been lived out daily in conversations, decisions, and choices across the system. We often talk about leadership as though it were embodied in a single person. In practice, it is culture that leads in their absence and shapes actions, behaviours, and possibilities. It is purposeful culture and meaningful direction that creates the constellation.

If this book has offered anything, I hope it is a new lens through which to see yourself as part of that constellation: not a follower awaiting orders, but a star oriented toward a shared purpose. The hive needs all of us.

ACKNOWLEDGMENTS

There's just one name on this book's cover. That might give you the idea that this is a solo effort. But nothing could be further from reality.

Writing a book is challenging – and it would not have been possible without an army of experts, ears and evangelists who volunteered their wisdom, their insights and their support (and a frankly obscene number of vanilla lattes) over the last four years, and those who have shaped my views on leadership for several decades before that.

First and foremost, my partner Charlene. She has weathered my ups and downs, been my lighthouse and my storm defence, and my biggest cheerleader. This book – indeed, my whole world today – could not be possible without her. Thank you.

The concept for Constellation Leadership began as part of my Masters' studies in 2021. I didn't go to university and it was a big jump from a 25-year corporate career into academia. To make it even more interesting, I began that journey at the age where getting out of bed makes my body sound like someone throwing wet wood on a fire.

Fellow student, Roy Dower (a true polymath completing, I believe, his sixth Masters), balanced wise words, debate and challenge to spur on my own thoughts and learnings. My thesis supervisor, David Witton, not only had patience; he gave me the freedom to explore the possibilities of leaderless leadership. Without their initial guidance, this research might never have seen the light of day. Thank you.

Of course, even getting into university wasn't a foregone conclusion. The last time I'd set foot in a classroom, you could still take shampoo in your in-flight hand luggage. Matt Birtles – a former manager of mine and a great leader himself – vouched for my capabilities. It might have been a small gesture objectively, but it changed my life and I became the first person in my family's history to go to university. Thank you.

Unbeknownst to me, Constellation Leadership had not been academically studied previously. During my research, I came across several examples of the practice in action. To the book's contributors – Marion Anderson, Callum Abbott, Ben Booth, Lt Col Samantha Brettell DL, and Dr. Ted Anders – thank you for the generous donation of your time, expertise and patience. When introducing a conceptual model, there is always a risk that it stays in the realm of theory. Your real-world insights have ensured this isn't the case. Thank you.

There is also a small but mighty band of advanced preview readers and proofreaders gave my eyes a rest and caught what I could not. Sometimes you just can't see the forest for the trees. Thank you.

For my insiders and my influencers – the people that have guided me (knowingly or unknowingly), whom I have admired, have cheered me on, let me learn from and alongside, and who work tirelessly to nurture purposeful cultures – thank you. Recognising everyone would take another book, but there are some that this acknowledgement section would be incomplete without: Martin Teasdale, Clayton Drotsky, Jo Garland, Ben Hammersley, Nikita Mikhailov, Tony Altham, Paul Banks, Matt Mytenka, John Lowe, Steve Cox-Voyle, Paula Brockwell, Adam Timmis, Judith Germain, Kayleigh Tait, Helen Beaumont Manahan, Kerry Sudale, Paul Jones, Louise Hunt, Ellie-Marie Wareham, Kerry Horton, Nick McCoy, Dr. Dawn Nicholson,

Deborah & Dr. Stewart Desson, Sarah Brennand, Kate Knowles, Prof. Bernd Vogel, Melanie Robinson, Nigel Howle, Sarah Farmer, Matt & Laura Smith, Sandra Brookes, Steve Rushton, Andy Hollins, the independent practitioner community of psychologists (Nikki, Kelly, Faye, Sanjay, and the gang), and, of course, my biggest fan and mum: Susan Reader. Thank you, all.

Finally, my first and my last: my Charlene. She's been with me before this journey even started. From overworked employee to excited Masters graduate to distracted writer – and all the steps in between (not least starting a consultancy practice, and the emotional rollercoaster that comes with running a small business) – she has been my haven and my heaven. She has picked me up more times than we can count, and never let me defeat myself. None of this would exist without her.

Love always – and thank you.

REFERENCES
INTRODUCTION

WHO LEADS WHEN THE LEADER IS NOT IN THE ROOM?

Office politics reduced in remote working – Elron, E., & Vigoda-Gadot, E. (2006). Influence and Political Processes in Cyberspace. *International Journal of Cross Cultural Management*, 6(3), 295–317. https://doi.org/10.1177/1470595806070636

Managers do thing right – Drucker, P. (1963) 'Managing for Business Effectiveness', *Harvard Business Review*, Available at: https://hbr.org/1963/05/managing-for-business-effectiveness (Accessed 18 August 2025).

Leaders do the right things – Drucker, P. (1965, March 6) 'Do you do things right, or do the right things?', *The Financial Post: Toronto Edition*, p.7.

Culture influences behaviour – Trickett, E. J. (2009). Community Psychology: Individuals and Interventions in Community Context. *Annual Review of Psychology*, 60(1), 395–419. https://doi.org/10.1146/annurev.psych.60.110707.163514

Culture tells us how to behave – Frei, F. and Morriss, A. (2012) 'Culture Takes Over When the CEO Leaves the Room', *Harvard Business Review*, Available at: https://hbr.org/2012/05/culture-takes-over-when-the-ce (Accessed: 18 August 2025).

Employee tenure trends – Copeland, C., & Thephasit, S. (2024). *Trends in Employee Tenure, 1983–2024*. Ebri.org. https://www.ebri.org/content/trends-in-employee-tenure--1983-2024

Labour market a volume of career roles – ONS. (2025). *Labour market overview, UK*. Ons.gov.uk; Office for National Statistics. https://www.ons.gov.uk/employmentandlabourmarket/peopleinwork/employmentandemployeetyp es/bulletins/uklabourmarket/august2025

ONE

A HISTORY OF LEADERSHIP: THE PYRAMID PRISON

Our tools shape us – McLuhan, M., & Fiore, Q. (1967). '*The medium is the massage'*. Bantam Books.

Leadership as a definition – OED (2023) 'Leadership', *Online Etymology Dictionary. OED*. Available at: https://www.etymonline.com/word/leadership#etymonline_v_30153 (Accessed: 18 August 2025).

History of leadership – Arany, L. and Popovics, P. (2022) 'The modern leader: The history of leadership styles and the most important qualities of a modern leader', *Cross-Cultural Management Journal*, 24(2), pp. 91–95.

NATURE NOT NURTURE

Leadership evolution of great man – Benmira, S. and Agboola, M. (2021) 'Evolution of leadership theory', *BMJ Leader [Preprint]*. doi:10.1136/leader-2020-000296.

Leadership evolution of great man – Gronn, P. (2002) 'Distributed leadership as a unit of analysis', *The Leadership Quarterly*, 13(4), pp. 423–451. doi:10.1016/s1048-9843(02)00120-0.

Lectures on heroism – Carlyle, T. (1841) 'Lecture I: The Hero as Divinity. Odin. Paganism: Scandinavian Mythology', *On Heroes, Hero-Worship, & the Heroic in History: Six Lectures*. London: James Fraser. pp. 1–2.

Attila the leader – Britannica, E. (1911). The new Encyclopaedia Britannica (Eleventh edition). Chicago: Encyclopaedia Britannica, Inc.

Traits are inherited – Galton, F. (1869). 'Hereditary genius: An inquiry into its laws and consequences', Macmillan and Co. https://doi.org/10.1037/13474-000

Most important leadership skills – Knight, R. (2023) '8 essential qualities of successful leaders', *Harvard Business Review*, Available at: https://hbr.org/2023/12/8-essential-qualities-of-successful-leaders

Most important leadership skills – Marr, B. (2022) '10 most important leadership skills for the 21st century workplace (and how to develop them)', *Forbes*, Available at: https://www.forbes.com/sites/bernardmarr/2022/07/26/10-most-important-leadership-skills-for-the-21st-century-workplace-and-how-to-develop-them/

EVOLVING THE GREAT MAN

Opposition to great man - Spencer, H. (1873). The study of sociology (Vol. 5). Henry S. King.

Trait theory introduced – Judge TA, Bono JE, Ilies R, Gerhardt MW (2002). "Personality and leadership: A qualitative and quantitative review". *Journal of Applied Psychology*. 87 (4): 765–780. doi:10.1037/0021-9010.87.4.765.

Considering the situation – Stogdill, R. M. (1948). "Personal factors associated with leadership: A survey of the literature". *Journal of Psychology*. 25: 35–71. doi:10.1080/00223980.1948.9917362;

Situational leadership – Yukl, G, Van Fleet, D. D. (1992). "Theory and research on leadership in organizations". *Handbook of industrial and organizational psychology*. Vol. 3 (2nd ed.). Palo Alto, CA: Consulting Psychologists Press. pp. 147–197.; Hughes, R. L., Ginnett, R. C., Curphy, G. J. (1996). Leadership. Boston: Irwin McGraw-Hill.

Trait-based training for leadership – ILM (2025) 'Leadership and management qualifications', *ILM by City & Guilds*. Available at: https://www.i-l-m.com/learning-and-development/leadership-and-management-qualifications (Accessed: 18 August 2025).

Life cycle theory of leadership – Hersey, P., & Blanchard, K.H. (1969). Life cycle theory of leadership. *Training & Development Journal*, 23(5), 26–34.

WHAT ARE WE HERE FOR?

Transactional leadership – Burns, J. M. (1978). *Leadership*. New York: Harper & Row.

Carrot and stick – Bass, B. M.; Avolio, B. J. (1993). "Transformational leadership and organizational culture". *Public administration quarterly*: 112–121.

Theory X – Fischer, E. (October 1, 2009). "Motivation and Leadership in Social Work Management: A Review of Theories and Related Studies". *Administration in Social Work*: 356.

Theory Y – Morse, J. & Lorsch, J. W. (1970) 'Beyond Theory Y', *Harvard Business Review*, Available at: https://hbr.org/1970/05/beyond-theory-y (Accessed: 19 August 2025).

WON'T SOMEBODY THINK OF THE PEOPLE?

As many theories of leadership – Stogdill, R.M. (1974) Handbook of Leadership. *A survey of theory and research*. New York, NY: The Free Press.

Increase in consultancy – Kipping, M. (1999). 'American Management Consulting Companies in Western Europe, 1920 to 1990: Products, Reputation, and Relationships'. *Business History Review*. 73 (2). Cambridge University Press: 190–220. doi:10.2307/3116240.

LEADERSHIP IN A VACUUM

Contingency leadership approach – Fiedler, F. E. (1993). The contingency model: New directions for leadership utilization. *In Matteson and Ivancevich (Eds.), Management and Organizational Behavior Classics* (pp. 333-345).

Boom in proprietary models – Strategyu. (n.d.) 'A Brief History of Strategy Consulting: 100 years from Frederick Taylor to the "Next New Normal"', *strategyu*, Available at: https://strategyu.co/strategy-consulting-history/ (Accessed 18 August 2025).

Participative vs. job-oriented leadership styles (Michigan studies) – Likert, R. (1947). Kurt Lewin: A pioneer in human relations research. *Human Relations*, 1(1), 131-140.

Behaviour over personality (Ohio State studies) – Stogdill, R. M., & Shartle, C. L. (1948). Methods for determining patterns of leadership behavior in relation to organization structure and objectives. *Journal of Applied Psychology*, 32(3), 286.

Societal culture and leadership (GLOBE project) – House, R. J., Dorfman, P. W., Javidan, M., Hanges, P. J., & De Luque, M. F. S. (2013). *Strategic leadership across cultures: The GLOBE study of CEO leadership behavior and effectiveness in 24 countries*. Sage publications.

A FORGOTTEN HEROINE

Rowntree strategy – Fitzgerald, R. (1989). "Rowntree and Market Strategy". *Business and Economic History*. 18: 45–58.

Urwick and Follett – Brech, E.F.L., Thomson, A., Wilson, J.F., Urwick, L. (2010) *Management Pioneer: A Biography.* New York: Oxford University Press

Mary Parker Follett's impact – Mendenhall, M.E. and Marsh, W.J. (2010) 'Voices from the past: Mary Parker Follett and Joseph Smith on collaborative leadership', *Journal of Management Inquiry*, 19(4), pp. 284–303. doi:10.1177/1056492610371511.

Leadership impact of Parker-Follett – Metcalf, H.C. and Urwick, L. (2004) Dynamic administration: The collected papers of mary parker follett. 1st edn. Boca Raton, FL: Routledge.

Shared leadership approaches – Hoch, J.E. (2012) 'Shared leadership and innovation: The role of Vertical Leadership and Employee integrity', *Journal of Business and Psychology*, 28(2), pp. 159–174. doi:10.1007/s10869-012-9273-6.;

Shared leadership theory – Pearce, C.L., Conger, J.A. and Locke, E.A. (2008) 'Shared leadership theory', The Leadership Quarterly, 19(5), pp. 622–628. doi:10.1016/j.leaqua.2008.07.005.

Distributed leadership in education – Spillane, J.P., Halverson, R. and Diamond, J.B. (2001) 'Investigating School Leadership Practice: A distributed perspective', *Educational Researcher*, 30(3), pp. 23–28. doi:10.3102/0013189x030003023.

Haudenosaunee society – Birch, J. and Hart, J.P. (2017) 'Social networks and northern Iroquoian confederacy dynamics', *American Antiquity*, 83(1), pp. 13–33. doi:10.1017/aaq.2017.59.

Haudenosaunee society – Roesch Wagner, S. (2020) How Native American women inspired the women's rights movement (U.S. National Park Service), *National Parks Service*. Available at: https://www.nps.gov/articles/000/how-native-american-women-inspired-the-women-s-rights-movement.htm (Accessed: 15 August 2025).

Finding all skills within one individual unrealistic – Burke, V. (2022) Author talks: Attributes-not skills-determine whether you 'cut it' or not, *McKinsey & Company*. Available at: https://www.mckinsey.com/featured-insights/mckinsey-on-books/author-talks-attributes-not-skills-determine-whether-you-cut-it-or-not (Accessed: 16 August 2025).

Finding all skills within one individual unrealistic – Mishra, A.K. and Mishra, K.E. (2013) 'The research on trust in leadership: The need for context', *Journal of Trust Research*, 3(1), pp. 59–69. doi:10.1080/21515581.2013.771507.

Finding all skills within one individual unrealistic – Malloy, R. (2012) *Managing effectively in a matrix, Harvard Business Review*. Available at: https://hbr.org/2012/08/become-a-stronger-matrix-leade

Distributed leadership model – Wareham, D. (2023) 'Creating Constellations: The influence of Constellation Leadership on Agile methodology-led project delivery success'. *ResearchGate*, Doi: 10.13140/RG.2.2.23440.79368

WHO'S THE MAN?

Psychological or sociological – Bratton, J. (2020) *Organizational leadership*. 1st edn. Los Angeles, CA: Sage.

A leader has always been a man – Arany, L. and Popovics, P. (2022) 'The modern leader: The history of leadership styles and the most important qualities of a modern leader', *Cross-Cultural Management Journal*, 24(2), pp. 91–95.

Leaders need new skills for matrixed organisations – Burke, C.S. et al. (2007) 'Trust in leadership: A multi-level review and Integration', *The Leadership Quarterly*, 18(6), pp. 606–632. doi:10.1016/j.leaqua.2007.09.006.

Complex organisations need context – Mishra, A.K. and Mishra, K.E. (2013) 'The research on trust in leadership: The need for context', *Journal of Trust Research*, 3(1), pp. 59–69. doi:10.1080/21515581.2013.771507.

Matrix environment behaviours – Wellman, J. (2007) 'Leadership behaviors in matrix environments', *Project Management Journal*, 38(2), pp. 62–74. doi:10.1177/875697280703800207.

We rearrange the pyramid – Nayar, V. (2009) 'Look for Leadership at the Bottom of the Pyramid', *Harvard Business Review*. Available at: https://hbr.org/2009/01/leadership-at-the-bottom-of-th (Accessed: 12 August 2025)

THE ROLE OF A LEADER

Culture is considered an afterthought – Yohn, D. L. (2021) 'Culture is everyone's responsibility', *Harvard Business Review*, Available at: https://hbr.org/2021/02/company-culture-is-everyones-responsibility (Accessed: 02 August 2025)

Lack of consensus of management – Kellermanns, F. W., Walter, J., Lechner, C., & Floyd, S. W. (2005). 'The Lack of Consensus About Strategic Consensus: Advancing Theory and Research'. *Journal of Management*, 31(5), 719-737. Doi: 10.1177/0149206305279114

Leader etymology – OED (2025) 'Leader', *Online Etymology Dictionary. OED*. Available at: https://www.etymonline.com/word/leader (Accessed: 18 August 2025).

Manager etymology – OED (2025) 'Manager', *Online Etymology Dictionary. OED*. Available at: https://www.etymonline.com/word/manager (Accessed: 18 August 2025).

Leader is a person – Wareham, D. (2023) 'Creating Constellations: The influence of Constellation Leadership on Agile methodology-led project delivery success'. *ResearchGate*, Doi: 10.13140/RG.2.2.23440.79368

EXITING THE PYRAMID

Distributed leadership in sports – Wilson, N. (2017). 'Developing distributed leadership: Leadership emergence in a sporting context.', In *Challenging leadership stereotypes through discourse: Power, management and gender* (pp. 147-170). Singapore: Springer Singapore.

Distributed leadership in SEAL teams – Diviney, R. (2021) *'The attributes: 25 hidden drivers of optimal performance'*, 1st edn. London, UK: Ebury Press.

Leadership as a shared method – Surman, T. and Surman, M. (2008) 'Open sourcing social change: Inside the constellation model', *Technology Innovation Management Review*. Available at: https://doaj.org/article/04c410ff708a441688f5bdad7b3e11ce (Accessed: 25 July 2025).

Culture is shared behaviours – Matsumoto, D. (1996). '*Culture and psychology*'. Pacific Grove, CA: Brooks Cole.

TWO

THE CULTURAL CURRENT: THE SILENT SOCIAL PRESSURE

Just followed the crowd – Reiner, R. (Director). (1992). *'A Few good men' [Film]*. Columbia Pictures; Castle Rock Entertainment.

Culture doesn't eat strategy for breakfast – Drucker, P. (1991). 'Don't change corporate culture: use it', *Wall Street Journal*, Available at: https://drucker.institute/wp-content/uploads/2021/09/Drucker-1991-Dont-Change-Corporate-Culture-Use-It.pdf (Accessed: 04 August 2025)

Biggest competitive advantage – Lawrence, T. (2025) 'Company Culture Is Your Competitive Advantage — Unless You Ignore It', *Forbes*, Available at: https://www.forbes.com/sites/tracylawrence/2025/02/03/company-culture-is-your-competitive-advantage-unless-you-ignore-it/ (Accessed: 19 August 2025).

Culture improves commercial performance – Laker, B. (2021) 'Culture Is A Company's Single Most Powerful Advantage. Here's Why', *Forbes*, Available at: https://www.forbes.com/sites/benjaminlaker/2021/04/23/culture-is-a-companys-single-most-powerful-advantage-heres-why/ (Accessed: 19 August 2025).

What makes a commercial culture? – Mankins, M. (2021) 'The defining elements of a winning culture', *Bain*, Available at: https://www.bain.com/insights/the-defining-elements-of-a-winning-culture-hbr/ (Accessed: 19 August 2025).

You cannot connect and elevate leadership – Seidman, D. (2016) 'Don't Engage, Elevate', *Forbes*, Available at: https://www.forbes.com/sites/dovseidman/2016/03/15/dont-engage-elevate/ (Accessed: 19 August 2025)

STRATEGY. STRATEGY. STRATEGY.

Strategy before culture – Kaul, A. (2019). 'Culture vs strategy: which to precede, which to align?'. *Journal of Strategy and Management*, *12*(1), 116-136.

GOOD OR BAD?

Culture is built on foundational assumptions – Denison, D.R., Haaland, S. and Goelzer, P. (2004) 'Corporate culture and Organizational Effectiveness', *Organizational Dynamics*, 33(1), pp. 98–109. doi:10.1016/j.orgdyn.2003.11.008.

The cultural web – Whittington, R. et al. (2021) *Fundamentals of strategy*. 5th edn. Hoboken, NJ: Pearson.; Johnson, G & Scholes, K. (1999). *Exploring Corporate Strategy*. (5th ed). Prentice Hall.

GOING OFF THE RAILS

Avanti West Coast reviews – Trustpilot (2025) 'Avanti West Coast Reviews'. *Trustpilot,* Available at https://uk.trustpilot.com/review/avantiwestcoast.co.uk (Accessed: 28 July 2025)

Virgin customer performance – Global Railway Review (2017), 'Virgin Trains leads in the new Rail Reputation Index'. *Global Railway Review,* Available at: https://www.globalrailwayreview.com/news/61742/virgin-trains-rail-reputation-index/ (Accessed: 28 July 2025)

Virgin customer performance – Transport Focus (2018) 'Rail passenger satisfaction at a glance: Virgin Trains – Autumn 2018'. *Transport Focus: National Rail Passenger Survey – NRPS – Autumn 2018*

Virgin customer performance – Premier Construction News (2018) 'Virgin Trains Wins at UK Rail Industry Awards 2018', *Premier Construction News,* Available at: https://premierconstructionnews.com/2018/03/29/virgin-trains-wins-uk-rail-industry-awards-2018/ (Accessed: 28 July 2025)

Virgin refund tickets – Global Railway Review (2019), 'Virgin Trains to launch new customer-focused train service'. *Global Railway Review,* Available at: https://www.globalrailwayreview.com/news/83515/virgin-customer-focused-service/ (Accessed: 28 July 2025)

Industrial action for AWC – Sweney, M. (2025) 'Avanti West Coast passengers face severe disruption as rail strikes resume'. *The Guardian*

Staff transferred from Virgin to AWC – Jolly, J. and Davies, R. (2019) 'Branson: Virgin trains will vanish from UK after Stagecoach ban'. *The Guardian*

Staff transferred from Virgin to AWC – BBC (2019) 'Virgin Trains: Final service departs as UK's longest-running rail franchise ends'. *BBC News*

Staff transferred from Virgin to AWC – BBC (2019) 'Avanti starts running West Coast Main Line after Virgin franchise ends'. *BBC News*

Virgin focus on employee experience – Bird, J. (2018) 'Virgin Trains conducts in-depth investigation into employee experience'. *Employee Benefits,* Available at: https://employeebenefits.co.uk/benefits-technology/virgin-trains-conducts-in-depth-investigation-into-employee-experience/189451.article (Accessed on: 25 July 2025)

Virgin set standards in service – Inspiring Workplaces (2017) 'The 2017 Employee Engagement Awards in association with People Insight opens for entries across UK & Europe'. *Inspiring Workplaces,* Available at: https://www.inspiring-workplaces.com/content/the-2017-employee-engagement-awards-in-association-with-people-insight-opens-for-entries-across-uk-europe (Accessed on: 25 July 2025)

A railway that generates prosperity – Avanti West Coast (2025) 'Welcome to Avanti West Coast'. *Avanti West Coast,* Available at: https://www.avantiwestcoast.co.uk/about-us/welcome-to-avanti (Accessed on: 25 July 2025)

Change the paradigm; change the culture – Johnson, G & Scholes, K. (1999). *Exploring Corporate Strategy*. (5th ed). Prentice Hall.

Metropolitan Police to stop attending mental health incidents – Met Police (2023) 'Mental Health incidents attended by the MPS in January 2023'. *Metropolitan Police,* Available at: http://met.police.uk/foi-ai/metropolitan-police/disclosure-2023/june-2023/mental-health-incidents-attended-mps-january2023/ (Accessed on: 25 July 2025)

Public outcry at MET decision – RCPsych (2023) 'RCPsych reaction to Met police plans not to attend 999 mental health incidents'. *Royal College of Psychiatrists,* Available at: https://www.rcpsych.ac.uk/news-and-features/latest-news/detail/2023/05/29/rcpsych-reaction-to-met-police-plans-not-to-attend-999-mental-health-incidents (Accessed on 25 July 2025)

MET's plans unpopular – Seddon, S. and Dilley, S. (2023) 'Metropolitan Police: Move to attend fewer mental health calls sparks alarm'. *BBC News,* Available at: https://www.bbc.co.uk/news/uk-65741824 (Accessed on: 25 July 2025)

Ethnicity Facts and Figures: Stop and Search (England and Wales) – Race Disparity Unit. (2024). Stop and search: Ethnicity facts and figures – Crime, justice and the law. *GOV.UK.* Available at: https://www.ethnicity-facts-figures.service.gov.uk/crime-justice-and-the-law/policing/stop-and-search/latest/ (Accessed: 25 August 2025)

Ethnicity Facts and Figures: The Macpherson Report – House of Commons Home Affairs Committee. (2023). The Macpherson Report: Twenty-two years on [Stop and Search section]. In *House of Commons publications.* UK Parliament. Available at: https://publications.parliament.uk/pa/cm5802/cmselect/cmhaff/139/13909.htm (Accessed: 25 August 2025)

Ethnicity Facts and Figures: Geographical Differences – Race Disparity Unit. (2021, March 31). Stop and search data and the effect of geographical differences. *GOV.UK.* Available at: https://www.gov.uk/government/publications/stop-and-search-data-and-the-effect-of-geographical-differences/stop-and-search-interpreting-and-describing-statistics (Accessed: 25 August 2025)

IF IT LOOKS LIKE A DUCK

Artefacts in psychological research – Lexicon of Psychology. (n.d.) 'Artifact', *Lexicon of Psychology,* Available at: psychology-lexicon.com/cms/glossary/34-glossary-a/6090-artifact.html

Artefacts in cultural psychology – Science Direct. (n.d.) 'Cultural Artifact', *Science Direct,* Available at: https://www.sciencedirect.com/topics/psychology/cultural-artifact

QUACKING AWAY

Significant manufacturing centre – Weber, A (2002) 'The Hawthorne Works', *Assembly Magazine,* Available at: https://www.assemblymag.com/articles/88188-the-hawthorne-works

Specialised and precise processes – Juran (1995). *A History of Managing for Quality.* ASQC Quality Press. p. 557.

Ford introduces the production line – Abrams, D. (2011) 'The Inventions of the Moving Assembly Line: A Revolution in Manufacturing', *Chelsea House,* p.68-71; Library of Congress (n.d.) 'Ford Implements the Moving Assembly Line'. *Library of Congress Research Guides,* Available at: https://guides.loc.gov/this-month-in-business-history/October/Ford (Accessed: 25 July 2025)

William Dickson experiments – Dickson, W. J. (1945). The Hawthorne plan of personnel counseling. *American Journal of Orthopsychiatry, 15(2), 343.*

Multiple Hawthorne studies – Jensen, S. H. (2021), Szabla, D. B. (ed.), 'Roethlisberger, Fritz J.: A Curious Scholar Who Discovered Human Relations', *The Palgrave Handbook of Organizational Change Thinkers, Cham: Springer International Publishing,* pp. 1479–1493, doi:10.1007/978-3-030-38324-4_22

Lightbulb luminosity results – Sedgwick, P., & Greenwood, N. (2015). Understanding the Hawthorne effect. *Bmj, 351.*

The impacts of observation – Mayo, E. (1949) 'Hawthorne and the Western Electric Company, The Social Problems of an Industrial Civilisation', *Routledge.*

Performance reductions after effect wanes – Diaper, G. (1990). The Hawthorne effect: A fresh examination. *Educational studies, 16(3), 261-267.*

Climate versus culture definitions – Schneider, B., Ehrhart, M. G., & Macey, W. H. (2013). 'Organizational climate and culture'. *Annual review of psychology, 64(1)*, 361-388.

Culture is about performance, not perks – Gagnon, C., Jansen, A., & Michaud, C. (2023, June 21). *Culture: 4 keys to why it matters.* McKinsey & Company. https://www.mckinsey.com/capabilities/people-and-organizational-performance/our-insights/the-organization-blog/culture-4-keys-to-why-it-matters

Culture is about great work – Deloitte. (2016). *Culture: The ultimate differentiator.* In *Global human capital trends 2016: The new organization – Different by design* (pp. 126–134). Deloitte University Press. https://www2.deloitte.com/us/en/insights/focus/human-capital-trends/2016/impact-of-culture-on-business-strategy.html

LEADERSHIP AND TOXICITY

Culture influences language – Pschaid, P. (1993). *Language and Power in the Office* (Vol. 7). Gunter Narr Verlag.

Humans are wired for conformity – Bose, G., Dechter, E., & Ivancic, L. (2023). Conformity and adaptation in groups. *Journal of Economic Behavior & Organization, 212*, 1267-1285.

Toxicity is subjective to the individual – Horwitz, S. (1994). Subjectivism. *The Elgar companion to Austrian economics*, 17-22.

Musk demands return to office – Nanji, N. (2022) 'Elon Musk tells Twitter staff to work long hours or leave'. *BBC News*, Available at: https://www.bbc.co.uk/news/business-63648505

Musk sets expectations of return – Rushe, D. (2022) 'Elon Musk tells employees to return to office or 'pretend to work' elsewhere'. *The Guardian*, Available at: https://www.theguardian.com/technology/2022/jun/01/elon-musk-return-to-office-pretend-to-work-somewhere-else

Musk sets office working expectations – Bloomberg (2022) 'Musk's first email to Twitter staff ends remote work'. *Bloomberg*, Available at: https://www.bloomberg.com/news/articles/2022-11-10/musk-s-first-email-to-twitter-staff-ends-remote-work

Musk increases hours for RTO – Business Insider (2022) Elon Musk told Twitter staff to expect 80-hour work weeks and fewer office perks. *Business Insider. Available at:* https://www.businessinsider.com/elon-musk-twitter-staff-expect-80-hour-work-weeks-report-2022-11

Psychological contract creation – Rousseau, D. (1990) 'New hire perceptions of their own and their employer's obligations: A study of psychological contracts'. *Journal of Organizational Behavior*, 11(5), pp. 389-400.

Psychological contract damage and repair – Solinger, O., Hofmans, J., Bal, P. and Jansen, P. (2015) 'Bouncing back from psychological contract breach: How commitment recovers over time'. *Journal of Organizational Behavior*, 37(4), pp. 494-514.

Cognitive dissonance – Cooper, J. (2012). Cognitive dissonance theory. *Handbook of theories of social psychology, 1*, 377-397. ; Festinger, L. (1957). *A Theory of Cognitive Dissonance*. Stanford, CA: Stanford University Press.

Self-determination theory – Deci, E. L., & Ryan, R. M. (2012). Self-determination theory. *Handbook of theories of social psychology, 1*(20), 416-436.

Self-determination theory – Deci, E. L., & Ryan, R. M. (1985). The general causality orientations scale: Self-determination in personality. *Journal of research in personality, 19*(2), 109-134.

Agreeableness in HR professionals – Lounsbury, J. W., Steel, R. P., Gibson, L. W., & Drost, A. W. (2008). Personality traits and career satisfaction of human resource professionals. *Human Resource Development International, 11*(4), 351–366. https://doi.org/10.1080/13678860802261215

Person-orientated fit – Ng, C., & Sarris, A. (2009). Distinguishing between the effect of perceived organisational support and person–organisation fit on work outcomes. *The Australasian Journal of Organisational Psychology, 2*, 1-9.

Person-orientated fit – Tyagi, R., & Gupta, M. (2005). Person-Organisation Fit: Practices and Outcomes. *Indian Journal of Industrial Relations*, 64-78.

Person-orientated fit – Kristof, A. L. (1996). Person-organization fit: An integrative review of its conceptualizations, measurement, and implications. *Personnel psychology*, 49(1), 1-49.

We experience the world subjectively – Jackowska, M., Brown, J., Ronaldson, A., & Steptoe, A. (2016). The impact of a brief gratitude intervention on subjective well-being, biology and sleep. *Journal of Health Psychology*, 21(10), 2207–2217. https://doi.org/10.1177/1359105315572455

We experience the world subjectively –Siedlecki, K. L., Salthouse, T. A., Oishi, S., & Jeswani, S. (2013). The relationship between social support and subjective well-being across age. *Social Indicators Research*, 117(2), 561–576. https://doi.org/10.1007/s11205-013-0361-4

We experience the world subjectively –Meskelis, S., & Whittington, J. L. (2020). Driving employee engagement: How personality trait and leadership style impact the process. *Journal of Business & Industrial Marketing*, 35(10), 1457–1473. https://doi.org/10.1108/jbim-11-2019-0477

LIVED, NOT LAMINATED

Leaders amplify culture – Schein, E. H., & Schein, E. H. (1970). *Organizational psychology* (p. 59). Englewood Cliffs, NJ: Prentice-Hall.

Rude to sit where food is prepared in New Zealand – Conscious Explorer (n.d.) 'The land of the long white cloud: New Zealand etiquette for tourists', *Conscious Explorer,* Available at: https://conscious-explorer.com/magazine/before-new-zealand-etiquette-for-tourists

Values can highlight what we don't do – Schwartz, S. H. (2014). Values and culture. In *Motivation and culture* (pp. 69-84). Routledge.; Heal, A (2021) 'Do we really need company values?', *People Management (09 December)*

Nearly 90% of FTSE 100 companies cite 'ethics' as a value – Peters, I (2023) 'More top firms than ever before have a code of ethics but staff need more support'. *Institute of Business Ethics (20 March)*

Boeing dominated the market – Spokesman Review (1996) 'Boeing Increases Market Share Aerospace Giant Captured Nearly 70 Percent Of Market Last Year'. *The Spokesman Review* (05 January)

Boeing McDonnell Douglas merger – Skapinker, M. (1997) 'Boeing completes McDonnell Douglas takeover'. *Financial Times*. London (05 August)

Clash of cultures following merger – Frost, N. (2020) 'The 1997 merger that paved the way for the Boeing 737 Max crisis'. *Quartz,* Available at: https://tech.yahoo.com/transportation/articles/1997-merger-paved-way-boeing-090042193.html (Accessed: 17 August 2025)

Relocation of headquarters – Wilma, D. (2018) 'On this day: Boeing moves corporate headquarters to Chicago in 2001'. *KIRO Historylink.org*

Whistleblower Ed Pierson – Smiley, L. (2025) 'The Worst 7 Years in Boeing's History—and the Man Who Won't Stop Fighting for Answers'. *Wired,* Available at: https://www.wired.com/story/boeing-whistleblower-737-max/ (Accessed on: 25 July 2025)

Whistleblower Ed Pierson – Pierson, E. (n.d.) 'Ed Pierson', *edpierson.com,* Available at: https://www.edpierson.com/

The military is not a profit-making organisation – Isidore, C. (2024) 'Boeing was once known for safety and engineering. But critics say an emphasis on profits changed that', *CNN,* Available at: https://edition.cnn.com/2024/01/30/business/boeing-history-of-problems

Lion Air Flight 610 – National Transportation Safety Board. (2019). Assumptions used in the safety assessment process and the effects of multiple alerts and indications on pilot performance, *NTSB Safety Recommendation Report No. DCA19RA017/DCA19RA101.* https://www.ntsb.gov/investigations/AccidentReports/Reports/ASR1901.pdf

Lion Air Flight 610 – McKirdy, E.; Faridz, D.; McKenzie, S. (2018). "Lion Air flight crashes en route from Jakarta to Pangkal Pinang". *CNN.*

Investigation into Lion Air incident – Federal Aviation Administration. (2022). Summary of the FAA's review of the Boeing 737 MAX (RTS Summary). *U.S. Department of Transportation.* https://www.faa.gov/sites/faa.gov/files/2022-08/737_RTS_Summary.pdf

When a sensor failed – Suhartono, M. & Ramzy, A. (2019). "Indonesian Report on Lion Air Crash Finds Numerous Problems". *The New York Times.*

MCAS categorised as an update – Laris, M. (2019). 'Changes to flawed Boeing 737 Max were kept from pilots, DeFazio says'. *The Washington Post*

MCAS issue known for a year – O'Kane, S. (2020) 'FAA and Boeing manipulated 737 Max tests during recertification', *The Verge*. Available at: https://www.theverge.com/2020/12/18/22189609/faa-boeing-737-max-senate-report-coverup-tests-whistleblowers

Training information withheld – Paris, F. & Romo, V. (2019). 'Preliminary Crash Report Says Ethiopian Airlines Crew Complied With Procedures', *NPR*

Incentives for expediting the MAX 8 to market – Shepardson, D. & Rucinski, T. (2019). "U.S. lawmakers question Boeing's $1 mln rebate clause for Southwest 737 MAX orders". *Reuters*.

Costs, fines and lost orders – Isidore, C. (2020) 'Boeing's 737 Max debacle could be the most expensive corporate blunder ever'. *CNN*.

WALKING THE TALK

Cultural drift disrupting strategy – Slater, D. H., & Ale, B. J. (2022). Organisations: Drifting or dysfunctional. In *Proceedings of the 32nd European safety and reliability conference (ESREL 2022)* (pp. 3173-3180). Research Publishing.

Amazon to acquire Whole Foods – Whole Foods Market. (2017, June 16). *Amazon to Acquire Whole Foods Market*. Whole Foods Market. https://media.wholefoodsmarket.com/amazon-to-acquire-whole-foods-market/

The bold fusion of Amazon and Whole Foods – Butler, S., & Wood, Z. (2017, June 16). *Amazon to buy Whole Foods Market in $13.7bn deal*. The Guardian; The Guardian. https://www.theguardian.com/business/2017/jun/16/amazon-buy-whole-foods-market-organic-food-fresh

Whole Foods championed for decentralised management – Denning, S. (2013). *The New Management Paradigm & John Mackey's Whole Foods*. Forbes. Retrieved June 19, 2024, from https://www.forbes.com/sites/stevedenning/2013/01/05/the-new-management-paradigm-john-mackeys-whole-foods/

Whole Foods set the standard for trust – Cuenllas, A. (2013). *Whole Foods Case Study: A Benchmark Model of Management For Hospitality*. Hospitality Net; Hospitality Net. https://www.hospitalitynet.org/opinion/4059396.html

Amazon's process-driven mode – Alvarez, J. B., Lane, D., & Coughlin, J. (2017). Amazon Buys Whole Foods. *Www.hbs.edu*. https://www.hbs.edu/faculty/Pages/item.aspx?num=53656

I don't recognise Whole Foods anymore – Sainato, M. (2019). *Whole Foods workers say conditions deteriorated after Amazon takeover*. The Guardian; The Guardian. https://www.theguardian.com/business/2019/jul/16/whole-foods-amazon-prime-working-conditions

Removal of employee benefits – Tarasov, K. (2022). *Amazon bought Whole Foods five years ago for $13.7 billion. Here's what's changed at the high-end grocer*. CNBC. https://www.cnbc.com/2022/08/25/how-whole-foods-has-changed-in-the-five-years-since-amazon-took-over.html

Workers unionise at Whole Foods – Sainato, M. (2024). *Philadelphia workers at Amazon's Whole Foods file for first union election*. The Guardian; The Guardian. https://www.theguardian.com/business/2024/nov/26/amazon-whole-foods-union-drive

Whole Foods loses Best Place To Work label – Blanding, M. (2018). *Amazon vs. Whole Foods: When Cultures Collide*. Harvard Business School. https://www.library.hbs.edu/working-knowledge/amazon-vs-whole-foods-when-cultures-collide

Morale drops at Whole Foods – Rahaim, N. (2017). *Vox First Person: Thank God I don't work at Whole Foods anymore*. Vox. https://www.vox.com/first-person/2017/6/21/15847070/whole-foods-amazon-workers-automation

Speed, simplicity and trust – Glassdoor (2024). *Speed, Simplicity and Trust – Aspirations or Propaganda?* Glassdoor. https://www.glassdoor.com/Reviews/Employee-Review-Vodafone-E5775-RVW2465040.htm

Values provide a common language – Strubel, P. (2017). *Core values: a common language for all employees*. Medium. https://medium.com/@PascaleStrubel/core-values-un-common-language-for-all-employees-68e61a438501

FROM "FOLLOW ME" TO FARMING

When leaders create the wrong environment – Edmondson, A. C. (2023). *Right Kind of Wrong*. Simon and Schuster.

Mismatched values and behaviours create toxicity – Grandey, A. A. (2003). When "the show must go on": Surface acting and deep acting as determinants of emotional exhaustion and peer-rated service delivery. *Academy of Management Journal, 46*(1), 86–96. https://doi.org/10.5465/30040678

ENGAGEMENT AS A RESPONSIBILITY

Benefits of people engagement – CIPD. (2025). *Employee Engagement & Motivation | Factsheets*. CIPD. https://www.cipd.org/uk/knowledge/factsheets/engagement-factsheet/

Employee engagement impacts – Sorenson, S. (2023). *How Employee Engagement Drives Growth*. Gallup. https://www.gallup.com/workplace/236927/employee-engagement-drives-growth.aspx

The impact of meaningful work – Frankl, V. E. (1985). *Man's search for meaning*. Simon and Schuster.; Heintzelman, S. J., & King, L. A. (2014). Life is pretty meaningful. *American psychologist, 69*(6), 561.; Martela, F., & Steger, M. F. (2016). The three meanings of meaning in life: Distinguishing coherence, purpose, and significance. *The Journal of Positive Psychology, 11*(5), 531-545.

Societal impact of employee engagement – Boyd, N., Nowell, B., Yang, Z., & Hano, M. C. (2018). Sense of community, sense of community responsibility, and public service motivation as predictors of employee well-being and engagement in public service organizations. *The American Review of Public Administration, 48*(5), 428-443.

Low employee engagement and impact on families – Allen, T. D., Herst, D. E. L., Bruck, C. S., & Sutton, M. (2000). Consequences associated with work-to-family conflict: A review and agenda for future research. *Journal of Occupational Health Psychology, 5*(2), 278–308. https://doi.org/10.1037/1076-8998.5.2.278

Low employee engagement and impact on alcoholism – Baek, S., Lee, Y. J., & Kim, J. H. (2023). Job dissatisfaction and alcohol use disorder: Evidence from a nationally representative longitudinal study. *Addictive Behaviors, 139*, 107599. https://doi.org/10.1016/j.addbeh.2023.107599

Employee engagement and domestic violence – Breiding, M. J., Basile, K. C., Smith, S. G., Black, M. C., & Mahendra, R. R. (2015). Intimate partner violence surveillance: Uniform definitions and recommended data elements, version 2.0. *Centers for Disease Control and Prevention*. https://www.cdc.gov/violenceprevention/pdf/ipv/intimatepartnerviolence.pdf

THREE

LOOK TO THE STARS: CREATING CONSTELLATIONS

We do the best work ourselves – Tzu, L. (2020). *Tao te ching*. Courier Dover Publications.

Each professional is a star – Empson, L. (2017) *Leading professionals: Power, politics, and prima donnas*. 1st edn. Oxford, UK: Oxford University Press.

Distributed leadership emerges between leaders and followers – Spillane, J.P. (2005) 'Distributed leadership', *The Educational Forum*, 69(2), pp. 143–150. doi:10.1080/00131720508984678.

Vertical and shared leadership models – Hoch, J.E. (2012) 'Shared leadership and innovation: The role of Vertical Leadership and Employee integrity', *Journal of Business and Psychology*, 28(2), pp. 159–174. doi:10.1007/s10869-012-9273-6.

Performance as a method – Spillane, J.P., Halverson, R. and Diamond, J.B. (2001) 'Investigating School Leadership Practice: A distributed perspective', *Educational Researcher*, 30(3), pp. 23–28. doi:10.3102/0013189x030003023.

STARRING IN A PROJECT

Waterfall versus Agile projects – Thesing, T., Feldmann, C., & Burchardt, M. (2021). Agile versus waterfall project management: decision model for selecting the appropriate approach to a project. *Procedia Computer Science, 181,* 746-756.

Agile project benefits – Freedman, R. (2018) *What is Agile?* 1st edn. Sebastopol, CA: O'Reilly Media, Inc.

Structure of an Agile team – Girvan, L. and Girvan, S. (2022) *Agile from first principles.* 1st edn. Swindon, UK: BCS Learning & Development Limited.

Agile project responsibilities – Greene, J. and Stellman, A. (2017) *What is Agile?* 1st edn. Sebastopol, CA: O'Reilly Media, Inc.

Scrum Master as a servant leader – Greenleaf, R. (2007) 'The servant as leader', *Corporate Ethics and Corporate Governance*, pp. 79–85. doi:10.1007/978-3-540-70818-6_6. ; Greenleaf, R.K. (2002) *Servant leadership: A journey into the nature of legitimate power and Greatness.* 3rd edn. New York, NY: Paulist Press.

WHEN STARS ALIGN AND SHINE

Constellation Leadership has no chair – Wareham, D. (2023). *Creating Constellations: The influence of Constellation Leadership on Agile methodology-led project delivery success.* https://doi.org/10.13140/RG.2.2.23440.79368

Fluid leadership requires self-awareness – Dimeglio, P. C. (2024). *How Self-Awareness Elevates Leadership Effectiveness.* Forbes. https://www.forbes.com/sites/paolacecchi-dimeglio/2024/02/14/how-self-awareness-elevates-leadership-effectiveness/

Resilience and resiliency definition – Merriam-Webster. (2019). *Definition of RESILIENCY.* Merriam-Webster.com. https://www.merriam-webster.com/dictionary/resiliency

Flocking behaviour without a leader – Emlen, J. T. (1952). Flocking behavior in birds. *The Auk, 69*(2), 160-170.

Ambiguity between teams can cause silos – Bento, F., Tagliabue, M., & Lorenzo, F. (2020). *Organizational silos: A scoping review informed by a behavioral perspective on systems and networks.* Societies, 10(3), 56. https://doi.org/10.3390/soc10030056

Misinterpretations result in protectionism – Argyris, C. (1990). *Overcoming organizational defenses: Facilitating organizational learning*

Conflict and withdrawal in unclear organisational contexts – Rizzo, J. R., House, R. J., & Lirtzman, S. I. (1970). Role conflict and ambiguity in complex organizations. *Administrative Science Quarterly, 15*(2), 150–163. https://doi.org/10.2307/2391486

THE LAZY APE

Brain is 2% of body weight – Veerakone, R. (2024). *Do we only use 10 percent of our brain?* MIT McGovern Institute. https://mcgovern.mit.edu/2024/01/26/do-we-use-only-10-percent-of-our-brain/

Brain uses 20% of energy – Raichle, M. E., & Gusnard, D. A. (2002). Appraising the brain's energy budget. *Proceedings of the National Academy of Sciences, 99*(16), 10237–10239. https://doi.org/10.1073/pnas.172399499

Thinking more uses more calories – Jabr, F. (2012). *Does Thinking Really Hard Burn More Calories?* Scientific American. https://www.scientificamerican.com/article/thinking-hard-calories/

Brain has barely changed in 160,000 years – Taylor, L. (2022). *Shape of human brain has barely changed in past 160,000 years.* New Scientist. https://www.newscientist.com/article/2331652-shape-of-human-brain-has-barely-changed-in-past-160000-year

'Good enough' biases and cognitive function – Tversky, A., Kahneman, D., & Slovic, P. (1982). *Judgment under uncertainty: Heuristics and biases* (pp. 3-20).

Heuristics and biases – Gilovich, T., Griffin, D., & Kahneman, D. (Eds.). (2002). *Heuristics and biases: The psychology of intuitive judgment.* Cambridge university press.

Face validity – Johnson, E. (2021). Face validity. In *Encyclopedia of autism spectrum disorders* (pp. 1957-1957). Cham: Springer International Publishing.

Validity and reliability – Mosier, C. I. (1947). A critical examination of the concepts of face validity. *Educational and Psychological Measurement, 7*(2), 191-205.

Over 170 cognitive biases – Wikipedia Contributors. (2019). *List of cognitive biases.* Wikipedia; Wikimedia Foundation. https://en.wikipedia.org/wiki/List_of_cognitive_biases

Cognitive biases – *Cognitive Biases Codex.* (2020). Unc.edu. https://www.sog.unc.edu/sites/www.sog.unc.edu/files/course_materials/Cognitive%20Biases%20Codex.pdf

We are blind to our blindness – Kahneman, D. (2011). *Thinking, Fast and Slow.* Farrar, Straus and Giroux.

10,000 hours of practice proposed – Gladwell, M. (2008). *Outliers: The story of success.* Little, Brown and Company.

10,000 hours of practice debunked – Ericsson, K. A., Krampe, R. T., & Tesch-Römer, C. (1993). The role of deliberate practice in the acquisition of expert performance. *Psychological Review, 100*(3), 363–406. https://doi.org/10.1037/0033-295X.100.3.363

Brainstorming sessions produce groupthink – Janis, I. L. (1972). *Victims of groupthink: A psychological study of foreign-policy decisions and fiascoes.* Houghton Mifflin.

Brainstorming is not useful – Peace, N. (2012). Why Most Brainstorming Sessions Are Useless. *Forbes.* https://www.forbes.com/sites/nataliepeace/2012/04/09/why-most-brainstorming-sessions-are-useless/

VAK learning styles debunked – Pashler, H., McDaniel, M., Rohrer, D., & Bjork, R. (2008). Learning styles: Concepts and evidence. *Psychological Science in the Public Interest, 9*(3), 105–119. https://doi.org/10.1111/j.1539-6053.2009.01038.x

Conscious cognition takes effort – Brady, S. T., Siegel, G. J., R Wayne Albers, & Price, D. L. (2012). *Basic neurochemistry : principles of molecular, cellular, and medical neurobiology.* Academic Press / Elsevier.

Out-group homogeneity – Ackerman, J. M., Shapiro, J. R., Neuberg, S. L., Kenrick, D. T., Becker, D. V., Griskevicius, V., ... & Schaller, M. (2006). They all look the same to me (unless they're angry) from out-group homogeneity to out-group heterogeneity. *Psychological science, 17*(10), 836-840.

Individuals' skills not being utilised – Webber, A. (2022). *Three in 10 workers' skill sets not being used to their full potential.* Personnel Today. https://www.personneltoday.com/hr/employees-secret-skills-research/

DRAWING THE CONSTELLATION

How we get things done around here – Deal, T. E., & Kennedy, A. A. (2000). *Corporate cultures : the rites and rituals of corporate life.* Basic Books. (Original work published 1982)

Social impacts in New York after 9/11 – Foner, N. and Foner, N. (2005) 'CHAPTER 1 The Social Effects of 9/11 on New York City: An Introduction', in *Wounded city: The social impact of 9/11.* 1st edn. New York, NY: Russell Sage Foundation (The September 11th Initiative), pp. 3–27.

Chilean miner timeline – Romero, S., & Barrionuevo, A. (2010). *Chilean miners are rescued after 69 days underground.* The New York Times. https://www.nytimes.com/2010/10/14/world/americas/14chile.html

Plan B is successful – Franklin, J. (2010). *Chilean miners rescue: Plan B drill hit the jackpot.* BBC News. https://www.bbc.com/news/world-latin-america-11511117

Unsung heroes of the Chilean miner rescue – Murphy, H. (2010). *The unsung heroes of Chile's rescue drama.* The Irish Times. https://www.irishtimes.com/news/the-unsung-heroes-of-chile-s-rescue-drama-1.868253

The distributed leadership of the Chilean miner rescue – Reardon, C. (2010). *The world watched Chile: Lessons from the rescue of the miners. Leadership in Action, 30*(6), 3–7. https://doi.org/10.1002/lia.1324

Greater difference within a generation than between generations – Schraiber, J. G., & Edge, M. D. (2024). Heritability within groups is uninformative about differences among groups: Cases from behavioral, evolutionary, and statistical genetics. *Proceedings of the National Academy of Sciences of the United States of America, 121*(12), e2319496121. https://doi.org/10.1073/pnas.2319496121

Generational differences are not as great as we think – Rudolph, C.W., Rauvola, R.S., Costanza, D.P. *et al.* (2021) Generations and Generational Differences: Debunking Myths in Organizational Science and Practice and Paving New Paths Forward. *J Bus Psychol* **36**, 945–967. https://doi.org/10.1007/s10869-020-09715-2

FOUR

THE STUDY: UNLOCKING CULTURAL INFLUENCE

Leaders manage and create culture - Schein, E. H. (2010). *Organizational culture and leadership* (Vol. 2). John Wiley & Sons.

Wikipedia is a self-governing network – Konieczny, P. (2010). *Adhocratic Governance in the Internet Age: A Case of Wikipedia. Journal of Information Technology & Politics, 7*(4), 263-283. https://doi.org/10.1080/19331681.2010.489408

Wikipedia's focus on governance from bottom-up – Beschastnikh, I., Kriplean, T., & McDonald, D. W. (2008). Wikipedian Self-Governance in Action: Motivating Policy Discussion. In *Proceedings of the 1st International Workshop on Wikis and Open Collaboration (WikiSym '08)*. ACM.

Coordination in natural disasters – Aggarwal, V., & others. (2021). Institutional Coordination in Disaster Management in the [context]. *ASCE Natural Hazards Review*.

Removing the reliance on an individual leader – McKee, L. et al. (2013) '"new" and distributed leadership in quality and safety in health care, or "old" and hierarchical? an interview study with strategic stakeholders', *Journal of Health Services Research & Policy*, 18(2_suppl), pp. 11–19. doi:10.1177/1355819613484460.

RESEARCHING CONSTELLATIONS

First research into constellation leadership – Wareham, D. (2023). *Creating Constellations: The influence of Constellation Leadership on Agile methodology-led project delivery success.* https://doi.org/10.13140/RG.2.2.23440.79368

Research paradigm – Attard, N. (2018) 'WASP (write a scientific paper): Writing an academic research proposal', *Early Human Development*, 123, pp. 39–41. doi:10.1016/j.earlhumdev.2018.04.011.

Socially-constructed interpretive paradigm – Saunders, M., Lewis, P. and Thornhill, A. (2019) Research methods for business students. 8th edn. Harlow, England: Pearson.

Radical humanist paradigm – Hassard, J. (1991) 'Multiple paradigms and Organizational Analysis: A case study', Organization Studies, 12(2), pp. 275–299. doi:10.1177/017084069101200206.

Deductive thematic analysis of data – Casula, M., Rangarajan, N. and Shields, P. (2020) 'The potential of working hypotheses for deductive exploratory research', *Quality & Quantity*, 55(5), pp. 1703–1725. doi:10.1007/s11135-020-01072-9.

Mission command philosophy in the military – Ploumis, M. (2020). *Mission command and philosophy for the 21st century. Comparative Strategy, 39*(2), 209-218. https://doi.org/10.1080/01495933.2020.1718995

WHAT IS SUCCESS?

Philosophy of Shu Ha Ri – Bradić, S., Kariya, C., Callan, M., & Jones, L. (2023). Universality and applicability of shu-ha-ri concept through comparison in everyday life, education, judo and kata in judo. *The Arts and Sciences of Judo, 3*(2), 20-24.

As competence builds, confidence builds – Lucero, K. S., & others. (2020). What Do Reinforcement and Confidence Have to Do with It: Results from a Continuing Professional Development Intervention. *Frontiers in Psychology*, 11, Article 578183. https://doi.org/10.3389/fpsyg.2020.578183

Competence and self-esteem – Johnson, M. D., & others. (1995). Competence Strivings and Self-Esteem: An Experimental Investigation. *Journal of Personality and Social Psychology*, 68(4), 624-643. https://doi.org/10.1037/0022-3514.68.4.624

Freedom of action through mission command – British Army, Centre for Army Leadership. (2024). *Mission Command and Leadership on Operations Since 1991*. UK Ministry of Defence.

Employees hold multiple roles in smaller organisations – Harney, B., Millington, A., & others. (2022). Advancing understanding of HRM in small and medium-sized enterprises (SMEs): Employee practices, roles, and dynamics. *International Journal of Human Resource Management*. https://doi.org/10.1080/09585192.2022.2109375

In small companies, employees have overlapping responsibilities – Cardon, M. S., & Stevens, C. E. (2004). Managing Human Resources in Small Organizations: What Do We Know? *Human Resource Management Review*, 14(3), 295-323. https://doi.org/10.1016/j.hrmr.2004.06.001

Specialisation enhances competency – Shea, J. B., & Morgan, R. L. (1979). Contextual interference effects on the acquisition, retention, and transfer of a motor skill. *Journal of Experimental Psychology: Human Learning and Memory*, 5(2), 179–187. https://doi.org/10.1037/0278-7393.5.2.179

Scrum master approach as a servant leader – Holtzhausen, N. and de Klerk, J.J. (2018) 'Servant leadership and the Scrum team's effectiveness', Leadership & Organization Development Journal, 39(7), pp. 873–882. doi:10.1108/lodj-05-2018-0193.

Scrum improved with servant leadership – Ripley, R. and Miller, T. (2020) Fixing your scrum: Practical solutions to common scrum problems. 1st edn. Rayleigh, NC: O'Reilly.

Social group size impacts relationships – Muthukrishna, M., & Henrich, J. (2016). Innovation in the collective: Culture, cognition, and cooperation. *Philosophical Transactions of the Royal Society B: Biological Sciences, 371*(1690), 20150192.

HOW BIG IS TOO BIG?

Primates can maintain stable, meaningful social relationships – Dunbar, R. I. (1992). Neocortex size as a constraint on group size in primates. *Journal of human evolution, 22*(6), 469-493.

Maintaining stable, meaningful social relationships – Hill, R. A., & Dunbar, R. I. M. (2003). Social network size in humans. *Human Nature, 14*(1), 53-72

We can remember many more faces and names – Jenkins, R., Dowsett, A. J., & Burton, A. M. (2018). How many faces do people know?. *Proceedings of the Royal Society B, 285*(1888), 20181319.

Silos encouraged above certain group sizes – Casey, J., Simon, S., & Graham, W. (2021). Leading with the social brain in mind. *Australian Educational Leader, 43*(4), 16-24.

Basecamp employee experience suffers as company grows – Newton, C. (2021). *Inside the all-hands meeting that led to a third of Basecamp employees quitting*. The Verge. Retrieved from https://www.theverge.com/2021/5/3/22418208/basecamp-all-hands-meeting-employee-resignations-buyouts-implosion

Senior staff at Basecamp leave – Lyons, K. (2021). *Basecamp implodes as employees flee company, including senior staff*. The Verge. Retrieved from https://www.theverge.com/2021/4/30/22412714/basecamp-employees-memo-policy-hansson-fried-controversy

Gore-Tex intentionally silo teams – Spradlin, D. (2019). *The maker of GORE-TEX is experimenting with an artificial cornea. Bloomberg*. Retrieved from https://www.bloomberg.com/features/2019-gore-artificial-cornea/

Amazon's two-pizza rule – Amazon Web Services. (n.d.). *Amazon's two-pizza teams: The ultimate drivers of innovation*. AWS Executive Insights. Retrieved September 21, 2025, from https://aws.amazon.com/executive-insights/content/amazon-two-pizza-team/

British Army structure of battalions into companies – British Army. (n.d.). *Our people*. Ministry of Defence. Retrieved September 21, 2025, from https://www.army.mod.uk/who-we-are/our-people/

Headcount restrictions used in other armed services around the world – Watling, J. (2024). *Russian military objectives and capacity in Ukraine through 2024.* Royal United Services Institute (RUSI). Retrieved September 21, 2025, from https://www.rusi.org/explore-our-research/publications/commentary/russian-military-objectives-and-capacity-ukraine-through-2024

THE TOLERANCE OF FAILURE

NASA's Apollo 13 mission flexibility – NASA. (2009). *Apollo 13: Mission Details.* NASA. https://www.nasa.gov/missions/apollo/apollo-13-mission-details/

PIXAR story development through 'brain trust' – Satell, G. (2015). *The Little Known Secret To Pixar's Creative Success.* Forbes. https://www.forbes.com/sites/gregsatell/2015/05/29/the-little-known-secret-to-pixars-creative-success/

Toy Story 2 rewriting due to feedback – Catmull, E. (2008). *How Pixar Fosters Collective Creativity.* Harvard Business Review. https://hbr.org/2008/09/how-pixar-fosters-collective-creativity

Toy Story 2 box office success – The Numbers. (1999). *Toy Story 2 financial performance* [Review of *Toy Story 2 financial performance*]. The Numbers. https://www.the-numbers.com/movie/Toy-Story-2

THE GLUE OF LIFE

Trust as a key factor in distributed leadership systems – Al-Ani, B., & Redmiles, D. (2009). In strangers we trust? Findings of an empirical study of distributed teams. In *2009 Fourth IEEE International Conference on Global Software Engineering* (pp. 121-130). IEEE.

Definition of trust – Rotenberg, K. (2018). The psychology of trust. Routledge.

Trust and the psychological contract – Atkinson, C. (2007). Trust and the psychological contract. *Employee relations*, *29*(3), 227-246.

Blanchard's approach to trust – Blanchard, K. H., Blanchard, K., & Conley, R. (2022). *Simple truths of leadership: 52 ways to be a servant leader and build trust.* Berrett-Koehler Publishers.

BRAVING from Brene Brown – Brown, B. (n.d.). *The anatomy of trust* [Review of *The anatomy of trust*]. Brenebrown.com. https://brenebrown.com/podcast/the-anatomy-of-trust/

Trust is contextual and situational – Thielmann, I., & Hilbig, B. E. (2015). Trust: An integrative review from a person–situation perspective. *Review of General Psychology*, *19*(3), 249-277.

ADDITIONAL INSIGHTS

Illusory superiority bias in respondents – Hoorens, V. (1993). "Self-enhancement and Superiority Biases in Social Comparison". *European Review of Social Psychology*. **4** (1): 113–139. doi:10.1080/14792779343000040

Dunning-Kruger effect in individuals – Schlösser, T.; Dunning, D.; Johnson, K. L.; Kruger, J. (1 December 2013). "How Unaware Are the Unskilled? Empirical Tests of the 'Signal Extraction' Counter-Explanation for the Dunning–Kruger Effect in Self-Evaluation of Performance". *Journal of Economic Psychology*. 39: 85–100.

Ability dominates outcomes – Rousseau, D. M., Sitkin, S. B., Burt, R. S., & Camerer, C. (1998). Not so different after all: A cross-discipline view of trust. *Academy of management review*, *23*(3), 393-404.

Link between trust and risk-taking in organisational settings – Dirks, K. T. (1999). The effects of interpersonal trust on work group performance. *Journal of applied psychology*, *84*(3), 445.

Trust as confidence in competence – Zucker, L. G. (1986). Production of trust: Institutional sources of economic structure, 1840–1920. *Research in organizational behavior*.

WHEN CULTURE LEADS

Shared leadership moves authority under specific conditions – Conger, J.A. and Pearce, C. (2003) *Shared leadership: Reframing the hows and whys of leadership.* 1st edn. Thousand Oaks, CA: Sage.

Haier reorganised business into microenterprises – van der Lecq, B. (2019). *Haier: A company worth studying* [Review of *Haier: A company worth studying*]. Corporate Rebels. https://www.corporate-rebels.com/blog/haier-a-company-worth-studying

Constellation leadership can outperform traditional models – Bergman, J.Z. *et al.* (2012) 'The shared leadership process in decision-making teams', *The Journal of Social Psychology*, 152(1), pp. 17–42. doi:10.1080/00224545.2010.538763.

Constellation leadership can outperform traditional models – Ensley, M.D., Hmieleski, K.M. and Pearce, C.L. (2006) 'The importance of vertical and shared leadership within New Venture Top Management Teams: Implications for the performance of startups', *The Leadership Quarterly*, 17(3), pp. 217–231. doi:10.1016/j.leaqua.2006.02.002.

Constellation leadership can outperform traditional models – Harris, A. (2013) 'Distributed leadership', *Educational Management Administration & Leadership*, 41(5), pp. 545–554. doi:10.1177/1741143213497635.

Constellation leadership can outperform traditional models – Karriker, J.H., Madden, L.T. and Katell, L.A. (2017) 'Team composition, distributed leadership, and performance: It's good to share', *Journal of Leadership & Organizational Studies*, 24(4), pp. 507–518. doi:10.1177/1548051817709006.

FIVE

PERSONALITY & INDIVIDUAL DIFFERENCES

Our inability to recognise and celebrate differences – Lorde, A. (2023). The master's tools will never dismantle the master's house. In *Postcolonlsm* (pp. 1670-1673). Routledge.

Marshmallow challenge - Daoudy, H., & Verstraeten, M. (2013). Team Dynamics and the Marshmallow Challenge: studying team performance and personal satisfaction with a focus on verbal interactions. *Working Papers CEB, 13*.

Marshmallow challenge study and results – Wujec, T. (2010). The marshmallow challenge. *Retrieved November, 12*(2013), 1.

Verbal interaction in group influence outcomes – Webb, N. M. (1985). Verbal interaction and learning in peer-directed groups. *Theory into practice, 24*(1), 32-39.

Peer group verbal interactions influence success – Girolametto, L., Weitzman, E., & Greenberg, J. (2004). The effects of verbal support strategies on small-group peer interactions. *Language, speech, and hearing services in schools, 35*(3), 254-268.

THAT'S SUCH A RED THING TO DO

Individual differences and personality – Ashton, M. C. (2022). *Individual differences and personality*. Academic Press.

Alcmaeon of Croton proposes humours – Celesia, G. G. (2012). Alcmaeon of Croton's observations on health, brain, mind, and soul. *Journal of the History of the Neurosciences, 21*(4), 409-426.

Hippocrates links humours to personality – Hippocrates (c. 460 – c. 370 BC), *On the Sacred Disease*.

Galen connects mind to body – Kagan, J. (2018). *Galen's prophecy: Temperament in human nature*. Routledge.

The personality of Harry Potter houses – Crysel, L. C., Cook, C. L., Schember, T. O., & Webster, G. D. (2015). Harry Potter and the measures of personality: Extraverted Gryffindors, agreeable Hufflepuffs, clever Ravenclaws, and manipulative Slytherins. *Personality and Individual Differences, 83*, 174-179.

Humourism origins in ancient Egypt – van Sertima, I. (1992). *Golden age of the Moor*. Transaction Publishers.

Humourism origins in ancient Mesopotamia – Sudhoff, K. (1926). *Essays in the History of Medicine*. New York City: Medical Life Press. pp. 67, 87, 104.

Personality by bodily fluid colour – Karenberg, A. (2015). Blood, Phlegm and Spirits: Galen on Stroke. *History of Medicine/Ru, 2*(2). https://doi.org/10.17720/2409-5834.v2.2.2015.15k

HAPPY BIRTHDAY. YOU'RE STUBBORN

Changing personality with cucumber – Smith, M. (2013). *Balancing Your Humors* [Review of *Balancing Your Humors*]. Psychology Today. https://www.psychologytoday.com/gb/blog/short-history-mental-health/201311/balancing-your-humors

Babylonian astronomy and the twelve signs –Herschel Holden,J. (1996). *A history of horoscopic astrology /.* American Federation Of Astrologers.

Greek scholars gain star charts – Pingree, D. E. (1997). From astral omens to astrology: from Babylon to Bīkāner. *Serie Orientale Roma.*

The Tetrabiblos introduces the zodiac – Ptolemy, C., & Proclus. (1940). *Tetrabiblos* (p. 36). Cambridge, MA: Harvard University Press.

Scientific reliability and validity of horoscopes – Fichten, C. S., & Sunerton, B. (1983). Popular horoscopes and the "Barnum effect". *The Journal of Psychology, 114*(1), 123-134.

Horoscope accuracy – McGrew, J. H., & McFall, R. M. (1990). A scientific inquiry into the validity of astrology. *Journal of Scientific Exploration, 4*(1), 75-83.

Ubiquity of horoscopes in modern media – Neamțu, C. (2025) Astrological Discourse in Media: The Unique Language of Horoscopes. *Asian Journal of Social Sciences and Legal Studies*, 290–307. https://doi.org/10.34104/ajssls.025.02900307

SLOPING FOREHEAD? HOME, YOU GO!

Franz Joseph Gall and phrenology – Van Wyhe, J. (2002). The authority of human nature: the Schädellehre of Franz Joseph Gall. *The British journal for the history of science, 35*(1), 17-42.

The pseudoscience of phrenology – Wihe, J. V. (2002). "Science and Pseudoscience: A Primer in Critical Thinking". *Encyclopedia of Pseudoscience*. California: Skeptics Society. pp. 195–203.

Phrenology in an applied world – McCandless, P. (1992). Mesmerism and Phrenology in Antebellum Charleston: "Enough of the Marvellous." *The Journal of Southern History, 58*(2), 199. https://doi.org/10.2307/2210860

Less than 20% of women are gainfully employed – Yellen, J. (2020). *The history of women's work and wages and how it has created success for us all.* Brookings; The Brookings Institution. https://www.brookings.edu/articles/the-history-of-womens-work-and-wages-and-how-it-has-created-success-for-us-all/

Two million women working by 1910 – Red Kap. (2020). *History of women in the workforce.* Www.redkap.com. https://www.redkap.com/women-workforce-history.html

Phrenology resurgent as a personality consideration – Gallup Jr, G. G., Frederick, M. J., & Pipitone, R. N. (2008). Morphology and behavior: Phrenology revisited. *Review of General Psychology, 12*(3), 297-304.

WHO IS THE "YOUNG IAN?"

Biography of Carl Jung – Charet, F. X. (2000). Understanding Jung: recent biographies and scholarship. *Journal of Analytical Psychology, 45*(2), 195-216.

Carl Jung's youth – Wehr, G. (2002). *Jung & Steiner: The birth of a new psychology.* SteinerBooks.

A fascination with homo erectus – Clark. G. (2024) "Fossils, Anthropology and Hominin Brain Phylogeny". Chapter 2, pp. 38-40. In *Carl Jung and the Evolutionary Sciences: A New Vision for Analytical Psychology.* Routledge.

Astrology is essential to alchemy – Lachman, G. (2010). *Jung the Mystic.* Tarcher.

Twelve Jungian archetypes – Jung, C. G. (1968). *The Archetypes and the Collective Unconscious.* Princeton University Press.

Shy as a proxy for untrustworthy – Oxford University Press. (2023). *The Oxford English Dictionary.* Clarendon Press.

The Myers-Briggs Type Indicator – Pittenger, D. J. (1993). The Utility of the Myers-Briggs Type Indicator. *Review of Educational Research, 63*(4), 467–488. https://doi.org/10.3102/00346543063004467

DiSC is utilised millions of times per year – EverythingDISC. (2021). *What is DiSC.* Discprofile.com. https://www.discprofile.com/what-is-disc

THE WONDER(WOMAN) OF TYPING TOOLS

Biography of William Moulton Marsten – Bunn, G. C. (1997). The lie detector, Wonder Woman and liberty: The life and work of William Moulton Marston. *History of the human sciences, 10*(1), 91-119.

Educated at Harvard and graduating Phi Beta Kappa – Harvard. (1915) Harvard College Class of 1915: Twenty-fifth Anniversary Report. *The Cosmos Press*

The emotions of normal people – Marston, W. M. (2013). *Emotions of normal people.* Routledge.

People can be categorised along two axis – Ahn, R. (2023). *Knowing Yourself and the DiSC Profile.* Careerminds. https://careerminds.com/blog/knowing-disc-profile

History of Wonder Woman – Lyons, C. (2006). Suffering Sappho! A Look At The Creator & Creation of Wonder Woman. *Comic Book Resources.*

The history of the polygraph – National Research Council, Division of Behavioral, Social Sciences, Committee on National Statistics, Board on Behavioral, Sensory Sciences, & Committee to Review the Scientific Evidence on the Polygraph. (2003). *The polygraph and lie detection.* National Academies Press.

Nomothetic psychology approach – Harris, R. J. (2003). Traditional nomothetic approaches. *Handbook of research methods in experimental psychology*, 41-65.

Idiographic psychology approach – Piccirillo, M. L., & Rodebaugh, T. L. (2019). Foundations of idiographic methods in psychology and applications for psychotherapy. *Clinical psychology review, 71*, 90-100.

DiSC as pseudoscience – Sumpter, D. (2020). How Swedes were fooled by one of the biggest scientific bluffs of our time. *Medium. Artikkeli, 14*, 2020.

Myers-Briggs as pseudoscience – Lilienfeld, S. O., Lynn, S. J., Lohr, J. M., & Tavris, C. (2015). *Science and pseudoscience in clinical psychology.* The Guilford Press.

CHARACTERISTICS CLING TO FAMILY

Francis Galton biography – Langkjær-Bain, R. (2019). The troubling legacy of Francis Galton. *Significance, 16*(3), 16–21. https://doi.org/10.1111/j.1740-9713.2019.01275.x

First industrial revolution – Deane, P. (1979). *The first industrial revolution.* Cambridge University Press.

Second industrial revolution – Mokyr, J., & Strotz, R. H. (1998). The second industrial revolution, 1870-1914. *Storia dell'economia Mondiale, 21945*(1), 219-245.

The works of Francis Galton – Bulmer, M. G. (2003). *Francis Galton: pioneer of heredity and biometry.* JHU Press.

Galton's contributions to psychology – Burt, C. (1962). Francis Galton and his contributions to psychology. *British Journal of Statistical Psychology, 15*(1), 1-49.

Anthropometry and measurement – Norton, K., Whittingham, N., Carter, L., Kerr, D., Gore, C., & Marfell-Jones, M. (1996). Measurement techniques in anthropometry. *Anthropometrica, 1*, 25-75.

Improving human breeding with desirable traits – Saini, A. (2019). *In the twisted story of eugenics, the bad guy is all of us.* The Guardian; The Guardian. https://www.theguardian.com/commentisfree/2019/oct/03/eugenics-francis-galton-science-ideas

Founder of eugenics – Gillham, N. W. (2001). Sir Francis Galton and the birth of eugenics. *Annual review of genetics, 35*(1), 83-101.

Nature versus nurture – Sandall, R. (2008). Sir Francis Galton and the roots of eugenics. *Society, 45*(2), 170-176.

Galton's views shape the field for decades – Hall, J. (2023). *Francis Galton: Narrative of an explorer in the human sciences.* Royal College of Psychiatrists. https://www.rcpsych.ac.uk/news-and-features/blogs/detail/history-archives-and-library-blog/2023/02/22/francis-galton

Language and the lexical hypothesis – Caprara, G.V.; Cervone, D. (2000). *Personality: Determinants, Dynamics, and Potentials*. New York: Cambridge University Press.

Allport expands the lexical hypothesis –Allport, G. W.; Odbert, H. S. (1936). *Trait-names: A psycholexical study*. Albany, NY: Psychological Review Company.

The OCEAN model of personality – Roccas, S., Sagiv, L., Schwartz, S. H., & Knafo, A. (2002). The big five personality factors and personal values. *Personality and Social Psychology Bulletin, 28*(6), 789–801. https://doi.org/10.1177/0146167202289008

Facets within the Five Factor Model – Diener, E., & Lucas, R. E. (2019). Personality traits. *General psychology: Required reading, 278*, 3.

SO, YOU'VE GOT A PERSONALITY

Culture is the personality of a group – Choi, H., Gelfand, M. J., Hong, Y., Oishi, S., Rentfrow, J., Saucier, G., & Benet-Martinez, V. (2025). Culture & personality: Five expert visions. *Personality Science, 6*. https://doi.org/10.1177/27000710241309798

Influence of personality of behaviour – Webster, M. M., & Ward, A. J. (2011). Personality and social context. *Biological reviews, 86*(4), 759-773.

Influence of personality of behaviour – Schweiker, M., Hawighorst, M., & Wagner, A. (2016). The influence of personality traits on occupant behavioural patterns. *Energy and Buildings, 131*, 63-75.

Influence of personality of behaviour – Juhász, M. (2010). Influence of personality on Teamwork behaviour and communication. *Periodica Polytechnica Social and Management Sciences, 18*(2), 61-74.

Influence of personality of behaviour – Ajzen, I. (2005). *Attitudes, personality and behaviour*. McGraw-hill education (UK).

Influence of personality of behaviour – Budaev, S., & Brown, C. (2011). Personality traits and behaviour. *Fish cognition and behavior*, 135-165.

Influence of personality of behaviour – Mikhailov, N., & Yankov, G. (2024). *Personality: A User's Guide*. Robinson.

Typing tools sacrifice nuance and accuracy – haupt, angela. (2024). *Are Personality Tests Actually Useful?* TIME. https://time.com/6959682/are-personality-tests-useful/

Drawbacks of OCEAN model – Sutton, J. (2025). *Big Five Personality Traits: The OCEAN Model Explained [2019 Upd.]*. PositivePsychology.com. https://positivepsychology.com/big-five-personality-theory/

SIX

TEAM PSYCHOLOGICAL SAFETY & TRUST

Five dysfunctions of teams – Lencioni, P. M. (2012). *The five dysfunctions of a team: Team assessment*. John Wiley & Sons.

Defence approach of zebra – San Diego Zoo. (2012). *Zebra | San Diego Zoo Animals & Plants*. Sandiegozoo.org. https://animals.sandiegozoo.org/animals/zebra

THE ZEBRA KNOWS

Irving Janis coined the term groupthink – Janis, I. L. (1972). *Victims of groupthink: A psychological study of foreign-policy decisions and fiascoes*. Houghton Mifflin.

Groupthink definition – British Psychological Society. (2022, February 7). *Groupthink: A monument to truthiness. The Psychologist*. https://www.bps.org.uk/psychologist/groupthink-monument-truthiness

Humans are social beings hardwired to seek inclusion and avoid exclusion – Tajfel, H., & Turner, J. C. (1986). The social identity theory of intergroup behavior. In S. Worchel & W. G. Austin (Eds.), *Psychology of intergroup relations* (2nd ed., pp. 7–24). Nelson-Hall.

Agreeableness as a personality dimension – Costa, P. T., Jr., & McCrae, R. R. (1992). *Revised NEO Personality Inventory (NEO PI-R) and NEO Five-Factor Inventory (NEO-FFI) professional manual.* Psychological Assessment Resources.

Personality and obedience to authority – Bègue, L., Monpierre, S., Moussaoui, L., & Nadler, A. (2015). *Personality predictors of obedience to authority. Personality and Individual Differences, 76,* 24–29. Doi: 10.1016/j.paid.2014.11.054

Subtle impacts of groupthink in organisations – Cleary, M., Lees, D., & Sayers, J. (2019). Leadership, thought diversity, and the influence of groupthink. *Issues in Mental Health Nursing.*

DON'T SCARE THE ZEBRA

Groupthink threat responses – Turner, M. E., Pratkanis, A. R., Probasco, P., & Leve, C. (1992). Threat, cohesion, and group effectiveness: Testing a social identity maintenance perspective on groupthink. *Journal of Personality and Social Psychology, 63*(5), 781.

Homogeneity of groupthink under perceived threat – Bodrick, M. M., Alassaf, M. I., & Alrowaitea, F. A. (2025). Is Groupthink a Real or Perceived Threat? Refocusing on Originality and Diversity Versus Groupthink in Organizational Ecosystems. *British Journal of Philosophy, Sociology and History, 5*(2), 01-07.

Evolutionary origins of groupthink – Henriques, G. (2020). Groupthink and the evolution of reason giving. *Groupthink in science: Greed, pathological altruism, ideology, competition, and culture,* 15-25.

Social identity theory – Hogg, M. A. (2001). A social identity theory of leadership. *Personality and social psychology review, 5*(3), 184-200.

Reinforcing groupthink in organisations – Eaton, J. (2001). Management communication: the threat of groupthink. *Corporate Communications: An International Journal, 6*(4), 183-192.

Disagreement curtailed in remote communication tools – Fischer, U., Mosier, K., Orasanu, J., Fischer, U., Morrow, D., Miller, C., ... & Orasanu, J. (2013). Exploring communication in remote teams: Issues and methods. In *Proceedings of the Human Factors and Ergonomics Society Annual Meeting* (Vol. 57, No. 1, pp. 309-313). Sage CA: Los Angeles, CA: SAGE Publications.

Zoom interface and reactions – Zoom (n.d.). Using non-verbal feedback and meeting reactions. *Zoom Support.* https://support.zoom.com/hc/en/article?id=zm_kb&sysparm_article=KB0063323

WHEN CULTURE TURNS CULTISH

WeWork's startup culture – Sheftell, J. (2011). *WeWork gives alternative to working at home with swanky buildings across NYC.* New York Daily News. https://www.nydailynews.com/2011/07/22/wework-gives-alternative-to-working-at-home-with-swanky-buildings-across-nyc/

Balloons, slogans, and tequila – Ashley, S. (2018). *How #MeToo spread from Hollywood to the high court.* CNN. https://edition.cnn.com/2018/10/12/tech/wework-sexual-harassment/index.html

WeWork CEO Adam Neumann – Forbes. (n.d.). Adam Neumann. *Forbes.* https://www.forbes.com/profile/adam-neumann/

Toxic positivity culture at WeWork – McLellan, S. (2024). *Make it Human.* Biteback Publishing.

Affective culture and the shared emotional norms of a group – Wright, D. A. (2000). Culture as information and culture as affective process: A comparative study. *Foreign language annals, 33*(3), 330-341.

Elevate the world's consciousness – Neumann, A. (2019). *The beginning of a new story - wework newsroom.* Newsroom. https://www.wework.com/newsroom/wecompany

WeLive and WeGrow ventures – Leskin, P. (2019). *WeWork changes name to "The We Company" as Softbank invests $2 billion.* Business Insider. https://www.businessinsider.com/wework-changes-name-to-the-we-company-2019-1

WeWork's financial losses – Thorbecke, C. (2023, November 7). *WeWork files for bankruptcy | CNN Business.* CNN. https://www.cnn.com/2023/11/06/business/wework-bankruptcy/index.html

IPO cancelled – Sen, J. F., Anirban. (2019, September 17). WeWork delays IPO after frosty investor response. *Reuters*. https://www.reuters.com/article/us-wework-ipo/wework-parent-says-ipo-still-on-despite-setbacks-idUSKBN1W12T6

Definition of a cult – Thomas, A., & Graham-Hyde, E. (2024). *"Cult" Rhetoric in the 21st Century*. Bloomsbury Publishing.

Innovation requires cognitive diversity – Post, C., De Lia, E., DiTomaso, N., Tirpak, T. M., & Borwankar, R. (2009). Capitalizing on thought diversity for innovation. *Research-Technology Management, 52*(6), 14-25.

WE(DON'T)WORK

Structural misalignment of WeWork – Pendergraft, G. (2021). The rise and fall of WeWork.

Cultural strain on organisation of WeWork – Sigler, T. H., & Tyran, K. L. (2020). *WeWork*. Neilson Journals Publishing.

Valuation collapsed from $47 billion – Nguyen, B. (2023). *WeWork's Rise To $47 Billion —And Fall To Bankruptcy: A Timeline*. Forbes. https://www.forbes.com/sites/britneynguyen/2023/11/07/weworks-rise-to-47-billion-and-fall-to-bankruptcy-a-timeline/

GROUPTHINK'S KRYPTONITE

Edmondson's work on psychological safety – Edmondson, A. C. (1999). Psychological safety and learning behavior in work teams. *Administrative Science Quarterly, 44*(2), 350–383. doi: 10.2307/2666999

Devil's advocate approach to critique – Hoffman, B. (2023). *It's time to play the devil's advocate*. Forbes. https://www.forbes.com/sites/brycehoffman/2023/10/01/its-time-to-play-the-devils-advocate/

The role of red teams in ideation – Ackerman, G., & Clifford, D. (2021). Red teaming and crisis preparedness. In *Oxford Research Encyclopedia of Politics*.

Red teams and creative conflict – Mansfield-Devine, S. (2018). The best form of defence–the benefits of red teaming. *Computer Fraud & Security, 2018*(10), 8-12.

Red teams in creative industries – Shaw, R. B. (2017). *Extreme teams: Why Pixar, Netflix, Airbnb, and other cutting-edge companies succeed where most fail*. Amacom.

Project postmortem reviews and their benefits – Klein, G. (2007). *Performing a project premortem*. *Harvard Business Review*. https://hbr.org/2007/09/performing-a-project-premortem

Teams with greater cognitive diversity tend to generate more creative solutions – Wang, X.-H., Kim, T.-Y., & Lee, D.-R. (2016). Cognitive diversity and team creativity: Effects of team intrinsic motivation and transformational leadership. *Journal of Business Research, 69*(9), 3231–3239. https://doi.org/10.1016/j.jbusres.2016.02.026

Diversity stifled without inclusion – CIPD. (2019). *Building inclusive workplaces*. CIPD. https://www.cipd.org/uk/knowledge/evidence-reviews/building-inclusive-workplaces/

WHO'S GOT MY BACK?

Trust is older than agriculture – Kumar, A., Capraro, V., & Perc, M. (2020). The evolution of trust and trustworthiness. *Journal of the Royal Society Interface, 17*(169), 20200491.

Trust as an evolutionary benefit of the tribe – Cook, K. (Ed.). (2001). *Trust in society*. Russell Sage Foundation.

Trust distinguishes humans from other primates – Tamas David-Barrett. (2023). Human group size puzzle: why it is odd that we live in large societies. *Royal Society Open Science, 10*(8). https://doi.org/10.1098/rsos.230559

Primates do feel trust in some contexts – Costa, M., Gomez, A., Barat, E., Lio, G., Duhamel, J. R., & Sirigu, A. (2018). Implicit preference for human trustworthy faces in macaque monkeys. *Nature Communications, 9*(1), 4529.

Chimpanzees trust their friends – Engelmann, J. M., & Herrmann, E. (2016). Chimpanzees trust their friends. *Current Biology, 26*(2), 252-256.

Trust as a biochemical response – Riedl, R., & Javor, A. (2012). The biology of trust: integrating evidence from genetics, endocrinology, and functional brain imaging. *Journal of Neuroscience, Psychology, and Economics*, *5*(2), 63.

Reputation as a survival mechanism – Feng, K., Han, S., Feng, M., & Szolnoki, A. (2024). An evolutionary game with reputation-based imitation-mutation dynamics. *Applied Mathematics and Computation*, *472*, 128618.

Trust is foundational to distributed leadership systems – Smylie, M.A. *et al.* (2007) 'Trust and the development of distributed leadership', *Journal of School Leadership*, 17(4), pp. 469–503. doi:10.1177/105268460701700405.

Trust in a hybrid world – Cheng, X., Yin, G., Azadegan, A., & Kolfschoten, G. (2016). Trust evolvement in hybrid team collaboration: A longitudinal case study. *Group Decision and Negotiation*, *25*(2), 267-288.

TRUST IN A DISPARATE WORLD

Physical proximity can enhance comfort and trust in interactions – Hall, E. T. (1963). A system for the notation of proxemic behavior. *American anthropologist*, *65*(5), 1003-1026.

Trust diminishes as physical distance grows – Camara, F., & Fox, C. (2022, August). Extending quantitative proxemics and trust to HRI. In *2022 31st IEEE International Conference on Robot and Human Interactive Communication (RO-MAN)* (pp. 421-427). IEEE.

Eyesight affects trust formation – Rzayeva, E. (2025). The Role of Eye Contact and Proxemics in Building Rapport with Language Learners. *Porta Universorum*, *1*(4), 271-294.

Distance impacts trust – Rzayeva, E. (2025). The Role of Eye Contact and Proxemics in Building Rapport with Language Learners. *Porta Universorum*, *1*(4), 271-294.

Personality could mitigate trust reduction – Prochazkova, E., Venneker, D., de Zwart, R., Tamietto, M., & Kret, M. E. (2022). Conscious awareness is necessary to assess trust and mimic facial expressions, while pupils impact trust unconsciously. *Philosophical Transactions of the Royal Society B: Biological Sciences*, *377*(1863). doi: 10.1098/rstb.2021.0183

Brain areas associated with visual imagery are used in trust – Winston, J. S., Strange, B. A., O'Doherty, J., & Dolan, R. J. (2013). Automatic and intentional brain responses during evaluation of trustworthiness of faces. In *Social neuroscience* (pp. 199-210). Psychology Press.

Closeness moderates trust in social groups – Jiménez, S., Mercadillo, R. E., Angeles-Valdez, D., Sánchez-Sosa, J. J., Muñoz-Delgado, J., & Garza-Villarreal, E. A. (2022). Social closeness modulates brain dynamics during trust anticipation. *Scientific Reports*, *12*(1), 16337.

Remote working example behaviours – Sharp Emerson, M. (2020). How to Better Manage Your Remote Team. *Harvard DCE*. https://professional.dce.harvard.edu/blog/how-to-better-manage-your-remote-team/

BRIDGES, NOT BINOCULARS

Ambiguity encourages mistrust – Seanor, P., & Meaton, J. (2008). Learning from failure, ambiguity and trust in social enterprise. *Social Enterprise Journal*, *4*(1), 24-40.

Myth of open collaboration fostering creativity – Troyer, L., & Youngreen, R. (2009). Conflict and creativity in groups. *Journal of Social Issues*, *65*(2), 409-427.

Groupthink and decision making in teams – Janis, I. L. (2020). Groupthink. In *Shared experiences in human communication* (pp. 177-186). Routledge.

Dominant voices in groups tend to shape discussions – Baron, R. S. (2005). So right it's wrong: Groupthink and the ubiquitous nature of polarized group decision making. *Advances in experimental social psychology*, *37*(2), 219-253.

Ideation improved by independent thinking – Reid, L. N., & Moriarty, S. E. (1983). Ideation: a review of research. *Current issues and research in advertising*, *6*(2), 119-134.

Ideation approaches improved in individuals – Daly, S. R., Seifert, C. M., Yilmaz, S., & Gonzalez, R. (2016). Comparing ideation techniques for beginning designers. *Journal of Mechanical Design*, *138*(10).

Automattic's approach to remote working – Automattic. (2020). *How We Work*. Automattic. https://automattic.com/how-we-work/

Automattic working approaches and talent management – Vecchi, A. (2019). Global work arrangements and talent management in the born-virtual organization: The case of Automattic. In *Research Handbook of International Talent Management* (pp. 144-185). Edward Elgar Publishing.

Vision statement for Automattic – Automattic. (2005). Around the world, building the internet's operating system—and a better way to work. *Automattic*. https://automattic.com/about/

GitLab approach to all-remote working – GitLab. (2024). *GitLab's Guide to All-Remote*. The GitLab Handbook. https://handbook.gitlab.com/handbook/company/culture/all-remote/guide/

Shared vision is a key factor in distributed teams – Chin, P. (2024). Unlocking the Potential of Visionary Leadership: A Study on Shared Vision, Teamwork and Team Performance. *Education Quarterly Reviews*, *7*(2). https://doi.org/10.31014/aior.1993.07.02.578

PSYCHOLOGICAL SAFETY IS A JOKE

Comedy is relational – Yue, X., Jiang, F., Lu, S., & Hiranandani, N. (2016). To be or not to be humorous? Cross cultural perspectives on humor. *Frontiers in psychology*, *7*, 1495.

Beauty is in the eye of the beholder – Little, A. C. (2014). Facial attractiveness. *Wiley Interdisciplinary Reviews: Cognitive Science*, *5*(6), 621-634.

Charisma is granted by a third party – Antonakis, J., Fenley, M., & Liechti, S. (2011). Can charisma be taught? Tests of two interventions. *Academy of Management Learning & Education*, *10*(3), 374-396.

Charisma flows between group members – Katz-Navon, T., Delegach, M., & Haim, E. (2023). Contagious charisma: the flow of charisma from leader to followers and the role of followers' self-monitoring. *Frontiers in Psychology*, *14*, 1239974.

Comedian's relationship with the audience to improve experience – Miles, T. (2019). No greater foe? Rethinking emotion and humour, with particular attention to the relationship between audience members and stand-up comedians (5: 1). In *The Routledge Comedy Studies Reader* (pp. 115-123). Routledge.

A joke without a laugh is just a sentence – Carr, J. (2021). The Easiest Way To Live A Happier Life (S. Bartlett, Interviewer). In *Diary of a CEO*. https://www.youtube.com/watch?v=roROKlZhZyo

Leadership as a relational process – Wood, M., & Dibben, M. (2015). Leadership as relational process. *Process studies*, *44*(1), 24-47.

Social influence theory and the impact on trust – Rachmad, Y. E. (2025). Social Influence Theory. *United Nations Economic and Social Council*.

SAFETY WITHOUT A LEADER

Psychological safety is relational – CIPD. (2024). *Trust and psychological safety: An evidence review*. CIPD. https://www.cipd.org/uk/knowledge/evidence-reviews/trust-psychological-safety/

Intentional and deliberate psychological safety design – Edmondson, A. (2002). Managing the risk of learning: Psychological safety in work teams. International Handbook of Organizational Teamwork.

Make norms explicit then evolve – Edmondson, A. (1999). Psychological safety and learning behavior in work teams. *Administrative science quarterly*, *44*(2), 350-383.

Make norms explicit then evolve – Lenberg, P., & Feldt, R. (2018, May). Psychological safety and norm clarity in software engineering teams. In *Proceedings of the 11th international workshop on cooperative and human aspects of software engineering* (pp. 79-86).

Make norms explicit then evolve – Jones, M. S., Cravens, A. E., Zarestky, J., Ngai, C., & Love, H. B. (2024). Facilitating psychological safety in science and research teams. *Humanities and Social Sciences Communications*, *11*(1), 1-12.

Ritualise feedback loops as relational moments – Feldman, M. S., & Pentland, B. T. (2003). Reconceptualizing organizational routines as a source of flexibility and change. *Administrative science quarterly*, *48*(1), 94-118.

Ritualise feedback loops as relational moments – Hobson, N. M., Bonk, D., & Inzlicht, M. (2017). Rituals decrease the neural response to performance failure. *PeerJ*, *5*, e3363.

Ritualise feedback loops as relational moments – Kim, T., Sezer, O., Schroeder, J., Risen, J., Gino, F., & Norton, M. I. (2021). Work group rituals enhance the meaning of work. *Organizational Behavior and Human Decision Processes*, *165*, 197-212.

Normalise transparent mistakes as a shared practice – Edmondson, A. (1999). Psychological safety and learning behavior in work teams. *Administrative science quarterly*, *44*(2), 350-383.

Normalise transparent mistakes as a shared practice – Edmondson, A. C. (2004). Learning from mistakes is easier said than done: Group and organizational influences on the detection and correction of human error. *The journal of applied behavioral science*, *40*(1), 66-90.

Normalise transparent mistakes as a shared practice – Hobson, N. M., Bonk, D., & Inzlicht, M. (2017). Rituals decrease the neural response to performance failure. *PeerJ*, *5*, e3363.

Encourage peer recognition and micro-acknowledgements – Yang, T., & Jiang, X. (2023). When colleague got recognized: third-party's reaction to witnessing employee recognition. *Frontiers in psychology*, *14*, 968782.

Encourage peer recognition and micro-acknowledgements – Yang, T., Jiang, X., & Cheng, H. (2022). Employee recognition, task performance, and OCB: Mediated and moderated by pride. *Sustainability*, *14*(3), 1631.

Build transparent decision pathways – DeChurch, L. A., & Mesmer-Magnus, J. R. (2010). The cognitive underpinnings of effective teamwork: a meta-analysis. *Journal of applied psychology*, *95*(1), 32.

Build transparent decision pathways – Mathieu, J. E., Heffner, T. S., Goodwin, G. F., Salas, E., & Cannon-Bowers, J. A. (2000). The influence of shared mental models on team process and performance. *Journal of applied psychology*, *85*(2), 273.

Build transparent decision pathways – Tyler, T. R. (1987). Procedural justice research. *Social Justice Research*, *1*(1), 41-65.

Map influence dynamically, not hierarchically – Pearce, C. L., & Conger, J. A. (2002). *Shared leadership: Reframing the hows and whys of leadership*. Sage publications.

Map influence dynamically, not hierarchically – Wang, D., Waldman, D. A., & Zhang, Z. (2014). A meta-analysis of shared leadership and team effectiveness. *Journal of applied psychology*, *99*(2), 181.

Map influence dynamically, not hierarchically – Mesmer-Magnus, J., Niler, A. A., Plummer, G., Larson, L. E., & DeChurch, L. A. (2017). The cognitive underpinnings of effective teamwork: a continuation. *Career Development International*, *22*(5), 507-519.

Design asynchronous interaction as relational scaffolding – Walther, J. B. (2015). Social information processing theory (CMC). *The international encyclopedia of interpersonal communication*, 1-13.

Design asynchronous interaction as relational scaffolding – Rødsjø, E., Sjølie, E., & Van Petegem, P. (2024). Psychological safety in interdisciplinary virtual student project teams: A validation study. *Computers in Human Behavior Reports*, *14*, 100413.

Design asynchronous interaction as relational scaffolding – Netzer, J. (2023). *How to excel at asynchronous communication with your distributed team*. Work Life by Atlassian. https://www.atlassian.com/blog/communication/asynchronous-communication-for-distributed-teams

Reflect and evolve continuously as a collective practice – Argyris, C., & Schön, D. A. (1997). Organizational learning: A theory of action perspective. *Reis*, (77/78), 345-348.

Reflect and evolve continuously as a collective practice – Norton, I. (2021). Work group rituals enhance the meaning of work. *Organizational Behavior and Human Decision Processes*, *165*, 197-212.

IT'S THE LITTLE THINGS

Small acts build trust in distributed teams – Colvin, G. (2019). *Talent is overrated : what really separates world-class performers from everyone else*. Nicholas Brealey Publishing.

Small acts build love in relationships – Gupta, S. (2025). *The Little Things in Relationships That Matter the Most*. Verywell Mind. https://www.verywellmind.com/the-little-things-in-relationships-that-matter-the-the-most-6891165

SEVEN

APPLYING THE CONSTELLATION

Leadership creates the conditions that enable others to face challenge – Heifetz, R. A. (1994). *Leadership without easy answers*. Harvard University Press.

DIVERSITY AS AN OUTPUT OF INCLUSION

Representation versus diversity in ED&I – Nicole Schreiber-Shearer. (2022, October 25). *Representation and diversity: Main Differences | Gloat*. Gloat.com. https://gloat.com/blog/representation-versus-diversity/

Diversity as a component of inclusions – CIPD. (2019). *Building inclusive workplaces*. CIPD. https://www.cipd.org/uk/knowledge/evidence-reviews/building-inclusive-workplaces/

BUILDING THE TEAM

Cusco earthquake of 1950 – Ericksen, G. E., Concha, J. F., & Silgado, E. (1954). The Cusco, Peru, Earthquake of May 21, 1950*. *Bulletin of the Seismological Society of America, 44*(2A), 97–112. https://doi.org/10.1785/BSSA04402A0097

15th-century Inca walls stood firm – Cuadra, C., Sato, Y., Tokeshi, J., Kanno, H., Ogawa, J., & Rojas, J. (2005). Preliminary evaluation of the seismic vulnerability of the Inca's Coricancha temple complex in Cusco. *WIT Transactions on the Built Environment, 83*, 9-17. https://doi.org/10.2495/STR050241

Dry stone masonry is more resilient to seismic activity – Lipa, L., Tarque, N., Pelà, L., & Goicolea, J. M. (2024). Seismic numerical analysis of an Inca stone wall in Sacsayhuaman using rigid body dynamics within a finite element framework. *Engineering Failure Analysis, 161*, 108254.

Modern dwellings more susceptible to damage – Brando, G., Cocco, G., Mazzanti, C., Peruch, M., Spacone, E., Alfaro, C., ... & Tarque, N. (2021). Structural survey and empirical seismic vulnerability assessment of dwellings in the historical centre of Cusco, Peru. *International Journal of Architectural Heritage, 15*(10), 1395-1423.

Hiring managers look for transactional criteria first – Page, M. (n.d.). *What employers and recruiters look for in a CV*. Michael Page. https://www.michaelpage.co.uk/advice/career-advice/cover-letter-and-cv-advice/what-employers-and-recruiters-look-cv

Employee engagement improved when individuals can grow in-role – Gallup. (2025). *How to Improve Employee Engagement in the Workplace*. Gallup. https://www.gallup.com/workplace/285674/improve-employee-engagement-workplace.aspx

In-role development improves employee engagement – Kwon, K., Jeong, S., Park, J., & Yoon, S. W. (2024). Employee development and employee engagement: a review and integrated model. *Career development international, 29*(2), 169-184.

Confirmation bias – Oswald, M. E., & Grosjean, S. (2004). Confirmation bias. *Cognitive illusions: A handbook on fallacies and biases in thinking, judgement and memory, 79*, 83.

Status quo bias – Samuelson, W., & Zeckhauser, R. (1988). Status quo bias in decision making. *Journal of risk and uncertainty, 1*(1), 7-59.

THE JOURNEY DEFINED

The Mayflower sets sail – Philbrick, N. (2007). *Mayflower : a story of courage, community, and war*. New York Penguin Books.

Motivations for the Mayflower journey – Fraser, R. (2017). *The Mayflower : the families, the voyage, and the founding of America*. St. Martin's Press.

Britain adopts the Gregorian calendar – Baumgartner, F. J. (2003). Lee Palmer Wandel (ed.). "Popes, astrologers and Early modern calendar reform". *History Has Many Voices*. 63. Pennsylvania State University Press: 176.

Organisational vision is aspirational and provides direction – The Strategy Institute. (2024). *Strategic Vision: A Guide for Developing a Clear Roadmap for Your Organization*. Thestrategyinstitute.org. https://www.thestrategyinstitute.org/insights/strategic-vision-a-guide-for-developing-a-clear-roadmap-for-your-organization

Vision positively correlates with employee performance – Slåtten, T., Mutonyi, B. R., & Lien, G. (2021). Does organizational vision really matter? An empirical examination of factors related to organizational vision integration among hospital employees. *BMC health services research, 21*(1), 483.

Mission statements provide specific goals – Hill, C. W. L., & Jones, G. R. (2008). *Strategic management : an integrated approach*. Houghton Mifflin.

Organisational strategy delivers mission – Jensen, M. C. (2001). *Foundations of organizational strategy*. Harvard university press.

Mission as a strategic tool – Pearce II, J. A. (1982). The company mission as a strategic tool. *Sloan Management Review (Pre-1986), 23*(3), 15.

Company values and their influence – Thomsen, S. (2004). Corporate values and corporate governance. *Corporate Governance: The international journal of business in society, 4*(4), 29-46.

Defining organisational culture – Ouchi, W. G., & Wilkins, A. L. (1985). Organizational culture. *Annual review of sociology, 11*(1), 457-483.

Cultural drift and its impact on performance – Slater, D. H., & Ale, B. J. (2022). Organisations: Drifting or dysfunctional. In *Proceedings of the 32nd European safety and reliability conference (ESREL 2022)* (pp. 3173-3180). Research Publishing.

A SHARED NORTH STAR

Focusing on people without strategy can cause business to struggle – Vermeulen, F. (2017, November 13). *Executives fail to execute strategy because they're too internally focused*. Harvard Business Review. https://hbr.org/2017/11/executives-fail-to-execute-strategy-because-theyre-too-internally-focused

Strategic misalignment with people can result in bankruptcy – Heracleous, L. (2016). On the road to disaster: Strategic misalignments and organizational failure. *Journal of Business Research, 69*(10), 4137–4141. https://doi.org/10.1016/j.jbusres.2016.04.014

The rise and fall of Blackberry – Abel, C., & Kenechukwu, C. (2025). Strategic Failures and Organisational Learning: The Case of BlackBerry and Implications for Emerging Technology Firm.

Blackberry learnings – Trivedi, P. D. (2017). Consumer dictates the market: Lesson from blackberry. *Journal of Management Research and Analysis, 4*(4), 183-185.

Apple didn't have a vision statement – Podolny, J. M., & Hansen, M. T. (2020). How Apple is organized for innovation. *Harvard Business Review, 98*(6), 86-95.

Volvo's 2007 mission statement – Volvo. (2006). *By creating value for our customers, we create value for our shareholders*. Volvo Group. https://www.volvogroup.com/content/dam/volvo-group/markets/global/classic/investors/reports-and-presentations/annual-reports/Volvo-Group-Annual-Report-2006-EN.pdf

Volvo's current mission statement – Volvo. (2023). *Our story | Volvo Cars*. Volvocars.com. https://www.volvocars.com/intl/our-story/

FINDING THE NORTH STAR

Definition of a CIC in the UK – GOV.UK. (2024). *Community Interest Companies Guidance*. GOV.UK. https://www.gov.uk/government/publications/community-interest-companies-how-to-form-a-cic/community-interest-companies-guidance-chapters

IN SEARCH OF LEGACY

Defining social impact – Parrett, E. (2024). *What is Social Impact and How Do I Measure It?* | *Good Finance*. Www.goodfinance.org.uk. https://www.goodfinance.org.uk/latest/post/what-social-impact-and-how-do-i-measure-it

Defining cultural impact – Partal, A., & Dunphy, K. (2016). Cultural impact assessment: a systematic literature review of current methods and practice around the world. *Impact Assessment and Project Appraisal, 34*(1), 1-13.

Defining emotional impact – Mehrabian, A., & Russell, J. A. (1974). The basic emotional impact of environments. *Perceptual and motor skills, 38*(1), 283-301.

Defining environmental impact – Glasson, J., & Therivel, R. (2013). *Introduction to environmental impact assessment*. Routledge.

Defining economic impact – Lindberg, K. (2001). Economic Impacts. *The Encyclopedia of Ecotourism*, 363.

WHY DID WE BEGIN?

Start with why – Sinek, S. (2009). *Start with why: How great leaders inspire everyone to take action*. Penguin.

Organisational purpose as a driver of business – Reyes, J. R., & Kleiner, B. H. (1990). How to establish an organisational purpose. *Management Decision, 28*(7).

Microsoft democratises computing – Microsoft. (n.d.). *Microsoft at 50: Celebrating our journey*. Microsoft News. https://news.microsoft.com/microsoft-50/

Empower every person and every organisation – Nadella, S. (2016). *Empowering every person and every organization on the planet*. JD Meier. https://jdmeier.com/empowering-every-person/

Motivation in psychology – Brown, L. V. (2007). *Psychology of motivation*. Nova Publishers.

Locke's goal-setting theory – Locke, E., & Latham, G. (2015). Goal-setting theory. In *Organizational behavior 1* (pp. 159-183). Routledge.

Dweck's growth mindset – Dweck, C. (2015). Carol Dweck revisits the growth mindset. *Education week, 35*(5), 20-24.

McGregor's Theory X and Y – McGregor, D. (1960). Theory X and theory Y. *Organization theory, 358*(374), 5.

Lack of consensus on definition of motivation – Kleinginna Jr, P. R., & Kleinginna, A. M. (1981). A categorized list of motivation definitions, with a suggestion for a consensual definition. *Motivation and emotion, 5*(3), 263-291.

Extrinsic and intrinsic motivation – Bénabou, R., & Tirole, J. (2003). Intrinsic and extrinsic motivation. *The review of economic studies, 70*(3), 489-520.

Introducing extrinsic motivators becomes transactional – Deci, E. L. (1971). Effects of externally mediated rewards on intrinsic motivation. *Journal of Personality and Social Psychology, 18*(1), 105–115. https://doi.org/10.1037/h0030644

Attention redirection of extrinsic reward – Deci, E. L., & Ryan, R. M. (2000). The "what" and "why" of goal pursuits: Human needs and the self-determination of behavior. *Psychological Inquiry, 11*(4), 227–268. https://doi.org/10.1207/S15327965PLI1104_01

Reduction in blood donation when incentivised – Niza, C., Tung, B., & Marteau, T. M. (2013). Incentivizing blood donation: Systematic review and meta-analysis to test Titmuss' hypotheses. *Health Psychology, 32*(9), 941.

Children's reading reduced when incentivised – Small, R. V., Arnone, M. P., & Bennett, E. (2017). A hook and a book: Rewards as motivators in public library summer reading programs. *Children and Libraries, 15*(1), 7-15.

Self-determination theory framework – Deci, E. L., & Ryan, R. M. (2012). Self-determination theory. *Handbook of theories of social psychology, 1*(20), 416-436.

HOW WE MOVE

Constellation Leadership has no permanent leader – Wareham, D. (2023). *Creating Constellations: The influence of Constellation Leadership on Agile methodology-led project delivery success.* https://doi.org/10.13140/RG.2.2.23440.79368

Trust improves employee independence and performance – Sharkie, R. (2009). Trust in leadership is vital for employee performance. *Management research news*, *32*(5), 491-498.

FROM VALUES TO VELOCITY

Ad hoc company missions distract employees – Hai, S., & Daft, R. L. (2016). When missions collide. *Organizational Dynamics*, *4*(45), 283-290.

STAYING ON-TRACK

N/A

COORDINATION AND SELF-ORGANISATION IN ACTION

The swallows of San Juan Capistrano – Hallan-Gibson, P., Tryon, D., & Tryon, M. E. (2005). *San Juan Capistrano.* Arcadia Publishing.

Murmuration in the animal kingdom – King, A. J., & Sumpter, D. J. (2012). Murmurations. *Current Biology*, *22*(4), R112-R114.

PUTTING CONSTELLATIONS INTO PRACTICE

N/A

EIGHT

UTILISING CONSTELLATIONS

We learn by doing them – Crisp, R. (Ed.). (2014). *Aristotle: nicomachean ethics.* Cambridge University Press.

Constellation leadership is under-studied – Empson, L. (2017) *Leading professionals: Power, politics, and prima donnas.* 1st edn. Oxford, UK: Oxford University Press.

A paucity of information about constellations – Surman, T., & Surman, M. (2008). Open sourcing social change: Inside the constellation model. *Open Source Business Resource*, (September 2008).

STUDY 1: DISCIPLINED FREEDOM

Author interview – Brettell, S. (2025). Interview with Danny Wareham. 22 August 2025, virtual.

A favourable situation will never be exploited if commanders wait for orders – Dupuy, T. N. (1977). *A Genius for War.* Prentice Hall.

Helmuth Karl Bernhard Graf von Moltke – Barclay, C. (2020). Helmuth von Moltke | German general [1800–1891] | Britannica. In *Encyclopædia Britannica.* https://www.britannica.com/biography/Helmuth-von-Moltke

Auftragstaktik or mission tactics – Stewart, K. (2009, June). Command Approach: Problem Solving in Mission Command. In *Proceedings of the 14th International Command and Control Research and Technology Symposium, Washington, DC.*

Mission command in the British Army – King, A. (2011). Military command in the last decade. *International Affairs*, *87*(2), 377-396.

The US Army and mission command – Matzenbacher, M. B. (2018). The US Army and mission command. *Military review*, *2018*, 61-71.

UK's military response to the COVID-19 pandemic – National Army Museum. (n.d.). *Recording the Army's Covid response.* National Army Museum. https://www.nam.ac.uk/explore/collecting-pandemic

UK's military response to the COVID-19 pandemic – GOV. UK. (2022). *COVID Support Force: the MOD's continued contribution to the coronavirus response.* GOV.UK.

https://www.gov.uk/guidance/covid-support-force-the-mods-continued-contribution-to-the-coronavirus-response

Operation Rescript and COVID response force – BBC (2020). Coronavirus: Up to 3,000 armed forces reservists to aid military response. *BBC News.* https://www.bbc.co.uk/news/uk-52130121

Largest domestic operation in British military history – Ministry of Defence. (2020). *Military Aid to Civil Authorities: The COVID Support Force.* Medium. https://defencehq.medium.com/military-aid-to-civil-authorities-the-covid-support-force-acd80ec70099

Combat estimate philosophy – Ancker, I., Clinton, J., & Scully, M. A. (2013). Army Doctrine Publication 3-0: An Opportunity to Meet the Challenges of the Future.

Combat estimate philosophy – British Army. (n.d.). Army Doctrine Publication: Operations. *Ministry of Defence Development, Concepts and Doctrine Centre.* 2010. pp. 6–15.

STUDY 2: FROM NASA TO NEIGHBOURHOODS

Author interview – Anders, T. (2025). Interview with Danny Wareham. 26 August 2025, virtual.

Dr. Ted Anders biography – Podomatic. (2021). *Ted Anders Ph.D., Co-Founder/Pres. Nature's Nurse Inc.* Podomatic. https://www.podomatic.com/podcasts/howardholleypresents/episodes/2014-08-18T03_11_20-07_00

Partnership with Baroness Mone – Jenkin, E. (2025, May 25). *The Rise and Fall of Michelle Mone* (A. Broad, Ed.; No. 1) [Review of *The Rise and Fall of Michelle Mone*]. BBC2.

Providing respiratory support to first responders – Natures Nurse. (2017). *Best natural product to support respiratory and immune system function.* Natures Nurse. https://naturesnurse.com/

A common thread through purpose – Anders, T. (2024). *Home - Dr. Ted Anders.* Dr. Ted Anders. https://drtedanders.com/

History of Automation Direct – Automation Direct. (n.d.). *About Us | Who we are.* Automation Direct. https://about.automationdirect.com/pdfs/whoweare/whoweare-company-overview.pdf

Impact of Customer Driven Leadership – CDL. (2025). *Customer Driven Leadership.* Customer Driven Leadership. https://customerdrivenleadership.com/

Development of Customer Driven Leadership – Hammond, D., & Anders, T. (2022). *Customer Driven Leadership.* Merack Publishing

Focus on using influence to do good – Cooper, E. (2025, January 20). *Michelle Mone's life coach speaks out for the first time in explosive new documentary investigating the £200million PPE scandal.* Mail Online; Daily Mail. https://www.dailymail.co.uk/femail/article-14305237/michelle-mone-life-coach-speaks-ppe-scandal-documentary.html

STUDY 3: THE HEAT OF PLAY

Author interview – Abbott, C. (2025). Interview with Danny Wareham. 27 August 2025, virtual.

The bright lights of OG and esports – ONE Esports. (2019). *OG becomes first-ever two-time TI champion with a 3-1 victory over Team Liquid.* ONE Esports. https://www.oneesports.gg/dota2/og-becomes-first-ever-two-time-ti-champion-with-a-3-1-ti9-victory-over-team-liquid/

Staying calm under pressure – Red Bull Esports. (2019). *Ceb reveals how Team OG stayed strong under pressure at TI9.* Red Bull. https://www.redbull.com/gb-en/team-og-ti9-victory-ceb-interview

DOTA2 basics and introduction – McDonald, T. (2013). *A Beginner's Guide to Dota 2: Part One – The Basics.* PC Invasion.

Team cohesion, trust and shared mental models – Poulus, D. R., Coulter, T. J., Trotter, M. G., & Polman, R. (2022). A qualitative analysis of the perceived determinants of success in elite esports athletes. *Journal of Sports Sciences, 40*(7), 742-753. https://doi.org/10.1080/02640414.2021.2015916

Impact of communication in esports – Maier, T., & others. (2024). Talking to Win: The Impact of Communication on Performance in Esports. *Journal of Electronic Gaming and Esports, 2*(1). https://doi.org/10.1123/jege.2024-0036

Coping, managing stress and burnout in esports – Poulus, D. R., Sargeant, J., Zarate, D., Griffiths, M. D., & Stavropoulos, V. (2024). Burnout, resilience, and coping among esports players: A network analysis approach. *Computers in Human Behavior, 153*, 108139.

Team structure and dynamics of gaming – Gisbert-Pérez, J., García-Naveira, A., Marti Vilar, M., Acebes Sánchez, J. (2024). Key structure and processes in esports teams: a systematic review. *Current Psychology, 43*(23), 20355-20374. https://doi.org/10.1007/s12144-024-05858-0

Rocket League basics and introduction – O'Connor, A. (2014). *Car-To-Ball: Rocket League.* Rock Paper Shotgun. https://www.rockpapershotgun.com/rocket-league-trailer

OG wins back-to-back – Esports.net. (2019). *OG wins TI9, becoming the first Dota 2 team to win The International twice.* Esports.net. https://www.esports.net/news/dota/og-wins-the-international-2019/

STUDY 4: COOPERATIVE CONSTELLATIONS

History of Mondragon – Forcadell, F. J. (2005). Democracy, cooperation and business success: The case of Mondragón Corporación Cooperativa. *Journal of Business Ethics, 56*(3), 255-274.

Mondragon's performance and approach – Arando, S., Gago, M., Jones, D. C., & Kato, T. (2015). Efficiency in employee-owned enterprises: An econometric case study of Mondragon. *ILR Review, 68*(2), 312-345. https://doi.org/10.1177/0019793914564966

Advantages of cooperative over traditional approaches – Retegi, J., & Igartua, J. I. (2021). An analysis of the Mondragon case's competitiveness from a systemic perspective. *Intangible Capital, 17*(4), 320-336. https://doi.org/10.3926/ic.2261

Wage rations, wage solidarity and layoff avoidance – Las Heras, M., Carneiro, J., & Keating, L. (2021). Problematizing the cooperative firm: A Marxian view on paradoxes, dialectics, and contradictions. *Journal of Management Studies, 58*(6), 1576-1605. https://doi.org/10.1111/joms.13175

How democracy applies within cooperative businesses – Stikkers, K. W. (2011). Dewey, Economic Democracy, and the Mondragon Cooperatives. *European Journal of Pragmatism and American Philosophy, 1*(1). https://doi.org/10.4000/ejpap.833

Decision making in Mondragon – Malleson, T. (2013). What does Mondragon teach us about workplace democracy? In *Sharing Ownership, Profits, and Decision-Making in the 21st Century* (Advances in the Economic Analysis of Participatory & Labor-Managed Firms, Vol. 14, pp. 127-157). Emerald Group Publishing Limited.

Ownership and participation in Mondragon – Rodriguez-Oramas, A., Burgues-Freitas, A., Joanpere, M., & Flecha, R. (2022). Participation and organizational commitment in the Mondragon Group. *Frontiers in Psychology, 13.* https://doi.org/10.3389/fpsyg.2022.806442

Impact of corporate longevity – CIPD. (n.d.). Human values prevail over economics. In *What can we learn from corporate longevity?* CIPD. https://www.cipd.org/en/views-and-insights/thought-leadership/the-world-of-work/lessons-corporate-longevity

STUDY 5: THE OPERATING SYSTEM WITHOUT A BOSS

Request for help with a new operating system – Torvalds, L. (1991). *Marc Lehmann's Home.* Schmorp.de. https://oldhome.schmorp.de/marc/cites.html

History of Linux – Almesberger, W. (2000, June). Booting linux: The history and the future. In *Proceedings of the Ottawa Linux Symposium.*

A summary of Linux – Siever, E. (2009). *Linux in a nutshell : a desktop quick reference.* O'reilly.

Coordination in opensource teams – Markus, M. L., Manville, B., & Agres, C. (2000). *What makes a virtual organization work?* Sloan Management Review, 42(1), 13-26.

Reputation as a motivator in opensource development – Stewart, K., & Hyndman, J. (2010). *Open source software and public vs. private value creation: Do developers use free software projects to build their reputations?* In M. Fitzgerald, B. Scacchi, J. L. Feller, & K. R. Nordström (Eds.), *Making Sense of Free and Open Source Software* (pp. 67-87). MIT Press.

Modular architecture benefits to development cycle – Stol, K.-J., Ali Babar, M., & Avgeriou, P. (2011). The importance of architectural knowledge in integrating open source software. In *Open Source Systems: Grounding Research* (IFIP Advances in Information and Communication Technology, Vol. 365, pp. 129-143). Springer. https://doi.org/10.1007/978-3-642-24418-6_10

Community strategy in development teams – Linåker, J., Regnell, B., & Damian, D. (2022). A community strategy framework: How to obtain influence on requirements in meritocratic open source software communities? *arXiv*. https://arxiv.org/abs/2208.03302

Governance, creativity and control in software development – Germonprez, M., Kendall, J. E., Kendall, K. E., & Young, B. (2014). Collectivism, creativity, competition, and control in open source software development: reflections on the emergent governance of the SPDX working group. *International Journal of Information Systems and Management, 9*(2/3), 125-145. https://doi.org/10.1504/IJISAM.2014.062290

Opensource software survival through informal and formal governance – Yin, L., Chakraborty, M., Schweik, C., Frey, S., & Filkov, V. (2022). Open source software sustainability: Combining institutional analysis and socio-technical networks. *arXiv*. https://arxiv.org/abs/2203.03144

Meritocracy in remote opensource teams – Eckhardt, E., Kaats, E., Jansen, S., & Alves, C. (2014). The merits of a meritocracy in open source software ecosystems. In *Proceedings of the 19th International Conference on Evaluation and Assessment in Software Engineering* (EASE '14). ACM. https://doi.org/10.1145/2645690.2645697

STUDY 6: A HEAD OF STEAM

History of Gabe Newall – Chiang, O. (2011). The Master of Online mayhem. *Forbes*. https://www.forbes.com/forbes/2011/0228/technology-gabe-newell-videogames-valve-online-mayhem.html

History of Valve – Dunn, J. (2013). Full Steam ahead: The History of Valve. *GamesRadar*. https://www.gamesradar.com/history-of-valve/

Valve employee handbook and review – Denning, S. (2012). *A glimpse at A workplace of the future: Valve*. Forbes. https://www.forbes.com/sites/stevedenning/2012/04/27/a-glimpse-at-a-workplace-of-the-future-valve/

Financial performance of Valve – Chiang, O. (2011). *Valve and Steam worth billions. Forbes.* https://www.forbes.com/sites/oliverchiang/2011/02/15/valve-and-steam-worth-billions/

Estimated sales top $1 billion – Tassi, P. (2011). *Steam sales estimated close to $1 billion in 2010. Forbes.* https://www.forbes.com/sites/insertcoin/2011/02/04/steam-sales-close-to-1-billion-in-2010/

Year on year revenue growth – Kirsch, N. (2011). *Steam revenue up 42 percent – brings in $468 million 1H 2011. Legit Reviews.* https://www.legitreviews.com/steam-revenue-up-42-percent-468-million-1h-2011_11144

40 million accounts reached and 100% sales growth – DigitalSpy Staff. (2012, January 6). *Steam closes 2011 with 100% sales growth, 5 million simultaneous users. TechPowerUp.* https://www.techpowerup.com/158193/steam-closes-2011-with-100-sales-growth-5-million-simultaneous-users

Managing without leaders at Valve – Thornblad, D. (2018). Managing Innovation without Managers: Valve Corp. *Journal of Case Studies, 36*(2).

Flat hierarchy and culture – Warr, P. (2013). *Valve's flat management structure "like high school."* Wired. https://www.wired.com/story/valve-management-jeri-ellsworth/

STUDY 7: THE AGILE ADVANTAGE

Author interview – Booth, B. (2025). Interview with Danny Wareham. 29 August 2025, virtual.

Top 50 Most Ambitious Business Leaders for 2024 – LDC. (2024). The LDC Top 50 2024 | Ben Booth. *Lloyds Development Capital*. https://www.ldc.co.uk/top-50/ben-booth-2/

MaxContact history and company – MaxContact (n.d.). MaxContact. *MaxContact*. https://www.maxcontact.com/

Fastest growing companies in Contact Centre industry – Contact- Centres. (2022). *MaxContact One of the Fastest Growing UK Contact Centre Specialists*. Contact-Centres.com. https://contact-centres.com/maxcontact-one-of-the-fastest-growing-uk-contact-centre-specialists/

Partnership with Whistl – Whistl. (2023). *Meet the Partner: MaxContact*. Whistl. https://www.whistl.co.uk/insights/meet-partner-maxcontact

MaxContact acquires Curious Thing AI – FPE. (2025). *MaxContact Strengthens AI Capabilities Through Acquisition of Conversational AI Firm, Curious Thing*. FPE. https://www.fpecapital.com/news/maxcontact-strengthens-ai-capabilities-through-acquisition-of-conversational-ai-firm-curious-thing

Curious Thing AI sale completed – Freeman, X. (2025). *MaxContact Acquires Curious Thing's Tech to Expand AI Capabilities*. Call Centre Helper. https://www.callcentrehelper.com/maxcontact-acquires-curious-things-tech-257747.htm

Award-winning growth in North West – Hough, P. (2023). *MaxContact Top 50 Companies at Northern Tech Awards 2023*. MaxContact. https://www.maxcontact.com/resources/blog-insights/maxcontact-named-as-one-of-the-top-50-companies-at-the-northern-tech-awards-2023/

NINE

AN INVITIATION TO THE FUTURE

Constellation Leadership model and history – Wareham, D. (2023). *Creating Constellations: The influence of Constellation Leadership on Agile methodology-led project delivery success*. https://doi.org/10.13140/RG.2.2.23440.79368

Edmondson and psychological safety – Edmondson, A. C., & Lei, Z. (2014). Psychological safety: The history, renaissance, and future of an interpersonal construct. *Annu. Rev. Organ. Psychol. Organ. Behav., 1*(1), 23-43.

Medical staff report fewer issues where safety is low – O'Donovan, R., & McAuliffe, E. (2020). Exploring psychological safety in healthcare teams to inform the development of interventions: combining observational, survey and interview data. *BMC health services research, 20*(1), 810.

Increase in reported incidents where safety is high – Edmondson, A. C. (2004). Learning from failure in health care: frequent opportunities, pervasive barriers. *BMJ Quality & Safety, 13*(suppl 2), ii3-ii9.

Humans can spot threats to safety in groups – Dezecache, G. (2015). Human collective reactions to threat. *Wiley Interdisciplinary Reviews: Cognitive Science, 6*(3), 209-219.

Amygdala response to threat – Wood, K. H., Ver Hoef, L. W., & Knight, D. C. (2014). The amygdala mediates the emotional modulation of threat-elicited skin conductance response. *Emotion, 14*(4), 693.

THE GHOST OF INDUSTRY

Frederick Taylor's time-and-motion studies – Krenn, M. (2011). From scientific management to homemaking: Lillian M. Gilbreth's contributions to the development of management thought. *Management & Organizational History, 6*(2), 145-161.

Today's organisations are complex – Burke, V. (2022) *Author talks: Attributes-not skills-determine whether you 'cut it' or not, McKinsey & Company*. Available at: https://www.mckinsey.com/featured-insights/mckinsey-on-books/author-talks-attributes-not-skills-determine-whether-you-cut-it-or-not

Contemporary structures require new skills to navigate – Mishra, A.K. and Mishra, K.E. (2013) 'The research on trust in leadership: The need for context', *Journal of Trust Research, 3*(1), pp. 59–69. doi:10.1080/21515581.2013.771507.

Mission command only works because of exhaustive planning – Hill, A., & Niemi, H. (2017). The Trouble with Mission Command. *Flexive Command and the Future of Command and Control. JFQ, 86.*

THE FUTURE

Global challenges require collaboration – Francis, G. (2025). *Is there hope for global collaboration? 4 experts share their views.* World Economic Forum. https://www.weforum.org/stories/2025/02/geopolitical-challenges-global-collaboration/

Collaboration required for resolutions – Bouffard, S. (2025). *Today's Challenges Require Global Collaboration And Innovation.* Learning Forward - the Professional Learning Association. https://learningforward.org/journal/global-perspectives/todays-challenges-require-global-collaboration-and-innovation/

FUTURE CHALLENGES

Climate change demands cross-boundary coordination – Kark, S., Tulloch, A., Gordon, A., Mazor, T., Bunnefeld, N., & Levin, N. (2015). Cross-boundary collaboration: key to the conservation puzzle. *Current Opinion in Environmental Sustainability, 12,* 12-24.

AI required global standards – UNESCO. (2024). *Enabling AI governance and innovation through standards.* Unesco.org. https://www.unesco.org/ethics-ai/en/articles/enabling-ai-governance-and-innovation-through-standards

Fragility in global supply chains – Stonebraker, P. W., Goldhar, J., & Nassos, G. (2009). Weak links in the supply chain: measuring fragility and sustainability. *Journal of Manufacturing Technology Management, 20*(2), 161-177.

Rise of populist politics – Moffitt, B. (2016). *The global rise of populism: Performance, political style, and representation.* Stanford University Press.

Identity and populism in Europe – Noury, A., & Roland, G. (2020). Identity politics and populism in Europe. *Annual Review of Political Science, 23*(1), 421-439.

Global demographic shifts – Sardak, S., Korneyev, M., Dzhyndzhoian, V., Fedotova, T., & Tryfonova, O. (2018). Current trends in global demographic processes. *Problems and Perspectives in Management, 16*(1), 48-57.

Impact of global demographic changes – Bloom, D. E., & Canning, D. (2004). Global demographic change: Dimensions and economic significance.

SELECTED FURTHER READING

Barzun, M. (2021). *The power of giving away power: How the best leaders learn to let go.* Penguin.

Bolden, R. (2011). Distributed leadership in organizations: A review of theory and research. *International journal of management reviews, 13*(3), 251-269.

Coyle, D. (2018). *The Culture Code: The Secrets of Highly Successful Groups.* Random House Uk.

Diviney, R. (2021). *The attributes : 25 hidden drivers of optimal performance.* Random House.

Empson, L. (2017). *Leading professionals : power, politics, and prima donnas.* Oxford University Press.

Harris, A. (2013). *Distributed leadership matters: Perspectives, practicalities, and potential.* Corwin press.

Helgesen, S. (1995) *The Web of Inclusion.* 1st edn. New York, NY: Currency/Doubleday.

Leithwood, K. A., Mascall, B., & Strauss, T. (Eds.). (2009). *Distributed leadership according to the evidence.* London: Routledge.

Kouzes, J.M. and Posner, B.Z. (2017) *The leadership challenge.* 6th edn. Somerset, UK: John Wiley & Sons, Inc.

Spillane, J. P. (2006). *Distributed Leadership.* John Wiley & Sons.

ABOUT THE AUTHOR

Danny believes that happy bees make tasty honey. With a purposeful culture, strategy and support systems, high performance becomes a side effect.

He is a Certified Business Psychologist, accredited coach, and psychometrician whose work lies at the intersection of leadership, culture and personality, with a focus on individual differences – especially the "dark triad" traits of narcissism, psychopathy, and Machiavellianism.

An expert in culture and leadership dynamics, Danny has been recognised among the Global Top 25 Thought Leaders on Culture and the Top 50 in Leadership and has spent nearly 30-years in contact centre, retail and fintech industries, designing cultures, leadership systems, and strategies in which energy, clarity, and collaboration multiply success.

He is the founder of Firgun, a consultancy whose Hebrew name captures his core motivation: "the genuine, sincere and pure happiness for another person's accomplishment or experience", whose clients include Worldpay, M&G Investment Bank, and LEGO.

He lives in Stoke-on-Trent, UK, with his partner, Charlene.

dannywareham.co.uk
constellationleadership.co.uk

A NOTE ON ARTIFICIAL INTELLIGENCE

Artificial intelligence (AI) in writing is a hot topic today (and rightly so). Questions about copyright and creativity result in ambiguous answers, when large language models are involved in a book's creation and how that publication's content might be utilised in the future.

I made an intentional decision not to use generative AI in the writing of this work, due to three core reasons:

1. This work is based on new research that has been unavailable to 'train' AI models at the time;

2. It is unclear (to me) where any submitted data is utilised after posting to an AI model and how that might be used elsewhere without my knowledge; and

3. When the goal is the publishing of the work, we lose something in the creative process. The clichéd adage is that 'the best way to learn is to teach', and in composing a book, I have learned far more about my own research than through the research alone.

Now that the book is finished, its purpose is to start discussion, critique and further research to explore the opportunities, challenges and risks of constellation leadership. This, I believe, is made more accessible if this completed work is used to train AI models.

Whilst no AI was used in its creation, I'm comfortable that its contents become part of our new world and its data may be used to enhance the information available on leadership.

www.ingramcontent.com/pod-product-compliance
Lightning Source LLC
Chambersburg PA
CBHW071331210326
41597CB00015B/1416